O Come, Let Us Worship

O Come, Let Us Worship

CORPORATE WORSHIP IN THE EVANGELICAL CHURCH

Robert G. Rayburn

BAKER BOOK HOUSE
Grand Rapids, Michigan

To
ARTHUR C. STOLL
who proved to me that
"there is a friend that sticketh closer
than a brother"

Foreword

It was not until I had been in the pastoral ministry for a number of years that I began to learn some of the truths which are set forth in this book. Worship was a subject hardly touched on in the evangelical theological seminaries which I attended and in others with which I was familiar. After several pastorates and two extended periods of active duty in the army chaplaincy, I was called away from the pastoral ministry to teach young men preparing to be pastors. I determined that I would share with them what I had learned about worship and that I would study with them ways and means of making corporate worship more acceptable to God and more meaningful to the worshipers. It was in response to the urging of the men who have been my students that I undertook the preparation of this book. I am grateful for their enthusiasm and encouragement. Having worshiped with some of them in the churches of which they are now pastors, I have been greatly blessed in participating in deeply meaningful corporate worship under their leadership. These experiences have been a further encouragement to prepare this volume.

While I personally hold to the historic Reformed and Presbyterian position in theology, I have written this book for all evangelicals. I have attempted to refrain from emphasizing those elements of corporate worship which are distinctly Reformed, except in the consideration of the sacraments. I sincerely hope that those who differ with me theologically on the sacraments will still be willing to consider seriously what is contained in the other chapters.

Unless otherwise indicated, Scripture quotations are from the King James (Authorized) Version. The other versions quoted are the Revised Standard Version (RSV), New American Standard Bible (NASB), and New International Version (NIV).

I want to express my thanks to my son-in-law, Mark E. Pett, to my son, Robert S. Rayburn, and to my colleague on the faculty of Covenant Theological Seminary, John W. Sanderson, all of whom have made valuable suggestions concerning the manuscript.

I am especially grateful to my secretary of many years, Mrs. Eshmal Porter, who has so patiently and skillfully prepared the manuscript for publication.

Robert G. Rayburn
St. Louis, Missouri

Contents

Aids for the Preparation of
Corporate Worship Services

1

The Importance
of Worship

The worship of God is at once the true believer's most important activity and at the same time it is one of the most tragically neglected activities in the average evangelical church today. In the preaching and teaching of the churches, in conferences and in seminars, individual Christians have been encouraged to have their own daily "quiet time," for a period of personal devotion is an important part of every Christian life. They have been admonished to pray for their own needs and the needs of others. They have been taught to study the Bible for their own spiritual growth and for use in guiding and instructing others. There remains, however, among sincere believers today a woeful ignorance concerning the significance of true worship and the means of attaining the blessing of rich, rewarding corporate worship.

On the subject of worship I have interviewed scores of men and women who were reared in evangelical churches. In addition I have questioned literally hundreds of theological seminary students concerning the same matter. In all of these consultations I have discovered only a very few who have received any instruction concerning corporate worship in the house of God. The overwhelming majority of them were taught neither its importance in the life of the individual Christian nor what methods and techniques they should apply to achieve fulfilling individual and corporate worship. Most of them did not remember ever hearing a sermon on the subject of worship. Those who did could not usually recall any practical suggestions which were given as to how to make their worship in the church more meaningful.

In the light of the neglect of this all-important subject it is perhaps not surprising that multitudes of young people who in childhood regularly attended evangelical Sunday schools and churches have turned away from the church, freely expressing their loss of interest because of their failure to find meaning and significance in the services of worship. The perfunctory way in which many so-called worship services proceed leaves young people with an impression of meaninglessness. The pastor supplies no rubrics and the congregation is unaware of the connection of various parts of the service with one another. There is no obvious reason why a certain psalm is chosen for responsive reading, nor why a particular hymn is sung. The variable components of the service seem to have been chosen at random and the order of the various parts is followed simply because it is the order to which everyone is accustomed. Instead of the Sunday morning service being anticipated as the high point of the week, it has come to be regarded as a time to be bored. This is all the more tragic when one considers the fact that opportunities for corporate worship with other believers should be to the individual Christian among the highest, most joyous, and most deeply satisfying experiences of his life.

The emphasis in the services of most evangelical churches today is placed almost exclusively upon the sermon. Serious efforts are made in many churches to provide some special musical numbers by the choir or competent soloists which will sustain the interest of the congregation. Mere enjoyment of the music on the part of the listener, however, is not necessarily related directly to the worship of God. Perhaps somewhat unconsciously most church members go to the services of their churches to listen to the preaching. Their comments following the services indicate that the whole period of worship is appraised exclusively on the basis of the sermon. Certainly there has never been a greater need for faithful and powerful preaching of the Word of God than there is today. But there is an even greater need for the experience of uplifting and fulfilling corporate worship of the Triune God. Any Christian who visits frequently in a variety of evangelical churches will testify that he often hears an inspirational sermon but he is rarely spiritually stirred and refreshed by the rest of the service of worship.

What is the answer to the problem of less than meaningful and satisfying experiences of corporate worship? First, the individual Christian must have specific instruction as to the importance and meaning of worship, especially corporate (common) worship. Second, this instruction should include the means by which the worshiper can attain the desired end of true spiritual worship. Third, every minister must understand the basic scriptural principles of worship himself and must instruct his congregation therein. He must also recognize his own responsibility to both prepare and conduct services in which every participant can clearly understand the meaning of what is transpiring and will be aided in lifting his praise and prayers to God in fellowship with the other believers present. This book is written for both laymen and ministers. It is hoped that both may be encouraged to give fresh consideration to the subject of their own individual responsibilities in the services of their churches. Those who lead the services as well as the congregations must understand clearly the importance of corporate worship and the means by which believers can fulfill the demands of a holy God and be provided from week to week all the spiritual enrichment and growth which their worship services should impart. Basic to our understanding of the place of worship in the corporate life of the church is the witness of the Scripture concerning worship.

The Teaching of Jesus

As we turn to a consideration of what the Scripture teaches concerning the importance of worship we must first give heed to the words of our Lord Jesus Christ on the subject. The most salient are recorded in the fourth chapter of the Gospel of John. There we read that as Jesus was walking along the road on a journey from Judea into Galilee He passed through Samaria. As He came near to the city of Sychar, being physically weary, He sat down to rest on the edge of a well. The apostle John in describing the Lord's journey says that the Lord *"must needs* go through Samaria" (John 4:4). It was not a geographical necessity that forced Him to take this route. He could have circumvented Samaria by crossing the Jordan River. Necessity was laid upon Him, however, by the eternal decrees of His Father. There was a poor sinful woman to be rescued from a life of shame. There were many citizens of the city of Sychar who were to be reached by the saving grace of God through the testimony of that woman and the preaching of the Savior. Elect from the foundation of the world, they could not be bypassed.

In the eternal counsels of God one of the most important aspects of the Lord's brief stop in Sychar was His interview with the unnamed Samaritan woman at the well, for out of that interview the apostle John has recorded for us the most important single statement that was ever made concerning the vital subject of worship. In what seems to be an attempt on the part of the woman to divert the attention of Jesus from the condition of her own sinful heart, after He had revealed His knowledge of her past life and her then adulterous situation, she introduced the subject of worship. Perhaps she simply asked the Lord to settle the ancient argument between the Samaritans and the Jews as to the proper place of worship in the hope that she could keep him from probing deeper into the sinfulness of her life and making her more conscious of her spiritual needs. In His answer to the woman, however, the Lord made a statement of such importance that it should command the very careful attention of any believer who truly loves the Lord and wants to glorify Him in his daily life. The Savior pointed out that the place of worship was without particular significance at that time, although He well knew that God had ordained that Jerusalem was to be the center of the worship of His people because the temple was established there. Jesus Himself had already spoken of the significance of the temple. To the woman at Sychar He said, however, "Woman, believe me, the hour cometh, when ye shall neither in this mountain, nor yet in Jerusalem, worship the Father" (John 4:21). It was important that she should understand that it is the person who is the subject of worship that is important, not the place. He continued, "Ye worship ye know not what: we know what we worship: for salvation is of the Jews" (v. 22). He followed with a word which is without parallel in all His teaching: "The hour cometh, and now is, when the true worshipers shall worship the Father in spirit and in truth: for *the Father seeketh such to worship him.* God is a Spirit: and they that worship him must worship him in spirit and in truth" (vv. 23, 24).

These words of Jesus set forth in a striking manner the basic reason why I said that the worship of God is the most important single activity of the believer. Nowhere in all the Scriptures do we read of God's *seeking* anything else from the child of God. One often hears that Christians are "saved to serve," and there is a limited sense in which this is true, for throughout eternity as well as during our earthly life it will be our joy and privilege to serve the Lord God. But this heavenly service will itself be primarily worship (see Heb. 9:14; 12:28; Rev. 22:3). Nowhere in the Bible are we told that the Lord seeks our service. It is not servants He seeks, but true worshipers.

When ministers preach on the Great Commission, they stress the importance of witnessing; and, indeed, no student of the Word of God would deny the fact that it is important for every Christian to be a faithful personal witness to the saving love of Christ. However, nowhere do the Scriptures tell us that the Lord is seeking witnesses. It certainly could be argued that there are other expressions in the Bible which indicate an activity of God similar to "seeking." For example, II Chronicles 16:9 might be said to indicate that God seeks those "whose heart is perfect toward him," so that He might "shew himself strong" in their behalf. This is true, and we do not wish to press the matter too far. However, it is not without real significance that the only time in the Scriptures when the word *seek* is used of God's activity is in connection with seeking true worshipers.

The well-known first question of the Westminster Shorter Catechism is, "What is the chief end of man?" and the equally well-known answer is, "Man's chief end is to glorify God and to enjoy him forever." How easy it is to forget that man was created for the purpose of bringing glory to his eternal Creator God. The Word of God tells us that everything that a believer does is to be done to the glory of God. "Whether therefore ye eat, or drink, or whatsoever ye do, do all to the glory of God" (I Cor. 10:31). "For of him, and through him, and to him, are all things: to whom be glory forever. Amen" (Rom. 11:36). The Scriptures are full of additional evidence that the glory of God should be the believer's major concern. The apostle Paul has given us some very solemn words concerning the unbeliever in the first chapter of Romans: "The wrath of God is revealed from heaven against all ungodliness and unrighteousness of men . . . because that, when they knew God, they glorified him not as God" (vv. 18, 21). Their sinful indulgences and perverted desires are not mentioned first. These come because there is no willingness to give glory to God.

It should not be cause for amazement that the existentialist who rejects the Word of God and therefore lives for himself alone finds that the existence of man is meaningless and life is absurd. It is only the Christian who has discovered the true meaning of life and the inexhaustible springs of eternal joy, because he realizes that he was created for the high and holy purpose of bringing glory to his Creator God. Alas, that so many Christians have failed to recognize that their single most important means of realizing their true purpose in life is responding in continual spiritual worship to the seeking God who loves them and saved them. They are unaware that acceptable worship must always be offered according to God's express provisions and commands. Indeed all Christians must understand that the activity which is of primary importance in the life of every believer is true spiritual worship of God.

The Witness of the Scriptures

It must be added at this point that, besides the fact that the Lord Himself spoke of worship as the one thing which the Father seeks from man, there are many other indications in the Scriptures of the importance of worship. Consider how the psalmist emphasizes the indispensable character of worship. In Psalm 29:2 he calls upon us to "Give unto the Lord the glory due unto his name; worship the Lord in the beauty of holiness"; and in showing the importance of corporate worship he invites men to join him in worship: "O come, let us worship and bow down; let us kneel before the Lord our maker. For he is our God; and we are the people of his pasture, and the sheep of his hand" (Ps. 95:6, 7). Consider also, for example, the fact that worship alone of all the activities of the believer will continue in heaven and will occupy the redeemed host forever. Like the love and grace of God to which it is the only fitting response, it will endure when all other earthly activity has ceased (see Rev. 4:10, 11; 5:11-14; 19:1-7, 10; 22:8, 9). For this reason, if for no other, our worship should be kept under constant, close scrutiny. We should seek to learn all that we can about how to worship God in a manner that brings glory to Him. Seeing that God "made the world and all things therein, seeing that he is Lord of heaven and earth, dwelleth not in temples made with hands; neither is worshipped with men's hands, as though he needed any thing, seeing he giveth to all life, and breath, and all things" (Acts 17:24, 25), we must carefully ascertain how to offer worship in an acceptable manner. Those ministers who lead services of worship must constantly bring their formulations of the orders of worship and the component parts of the service as well as their method of leading the common worship of the Lord's people under the testing of the one infallible guide, the Holy Scriptures. It is an awesome responsibility to lead a congregation of the Lord's people in the worship of His holy name. Carelessness in the matter is inexcusable.

Another way in which God has emphasized the importance of worship is by His giving more specific and clear details as to the manner in which His children were to carry on their worship than He gave them concerning any other activity. Large sections of the Book of Exodus are given over to painstaking details concerning the construction of the place of worship for the children of Israel, the tabernacle. Almost the entire Book of Leviticus is taken up with instruction concerning the worship of the people of God and the regulations which they were to observe in order to make their worship acceptable. The Book of Psalms in its entirety is a book of worship. It has been properly designated as the inspired prayer and praise book of God's people.

Almost all of the prophets had much to say about the worship of Jehovah. They rebuked the people severely for the abuses which had crept into their worship. Isaiah cried out, "To what purpose is the multitude of your sacrifices unto me? saith the Lord. . . . Bring no more vain oblations; incense is an abomination unto me; the new moons and sabbaths, the calling of assemblies, I cannot away with; it is iniquity, even the solemn meeting. Your new moons and your appointed feasts my soul hateth; they are a trouble unto me; I am weary to bear them" (Isa. 1:11-14). Micah prophesied the destruction of idolatry in Israel, "Thy graven images also will I cut off, and thy standing images out of the midst of thee; and thou shalt no more worship the work of thine hands" (Mic. 5:13). Outstanding among those prophets who warned the Lord's people about the degeneration of their worship was Jeremiah, who cried out to the people in such words as these: "Will ye steal, murder, and commit adultery, and swear falsely, and burn incense unto Baal, and walk after other gods whom ye know not; and come and stand before me in this house, which is called by my name, and say, We are delivered to do all these abominations?'' (Jer. 7:9, 10). Again and again he reminded the people of the necessity of pure hearts in their worship of the Lord. Without purity of heart their pretense of worship was indeed an abomination. Even the divinely authorized ordinances themselves had become offensive to the God who had given them because of the way they had been abused. It was because the prophets recognized the supreme importance of the worship of the Lord that they cried out against those sins of the people which made their worship unacceptable. If God could not accept their worship He would not bless their nation.

If ever there has been a time when God's people needed to be warned about the wickedness of a presumptuous approach to God in worship, coming to Him without true understanding of what is involved in worship, without confession of sin and a cleansing of the life, it is today. Yet, having personally visited in a large number of churches in recent months and years, sometimes as a guest preacher, I have been amazed at the carelessness and insincerity that were evident in the services. The people were going through the motions of worship, singing the words of the hymns and maintaining quiet when prayers were being uttered, but with no apparent sincere worship of God. The pastors who conducted the services were also careless. In a number of services, for example, there was nothing to remind the congregation that it is only the pure in heart who shall see God and it is only those whose lives have been cleansed from evil who are able to pray with the confidence that the Lord will hear them. "If I regard iniquity in my heart, the Lord will not hear me" (Ps. 66:18), was the psalmist's warning. It is the repentant sinner whom the Lord will hear not only when he intercedes in prayer but also when his voice is lifted in praise and adoration. "The Lord is nigh unto them that are of a broken heart" (Ps. 34:18). They are the ones who know the reality of true worship. Since worship is the most important activity of all believers, every one of us needs to give careful attention to his own habits of worship.

The Definition of Worship

It is important at this point to ask what we mean by the worship of God. Unless we understand clearly what we are speaking about, we shall certainly err in our understanding of how we are to accomplish the desired end of true spiritual worship. Worship has been variously defined, and the definitions differ widely. Some are too broad. Evelyn Underhill offers this definition, "Worship in all its grades and kinds is the response of the creature to the Eternal."[1] This definition seems to me to be quite inadequate, for there are many responses which the creature makes which certainly could not be considered worship, especially Christian worship. Julius Melton says that "worship, in its most profound sense, is coextensive with the entirety of a Christian life."[2] Here we would insist that while what he says may certainly be true of the ideal Christian life, the statement does not clearly define worship. John Huxtable defined worship as "a dialogue between God and his people."[3] Certainly worship involves such a dialogue, but it includes more than this.

The limitations of time and space make it impossible for me to examine many more of the very numerous definitions of worship which have been offered in books on the subject. *Webster's Dictionary* says that to worship is "to pay divine honor, reverence and homage to the Supreme Being through adoration, confession, prayer, thanksgiving and the like." While this adds certain significant elements, it cannot be considered a definition of Christian worship. Let me therefore give you my definition of Christian worship so that you will understand clearly what is being discussed in this book. *Worship is the activity of the new life of a believer in which, recognizing the fullness of the Godhead as it is revealed in*

---

[1]Evelyn Underhill, *Worship* (Scranton: Harper & Row, 1936), p. 3.

[2]Julius Melton, *Presbyterian Worship in America* (Richmond: John Knox Press, 1967), p. 9.

[3]John Huxtable, *The Bible Says* (Richmond: John Knox Press, 1962), p. 109.

the person of Jesus Christ and His mighty redemptive acts,
he seeks by the power of the Holy Spirit to render to the liv-
ing God the glory, honor, and submission which are His due.
It could be argued that in the broadest sense this definition
describes the whole of the life of the sincere Christian and
that it would thus correspond to Melton's definition of worship cited above. However, we are particularly concerned
with the activity of the individual believer when he is consciously seeking to give to God acceptable worship. If our
definition of worship is true for the individual, then we can
say that corporate Christian worship is the activity of a congregation of true believers in which they seek to render to
God that adoration, praise, confession, intercession, thanksgiving, and obedience to which He is entitled by virtue of the
ineffable glory of His person and the magnificent grace of
His acts of redemption in Jesus Christ.

Faith and Worship

Worship is always regulated by faith. A man's worship is
governed by what he believes, for worship is man's means of
ascribing to God that adoration, reverence, praise, love, and
obedience of which he sincerely believes God to be worthy.
Worship which is truly Christian must of necessity declare
and demonstrate the believer's understanding of the attributes of the Triune God, Father, Son, and Holy Spirit, as
they are self-disclosed fully and finally in this world by
means of the written word of Holy Scripture. It is of utmost
importance that each of the three persons of the Godhead
should receive that special recognition in worship to which
His particular ministry entitles Him. God has said, "I am the
Lord: that is my name: and my glory will I not give to
another" (Isa. 42:8). Of fundamental importance, of course,
is the fact that the Christian understands that man can truly
know God only in and through Jesus Christ who is Lord and
Savior. Therefore only worship based upon saving faith in
Jesus Christ, the absolutely unique Son of God, is acceptable
to God. For the Christian the substitutionary death and
resurrection of Jesus Christ are at the very core of worship.

It is easy for men to distort the nature of the one true God even while they believe that they are offering worship to Him. Multitudes of professed Christians go to their churches each Sunday to worship a god who may be a poor imitation of the God of the Bible, a god who is actually the creation of their own imaginations and therefore nothing more than a false god, an idol of their own making. Literally thousands of congregations today are led in their worship by men whose god is not the God of the Bible, the Father of our Lord and Savior Jesus Christ, a personal God who is inflexibly righteous and just and at the same time infinitely loving and compassionate. Their god is a nonpersonal god who might be properly referred to as "the ground of being," to use the well-known description of his god given to us by the famous theologian, Paul Tillich.

The true worshiper will know that he cannot offer to God worship which is based upon man's reason nor upon man's own efforts of mind and body. Worship, if it be true worship, must be the offering back to God, by the power and ministration of His Holy Spirit, of that which He has first given unto us. As the apostle Paul put it, "Who has first given to Him that it might be paid back to him again? For from Him and through Him and to Him are all things. To Him be the glory forever. Amen" (Rom. 11:35, 36, NASB). The enabling of the Holy Spirit, so essential to true Christian worship, according to the Scriptures, means that worship is not just an act of man alone, but in it man is moved and enabled by the Spirit of God. If worshipers are not consciously dependent upon the Holy Spirit, their worship is not truly Christian. Thus, unless our response to God is formed by an appropriation by faith of who He is and what He has done and is doing for us, as those truths are recorded for us in the inerrant Scriptures, it is not properly Christian worship.

The Vocabulary of Worship

To understand better what worship entails, let us examine the meaning of the words used in our language and in the original languages of the Scripture to describe this activity. The English word *worship* is a contraction of the original Anglo-Saxon word *worth-ship*. Thus, originally, to give worship to anyone simply meant to accord him the proper recognition of his inherent dignity and value, or to put it another way, to accord him his worth or his worthiness. Therefore when the Englishman addresses the courtroom judge or the mayor as "your worship," he is not being sacrilegious. Neither is the man in error who promises in some traditional marriage services to worship his wife with his body. His promise is in line with the scriptural instruction which gives the wife the authority over her husband's body as it gives him in turn authority over her body (I Cor. 7:4). He renders to her that which is her due. The English word *worship* then is a fine one, for it forces our attention upon the intrinsic majesty of our God and the necessity of rendering to Him that recognition of the glory of His being and His wonderful redeeming work of which He is so worthy. The psalmist called out, "Give unto the Lord the glory *due* unto his name" (Ps. 29:2); and in the Revelation we read, *"Worthy* is the Lamb . . . to receive honor and glory and blessing" (Rev. 5:12).

We must recognize, of course, that what is even more important than the English word is the biblical terminology which is behind it. There are several words in the original Greek and Hebrew which are translated "worship." When our Lord was tempted by Satan and promised the kingdoms of this world if He would fall down and worship the Evil One, the Lord rebuked Satan with these words, "It is written, Thou shalt worship the Lord thy God, and him only shalt thou serve" (Matt. 4:10). In this statement are found two Greek words both of which may be translated "worship" and are so translated in English versions of the New Testament. The first of these is the word *proskynein,* which is the word translated "worship" in the Lord's statement, "Thou shalt worship the Lord thy God." It originally had the meaning of bowing down or prostrating oneself. It referred to the physical act of obeisance before an earthly ruler. It is the word used in the Septuagint (the early Greek version of the Hebrew Old Testament) to translate the Hebrew word *shachah,* which means the same thing.

The other Greek word which is in the Lord's statement to Satan is translated "serve" ("him only shalt thou serve"). This is the word *latreuein.* The original meaning of this word was simply to serve as a slave serves his master or a hired servant his employer. However, it became a word used for worship and is so translated in such passages as Acts 7:42; 24:14; Philippians 3:3; and Hebrews 10:2. The last case cited is a noun form of the verb. This word corresponds to the Hebrew word *'abadah,* which has the same root as the noun which is translated "servant." This is especially significant because the Suffering Servant of the Lord is in the Hebrew the *'Ebed Yahweh.* So the obedient service of the Lord which took Him to the cross must be seen as the worship which the Lord said must not be offered to anyone except God. Jesus, in resisting the temptation of Satan was, as J. S. McEwen has pointed out,[4] guarding jealously for God His right to be worshiped alone, in accordance with the Second Commandment. It is interesting in this connection also to note that Paul, as he expounds the meaning of Psalm 18:49 in Romans 15:8-10, tells us that Christ leads the worship of the people of the nations (Gentiles).

What is the significance of the biblical terminology? First, it makes very clear the fact that in true Christian worship the sincere believer is prostrating himself before the living God (even though this may not involve a physical act) in recognition of His glorious majesty, so that he may offer the adoration, the praise, the thanksgiving, the exaltation to which God alone is entitled. Second, it makes plain the fact that the true worshiper essentially is offering himself to God in submission as an obedient servant even as his Savior did. As I have indicated above, Jesus Christ is seen as the perfect worshiper, resisting every temptation, even the ultimate temptation to refuse the death of the cross. Since we who have

---

[4]J. S. McEwen, in *A Theological Word Book of the Bible,* ed. Alan Richardson (New York: Macmillan, 1955), p. 288.

believed in Him find our greatest fulfillment in the complete identification we have with Him individually as well as in His body, the church, we must see that as His worship took Him to the cross, so our worship of God takes us to the cross. We cannot die as the sinless Savior died, but we must know "the fellowship of his sufferings, being made conformable unto his death" (Phil. 3:10). He agonized over the lost condition of men. Our surrender to Him involves a willingness to sacrifice selfish interests and even to suffer for the salvation of the souls of men. The cross of Christ is at the very center of all truly Christian worship.

It must also be pointed out before we proceed further, although it will be treated again in connection with the brief study of worship in the Old Testament, that the Bible makes it clear that the worship of the true and living God, the Father of our Lord Jesus Christ, can be acceptably offered only by those who have been redeemed. We must remember that worship does not originate with man. We have already seen that God the Father seeks true worshipers to worship Him. In order that they could be true worshipers God took the initiative in redeeming them unto Himself. In the Old Testament God's redeeming grace is most clearly seen in His act of bringing the children of Israel out of their slavery in Egypt. The covenant on Mount Sinai was established by God with His people only after He had brought them out of their bondage in a foreign land. They were not yet in the Promised Land; there was a very difficult pilgrimage still ahead of them, but they were a redeemed nation. Great as this deliverance was, however, it was but a foretaste of that salvation under the new covenant whereby men are irresistibly drawn by the Holy Spirit unto Jesus Christ and are delivered from their slavery to the prince of this world and taken into the service of their Redeemer.

Christian worship then can take place only within the covenant of redemption, or the covenant of grace. This covenant was established by God and is based entirely upon His own redemptive acts on the cross of Calvary. When man worships he responds to the redemptive acts in Christ Jesus which God has already completed. All truly Christian worship, including all prayer, is offered "through Jesus Christ our Lord." Essentially this means that we are entering into the perfect worship of the Lord Himself even as our worship finds its basis in the redemption which Christ provided by His death and resurrection. William Nicholls has well said, "Christian worship is essentially eucharistia, thanksgiving, to the God who has given us full and final redemption and in the same act restored to us our broken relationship with all His creation, whose praise we are called to make articulate. We worship because we have seen the glory of God in the face of Jesus Christ."[5]

Now, if what we have said is true, it certainly follows that one of the greatest needs in most evangelical churches today is a genuine revival of true spiritual worship. Many such churches are following an order of worship which has been the same for many years, hardly modified over a period of generations and without any particular significance for the vast majority of the congregation. Other churches have recognized that something was lacking in their services. They have, however, listened to the impassioned plea of the young people for "relevance" and have introduced a wide variety of novelties into their worship services. All kinds of new liturgies have been invented in an attempt to reach those among the youth who have been alienated from the church. However, it is not young people alone who have brought indictments against the worship services of our day. Many liberal biblical scholars, proponents of social action, psychologists, and even devout ghetto clergymen have complained that modern worship services do not communicate the Christian faith to the contemporary mind. They have pled for services more relevant to man in the life situation in which he finds himself in the modern world. Hugh T. Kerr has insisted that "much of our Sunday worship, our pastoral prayers, our hymns and anthems, our pulpit homilies, our

---

[5]William Nicholls, *Jacob's Ladder: The Meaning of Worship* (Richmond: John Knox Press, 1958), p. 18.

sacramental ceremonies, our vested choirs and divided chancels, our processing and recessing . . . is simply unrelated to reality."

While this indictment may indeed be true of the services in many churches, the problem is most certainly not with the constituent parts of the services as such. Pastoral prayers, hymns, and anthems can, when properly used, contribute greatly to the expression of sincere worship on the part of a congregation of the Lord's people. Neither does the problem arise from having the choir vested, nor from its making its entry to the service in a processional. The problem arises both from the lack of careful planning and preparation of the liturgy (what is called the order of service in most evangelical churches today) and also from the congregation's lack of instruction in these matters, so that the worshipers fail to understand the relationship of the various components of the service, even when these components might be well selected and in a proper sequence. The worshipers are also unaware of what their own participation involves.

It must be added that to express dissatisfaction with a service because it does not communicate the Christian faith to contemporary man is to miss the point of what Christian worship essentially is, the offering to God of that honor, praise, thanksgiving, and obedience of which one who has already experienced true Christian faith is totally convinced He is worthy. While there is certainly need for special evangelistic meetings in which a clear communication of the essentials of the Christian faith is given, the corporate worship of true believers is basically different from a gathering designed for evangelistic purposes.

The term *relevance* as it is used today could properly be called a cliché. Many who use it freely would be at a loss to explain specifically what they mean by it. Unfortunately, many who speak of relevant worship mean worship which shows the influence of the secular world and has been adapted to the changing attitudes of the secular society of the day. For others, relevant worship is simply worship which they like because it pleases their individual artistic tastes. It is evident that most of those who express dissatisfaction with present-day worship services on the contention that they are not relevant are thinking exclusively in terms of what worship should do for the individual worshiper. Theirs is a utilitarian viewpoint of worship. The most basic consideration in Christian worship, however, is not the effect it has on the one who worships, but the effect it has on God! It is easy to forget when one goes to a worship service that our Lord indicated that the concern which should be uppermost in our minds is to "worship *him* in spirit and in truth," not to receive some kind of a lift ourselves. We need to be reminded often of the truth of a statement made by Herbert Farmer in a book about preaching, for it is certainly as true of every part of a worship service as it is of preaching: "It is not the necessities of *our* nature, even our redeemed nature, which are being satisfied in . . . preaching, but . . . the necessities of God in the prosecution of His own sovereign purpose."[6] Paul W. Hoon has also pointed out the important fact that worship "is as much an end as a means—as much the 'summit' toward which the life of the church is directed as the 'fount' from which her activity flows." He has very aptly indicated the error of an abnormal emphasis on relevance with the statement that "to think of worship only in terms of 'relevance' is to deal simplistically with matters very complex, to risk obscuring deeper issues by stating only the surface problem, and to trap oneself into false postures at the outset by trying to understand them."[7]

Ministers who plan and conduct worship services must not be too much concerned that their services are lively, nor that they have enough "swing" in them to attract the non-Christian. The attitude of too many has been conditioned by the efforts of the movies and television to move everything at a rapid pace, to shock and then to soothe. Instead, pastors

---

[6]Herbert Farmer, *The Servant of the Word* (Philadelphia: Fortress Press, 1964), p. 11.

[7]Paul W. Hoon, *The Integrity of Worship* (Nashville: Abingdon Press, 1971), pp. 151-52.

must be careful so to prepare and then direct every service that those who have assembled to worship may be able to offer up to God pure uninterrupted devotion. This is possible only if those whose hearts overflow with love and gratitude to their Redeemer are not disturbed by distractions and meaningless activity as they offer their spiritual worship. Such worship always involves both listening reverently to the Word of God and responding to it with both mind and heart. One purpose of this book is to encourage thoughtful consideration of the methods of making the worship of the church more acceptable to God and more meaningful to the worshiper.

The Significance of Corporate Worship

We must turn now to a consideration of the subject of corporate worship as differentiated from the worship of the individual in the solitude of his own personal devotions. Corporate or common worship—and the terms are identical as used in the churches today—has been defined as "what we say and what we do when we stand together before God, realizing in high degree who He is and who we are."[8] To this we would need to add, "and what He has done for us," for as we have already pointed out, Christian worship can never be divorced from the cross. There are many in the churches today, however, who do not understand the significance of the corporate act of worship. While it is true that an individual can worship God sincerely and meaningfully in strict solitude and many of us do enjoy sweet communion with Him when we are alone, we can never know the full richness of worship unless we unite in common worship with other members of the body of Christ.

When there are a number of worshipers present, there is a participation in worship which is more intense than is the individual passion of any one of them when he is by himself. It

---

[8]Richard Davidson, "The Worship of the Reformed Churches," *Presbyterian Register,* vol. XVII, no. 10, p. 292.

is common knowledge that a mob is more cruel than any individual in it would be by himself. Similarly, the enjoyment of an elite company of music lovers at the symphony is more intense than that of a single music lover sitting by himself listening to the same music. God has so created man that there are deeper delights and more intense inspiration in the worshiping congregation than in individual devotion. Martin Luther spoke of his own appreciation for this fact when he said, "At home in my own house there is no warmth or vigor in me, but in the church when the multitude is gathered together, a fire is kindled in my heart, and it breaks its way through." It is not just that we might receive instruction in His Word that God has commanded us not to forsake "the assembling of ourselves together" (Heb. 10:25). He knows that every one of us needs the high experience of true corporate worship continually. As we bless and encourage one another in personal fellowship, so we are strengthened and uplifted by being together in common worship. To unite one's heart and one's voice with believers all around him as songs of praise are sung, prayers are offered up, confession is made, and the Scriptures are read, is indeed an experience which carries the soul beyond the reaches of individual worship and unites it with the Son of God who Himself leads the worship of those who gather in His name. He promised that "where two or three are gathered together in [unto] my name, there am I in the midst of them" (Matt. 18:20). While God's presence is certainly not limited to times of corporate worship in the church, this promise means that He will be present in a very special way when His children assemble to give Him common worship. How sad it is then that so many professing Christians find it easy to excuse themselves from the worship services of their churches.

The New Testament mentions no other requisite in connection with corporate worship. The Scriptures lay down no rules regarding numbers, the place of assembly, or official requirements for those who lead. The one significant thing is the presence of Jesus Himself. I can testify personally that some of the richest worship experiences of my life took place when I was a combat chaplain in the United States Army with just a few men, infantrymen and artillerymen, gathered together with me in the open air during a lull in battle which afforded them an opportunity to assemble themselves in the name of the Lord. It was His presence that made those times so sweet. His presence is always a gift of His love. It can neither be worked up nor prevented by the efforts of men. It is not brought about by the church, nor is it dependent upon the strength of the faith of those who come together. It is the fulfillment of His own promise. When His children assemble themselves to worship Him, there is nothing more certain than His promised presence. This is the same presence of Christ which is experienced in the observance of the Lord's Supper, and His presence on either occasion is based upon the unconditional saving love of God. The promise was made, however, for the assembly of believers, no matter how small. It was not made for the solitary worshiper.

Another consideration which gives import to corporate worship as distinct from individual worship is the fact that every believer is a member of the body of Christ. He is never merely an individual but is part of a divine society. He is a child of God, and that makes him a member of the family of God and of the body of Christ. He functions properly only when discharging his own responsibilities in the body. God has made no provision for a believer living in isolation from other believers. When one becomes a Christian he immediately becomes a member of the body. We must remember, moreover, that that body will have its local manifestation in a church, even though it be composed of only a small group of believers. The apostle Paul, in discussing the problem of spiritual gifts which had arisen in the Corinthian church, reminded the believers there that "the body is not one member but many" (I Cor. 12:14). The "many" members he referred to were not the members of the entire Christian church in existence in that day. Paul was dealing with a local situation. There were apparently individual Christians who considered themselves quite detached from the other believers. He made it clear that no Christian is to think of himself as the body of Christ. Each Christian is to remember that he is but one member of that body in one locality and must forward the work of Christ within that body.

The inspired apostle reminded the Corinthians that one member of the body could not excuse himself from his place in the body because he did not have the same function as some other member (I Cor. 12:15-17). Neither could one member profess to have no need of some other member (v. 12). That no believer can exist in isolation from other believers is clear from Paul's emphatic statement, "Now hath God set the members every one of them in the body, as it hath pleased him. And if they were all one member, where were the body? But now are they many members, yet but one body" (vv. 18-20). It has already been established that the highest and holiest function of the believer is the worship of the living God. Since this is true, the highest and holiest function of the body of believers in any place is Christian corporate worship. Thus every believer must participate in the worship of the body and must perform his proper obligations in that worship.

The importance of the corporateness of worship is also emphasized by the doctrine of the church universal, the body of Christ which is made up of all believers of the past, present, and future. It was not our action but that of Christ which first constituted the church; and since it is His body, responding to His initiative in worship, a sense of the universal and corporate is always necessary if worship is to be authentically Christian. Because this is true, traditional forms in the liturgy of the church have great value when they are properly used and understood for what they are by the worshipers. Of course, there is danger in the use of traditional components in a worship service. To focus attention on forms of prayer or upon hymns which come out of the ancient church might arouse an excitement and interest which will draw the attention of the worshiper away from the living God, who is the object of worship and who alone makes forms meaningful. However, tradition should never be discarded out of hand by the believers in any age. It does aid in the communication of a sense of the universal and corporate nature of the church. This it accomplishes by conveying to the individual a sense of the rich blessing of his great heritage and by making it possible for him as he appropriates for his own the devotion of the saints of past ages to sense in a deeper way his union with them. It is enriching to any individual when a prayer of Chrysostom, of Augustine, of Calvin, or of Cranmer becomes his own prayer. He is united with the faithful company of those who have gone before as he sings the hymns of the ancient Greek patriarchs, of the German Reformers, of the English Puritans, or even of the American evangelists. Indeed, through the use of traditional elements in our worship services we can make more real the communion of saints, and believers can sense in a deeper way their own place in the church triumphant as well as in the church militant.

The significance of corporate worship, therefore, must not be overlooked; and any Christian who wishes to experience the richest blessing in worship must enter into a deliberate self-identification with his fellow believers as they worship with him in the church. As we have indicated, the specific promise of the presence of Christ in the midst of those who are gathered in His name clearly indicates an essential element of corporate worship which is not in the same sense present in individual worship or devotion.

The Relationship of Theology and Worship

Before we proceed further in this subject, it is necessary for us to make clear the fact that, for the Christian, worship must always be under the judgment of theology. Neville Clark has correctly said that "what is believed will and must govern what is done in worship."[9] We must be constantly mindful of those suppositions which determine our theology and therefore our worship. The character of a man's worship is determined first by the character of the God in whom he

---

[9]Neville Clark, *Call to Worship* (London: SCM Press, 1960), p. 38.

believes, and second by his understanding of the way God has established a personal relationship with him. A third matter of considerable importance also is the individual's faith in the established means of communication between God and himself. If the first person of the Trinity is given first rank in the service in such a way that mere theism assumes a place of superiority over Christian revelation, there is grave danger of removing from Christian worship that which makes it Christian, the Lord Jesus Christ Himself. Similarly an unbalanced emphasis on one aspect of God's character or His work can render a service something less than Christian. If too much stress is laid on the sovereignty of God and the awesome character of His eternal decrees, it is easy to see how a worship service can feature almost exclusively the holy precepts of divine law and become overly didactic and purely intellectual. It is important that attention should be paid to God as Creator, but this emphasis should always accompany the truth of God as Savior.

The integrating reality of all true Christian worship is Jesus Christ. In our worship of Him we must not eliminate any of the essential elements of His being, His life, and His work—the deity, the incarnation, the sinless life, the atonement, the resurrection, the eschatological hope, and the sacraments which He has established for His church. The fact of the incarnation itself must always underlie our worship if we are to be faithful to the biblical revelation. Jesus Christ is indeed the Son of man, but He is just as truly the Son of God. There seems to be a tendency in the human mind to be overattracted to either the humanity or the deity of Jesus Christ. In the early history of the Christian church these attitudes appeared in the Docetic and Ebionite heresies. The Docetists maintained the deity of Jesus Christ at the expense of His humanity, and the Ebionite doctrine held firmly to His humanity at the cost of His deity. In the present day we do not have these heresies in the evangelical churches, but it is necessary to guard against an overemphasis on one or the other of the natures of Christ. In some evangelical churches the emphasis is so evidently on the divine nature of Christ that the worship service is focused almost exclusively upon the salvation provided by the death of the Son of God. There is little if any heed given to His work in creation, to the great ministries of mercy and kindness which characterized His earthly life and labors, and to the ethical and spiritual responsibilities that fall upon those who become His children through faith. Not long ago an attractive young married lady told me that she had been a member of an evangelical church all her life. She had never heard anything in the church except the simple gospel of salvation. Since she had received Jesus Christ as Savior and listened to essentially the same message every Sunday, she assumed that she had experienced all that there is in the Christian life. It is unfortunate that some churches never preach any biblical truth other than the gospel of salvation.

On the other hand, there are churches which have reacted so strongly against the otherworldly emphasis which they have observed among the more evangelistically inclined Christians that their worship services are characterized by the absence of the soteriological element and an almost exclusive concentration upon the humanitarian aspects of the Christian life. Believers are exhorted to follow Jesus as their example, but little is heard about the richness and fullness of their salvation in Him. We will perhaps never find the perfect theological blend of the elements of a Christian worship service, but as we are obedient to the Word of God we shall find that He leads us into a deeper and fuller understanding of His grace and a clearer participation with Him in the worship which we offer in His name.

Before leaving the subject of the worship of the Trinity, a word needs to be said concerning the place of the Holy Spirit in our worship services. If the Holy Spirit's true ministry in worship is not recognized, that which is called a service of worship may be little more than a jolly social gathering. Such gatherings offer an experience so subjective that there is little in it which makes the God of the Bible more real or which gives the worshiper a clearer understanding of the revealed will of God and a desire for a higher obedience to it. The ministry of the Holy Spirit is inseparably related to Jesus Christ; it is His ministry to take the things of Christ and show them to the believers. This means that He will be teaching all the thrilling doctrines which have to do with the person of Christ. His ministry is thus essential to the corporate worship of the people of God. It is He who in regeneration brings men to the new life that is in Christ Jesus. His abiding presence in the believer is the earnest of his inheritance. He is the divine seal which ratifies the salvation unto eternal life which every true Christian has received. It is He who binds the members of the body of Christ into one body, thus making possible for them the high privilege of common worship. He must certainly be honored in our services of worship for He is the One who makes us acceptable to God.

The Need for Instruction in Worship

I have mentioned several times the fact that the average worshiper in evangelical churches today needs to be instructed, not only in the meaning and importance of corporate worship but also in the means to be employed in making that worship fulfill our Lord's requirements. Christian education programs have been sadly deficient in this matter. There have been some misguided efforts to make worship more meaningful to small children through the construction of "worship centers" with pictures of Jesus, open Bibles on small "altars," and other accouterments designed to help them to communicate with God. All these not only border on idolatry but actually in many cases are a hindrance rather than a help. Children at a very early age can learn to communicate with God entirely apart from any material aids. My experience as a father of four children has proved this to me. A child will often understand spiritual communion better than will an adult who has never attempted to communicate with God. The great need is for the church to provide education for both young and older people as well as the children. All members of the Christian household need to know the meaning and methods of acceptable Christian worship.

If the average worshiper were able to record accurately the

exact number of minutes out of an hour-long worship service in which he was actually worshiping God, the number would be surprisingly small. It is so easy for one's mind to be diverted from thoughts of worship. If many Christians were as unsuccessful in their witnessing as they are in their worshiping, they would be alarmed. All too many believers take a very casual attitude toward their attendance at the services of corporate worship. They are accustomed to the idea that much of the hour spent in the Sunday morning service is comparatively meaningless.

There is a sense in which worship can be considered hard work, for to worship intelligently and continually through a service of even an hour's length requires careful concentration. It is easy to daydream during parts of a service, especially if one sees no particular significance in what is transpiring. The thoughts and cares of the world press in upon all of us to such an extent that to sit quietly in a congregation of worshipers and keep from thinking about the activities of the past week or the plans for the future is very difficult.

Another problem presents itself to worshipers, a problem of which many are ignorant. This is the fact that it is possible for a person to think that he is worshiping God when actually he is not engaged in worship at all. To understand what is meant and how this is possible we must first consider the truth that there are several ways by which meaning can be conveyed in a worship service. What is conveyed is all-important; unfortunately, what is intended to be conveyed may be interfered with by the means of conveyance. Professor Hoon calls the means of conveyance "the language of worship," and indicates that this term denotes "all objects and actions in space and time employed [in worship] by man's physical senses and faculties of personality to express or apprehend meaning, including oral, visual, tactile, kinesthetic, and even olfactory and gustatory media as well as mental concepts and images."[10] He points out that while

---

[10]Hoon, *Integrity of Worship,* p. 215.

ministers may suppose that they have worked hard on their sermon, making sure their grammar was correct and taking pains to practice their delivery and to see that the acoustics were good, this is not all that is involved.

> Silence also is language. The shape of a chandelier is language . . . the symbols on the communion table—a cross, an open Bible, a picture, flowers, the form of bread used—whether thin disc, white cubes or brown crust—are language. Sitting and standing, the tempo in which the service is conducted, the deportment of the choir, the carpeting on the floor, the vestments of the clergy, the location of the font, the illumination of the windows—all these are language. Especially the order of service (even the style of type in which it is printed) is a powerful form of language. . . . In short, all the media of worship are pregnant with meaning to a greater or lesser degree, even if the meaning is a corruption of authentic meaning.[11]

This makes it easier for us to understand how men may deceive themselves or may be deceived by others into thinking that they are worshiping when they are not. Let us consider some of the ways in which this comes about.

First, it is easy to confuse an emotional reaction to certain stimuli with an act of worship. That in worship there is an emotional content to the believer's response to the love of God certainly cannot be denied. However, it is possible to be deeply stirred emotionally and still be without any worshipful response to God. A minister may tell a story so moving that half of his congregation are in tears, yet none of the tears have anything to do with God, His person, or His work.

Second, one can unconsciously confuse a purely aesthetic response to something beautiful with an expression of worship. That it is easier to worship God in a building properly designed for worship all will agree, but one can admire the beauty of a Gothic cathedral and remain unmoved spiritually. If the beauty of the building alone moves one sitting in a church, the response is not one of worship. Aesthetic responses are often quite emotional without being spiritual. Great care must be exercised in the use of the beautiful in a

---

[11]Ibid., pp. 215-16.

worship service to guard against stimulating merely an emotional response. Handel's "Hallelujah Chorus," from the great oratorio *Messiah,* can be sung by a chorus of unbelievers, accompanied by a great symphony orchestra, with such musical perfection that it sends a spine-tingling thrill through a vast audience, but there may be no worship of God in the hearts of most of the listeners. It is unfortunate that as a rule the liberal churches of our land are much more careful about the quality of the music that is performed in their services than are the evangelical churches. There are outstanding exceptions, of course. One large church with which I am very familiar, having served as its pastor some years ago, has a volunteer choir composed entirely of devout believers whose frequent renditions of Bach's cantatas, as well as extremely difficult anthems, would meet the most exacting standards of musical critics. On the other hand, the music performed at many evangelical churches which I have attended throughout the country would have to be classified as mediocre to poor in quality. I would insist, however, that a beautiful anthem beautifully rendered by a well-trained choir does not necessarily produce a worshipful response. Only if both the choir members and the worshipers who make up the audience participate in authentic praise to God as the music is offered is the anthem a real contribution to meaningful worship.

What has been said about music could also be said about other beautiful elements which may be introduced into the worship of God. Stained glass windows can be very beautiful. I myself have been moved by the world-famous windows of the Chartres Cathedral, but felt little constraint to worship God in that beautiful building not only because of my knowledge of the history of its construction, but also because of the evident bowing down before idols which was going on around me while I was enjoying the beauty of the windows and the architecture. Stained glass windows and Gothic arches may be beautiful to an awe-inspiring degree, but the worshiper must guard his response to them if he is participating in a worship service.

I have no personal objections to services of worship by

candlelight. My wife and I usually eat our dinner in the evening by candlelight. There is something soft and beautiful about it. However, candlelight does not of itself produce a spiritual response in the heart of man. Burning candles are far from essential to meaningful worship.

A third matter of importance has to do with man's great tendency to substitute activity which is purely of the flesh for that which is spiritual. The movements of our bodies do have a definite relationship to the attitudes of our minds and hearts, but it is quite possible to confuse a physical performance with a spiritual act of worship. Later in this book I shall strongly recommend the posture of kneeling in public prayer in the churches. However, it must be clearly understood that the physical act of kneeling in a church certainly does not of itself denote true worship. The raising of the hands above one's head does not necessarily indicate a sincere lifting of the heart in the worship of God, although it may be helpful to some in giving a more complete expression of their thanksgiving to God.

This brings me to a final difficulty which is to be faced in keeping the worship of the churches pure. It seems very easy for many believers to confuse being entertained with worshiping their almighty God and Savior. There is a vast amount of what might be called pure entertainment being offered in the services of churches whose pastors and people would be classified as soundly evangelical. Not long ago in a morning service I listened to a group of attractive young singers whose voices blended admirably and who were undoubtedly splendid Christians. Their music, however, was presented in a very theatrical way. When the young men sang of their love for Jesus, each young woman turned to gaze with almost adoring eyes upon the young man nearest to her, as though he were singing a tender love song especially for her. It was impossible for me to watch this performance and offer worship to God while the music was being sung. The music was sentimental and entertaining, but it did nothing to stir the hearts of the listener beyond sheer pleasure in the appeal of the young singers. To have exclaimed to them following the service, "I really enjoyed your music," would have been possible. To have said that they enabled me to worship God meaningfully as they sang would have been impossible. Christian entertainment may have its place in certain gatherings. It does not belong in a service of worship.

In concluding this discussion we must be reminded of the fact that false worship is not acceptable worship. No matter what our gatherings may be called at the heading of the church bulletin, if they are to be corporate worship services special care must be taken to insure that those who gather have every encouragement to make the most of the opportunity for fulfilling God's command to worship. Our Lord has said, "They that worship him *must* worship in spirit and in truth." There may be times when God accepts our good intentions in place of the deeds we did not do, but in worship we have no such case. God is truth; He has revealed Himself and His will to us clearly in the Scriptures. We must be very careful to worship Him in an acceptable manner.

The purpose of this book is practical. We have pointed out that the corporate worship of God is of supreme importance because it is the principal means by which God is glorified in His church. We have further observed that while it is the individual's only indispensable activity it is also that which gives fullest expression to the communion of the saints. In it the believer is united with the worshiping saints in heaven where he will someday continue forever his own worship of the eternal God, Creator and Redeemer. This book is written that the author might challenge the thinking of sincere Christians today so that they will bring their own worship practices under close scrutiny. It is also intended as an encouragement to pastors to be more diligent in teaching the principles of worship to their congregations and in leading their own services of worship in an enlightened way. In later chapters the order of worship as well as each of the component parts of a worship service will be discussed. Before taking up these practical matters, however, the reader should take a brief look at some of the most salient features of the worship of God as they are revealed to us in the Bible. The next two chapters will give consideration to some of the most significant features of worship in the Old Testament and in the New Testament.

2

Corporate Worship
in the Old Testament

If we are to understand more fully the attitudes and activities which are to be included in our corporate worship of God, it is important for us to learn all we can from the origins and development of worship as these are revealed to us in the Bible. The Scriptures are full of teaching on worship because it is of great import to the living God who gave us the Scriptures. The present study can by no means be exhaustive. It is the author's hope that what is pointed out will serve to stimulate believers to a deeper study of the subject so that their own worship will more fully express the praise of the eternal God. We will begin our examination where God begins His written revelation—at creation.

God created man in His own image, and in doing so He gave man the capacity to communicate with and to worship his Creator. God had made abundant provisions for man. These included his having dominion over all the living creatures of the earth as well as his having the unspoiled Garden of Eden in which to dwell. Such privileges gave to man much cause for offering praise and thanksgiving. The greatest of all his blessings, however, was the favor of continual personal fellowship with his divine Creator, who had made everything good for him to enjoy. Although the Scriptures do not specifically say so, worship of God must certainly have begun in the Garden of Eden before the fall as Adam and Eve enjoyed unbroken communion with their Creator God. They had the privilege of face-to-face encounter with their Maker. This is evident from the fact that after they had sinned they "hid themselves from the presence of the Lord God" (Gen. 3:8). God's very approach to them after the fall, not running hastily as one who is driven by anger, but walking in some visible form, and calling to them with a voice of tender concern, certainly indicates God's desire for the fellowship and worship of His children. The Book of Genesis gives us only momentary glimpses into the worship practices of the Lord's people and does not tell us how God gave them the directions for their worship. It was only after the exodus that God gave specific instructions concerning worship which were recorded in Scriptures. There are, however, some interesting and significant brief opportunities to observe the worship of God's people in Genesis, beginning in the Garden of Eden.

With the setting apart of the Sabbath day as blessed and sanctified, God established the first specific ordinance of worship. This happened immediately following the creation of man while he was still in a state of innocence. However, after the fall and the expulsion of sinful man from the garden, the record includes a definite suggestion of continuing worship on the Sabbath. The statement that "in the course [or process] of time" (Gen. 4:3), which is literally "in the end of days," Cain brought his offering would seem to indicate the end of the week or the Sabbath day.

The Sabbath later became the sign of Israel's special covenant relation to the Lord (Exod. 31:13). Its observance marked Israel as God's peculiar people and served as a reminder of the rest into which God desired to bring them. Because of unbelief the generation of Israelites that departed from Egypt with Moses perished in the wilderness. Joshua led the nation into Canaan, but we learn from Hebrews 4 that the rest which God has for His people was not realized with the conquest of Canaan, but was in its fullest sense to be realized only through the person and work of Christ. How wonderful it would be if the people of God in this our day could be identified as God's own covenant people by their faithful keeping of the Sabbath.

The Beginning of Sacrifice

It is also in Genesis 4:3 that we read of the beginning of sacrifice in worship. Some, of course, will insist that God introduced the principle of sacrifice when He made garments of skin for Adam and Eve and clothed them. Whether this be true or not, it is clear that from this time forward the element of sacrifice was predominant in all the worship of the Old Testament. In the light of the full biblical revelation, we know that every sacrifice pointed forward to the one perfect and final sacrifice which would be made by the Son of God Himself.

How much the early generations of man understood concerning the prophetic and typical aspects of their sacrifices we do not know. The Old Testament Scriptures give us little detailed information about the content of the faith of the godly seed in pre-Abrahamic days. We do know that God had revealed to Adam the promise of the coming Redeemer and His triumph over Satan, although even this great announcement was veiled in symbolic language (Gen. 3:15). It was through the medium of sacrifice that God chose to provide for man not only a visible means of worship but also a means of comprehending at least in part those deep theological truths concerning the awful gulf which separates man in his sin from a holy God. Through blood sacrifices was also set forth the fact, later to be fully revealed, that "without shedding of blood there is no forgiveness" (Heb. 9:22, NASB). Animal sacrifice is today completely outside our experience and practice, but we must not forget that in the wisdom of God it was given a dominant place in the worship of the Old Testament because of the central fact of salvation history to which every sacrifice pointed, God's offering of His own Son as a sufficient sacrifice for the sins of man. We shall have more to say about the place of sacrifice in contemporary Christian worship. At this point it is sufficient to point out that it occupied a predominant place in the worship of the children of God from the earliest time until the death of Christ.

A proper place of worship is suggested in the fact that Cain *"brought* an offering to the Lord of the fruit of the ground. And Abel, on his part also *brought* of the firstlings of his flock" (Gen. 4:3, 4, NASB). That they brought an offering implies that there was a specific place of worship designated as a place of sacrifice. A further indication of a designated place of worship is given in the statement that "Cain went out from the presence of the Lord" (Gen. 4:16).

God had given the sons of Adam specific instructions about their worship. He has never been pleased when men have sought to worship Him in their own ways according to their own purposes and pleasure. That He had provided guidance for Cain and Abel as to the substance of their offerings, and perhaps as to the place of their sacrifice, is evident from the statement in Hebrews 11:4 that Abel's offering was "by faith" and was a more acceptable or better sacrifice than Cain's. The fact that it was offered by faith means that it was offered according to the revealed Word of God, for the Scriptures tell us that "faith cometh by hearing, and hearing by the word of God" (Rom. 10:17). In all probability the children of Adam received the instruction of the Lord's Word from their parents, Adam and Eve. Without God's instruction Abel's offering could not have been offered "by faith." Cain's willful disobedience in bringing a sacrifice of his own choosing demonstrates from the very earliest days the attitude of the rebellious heart of the natural man who feels that God should accept whatever a man chooses to bring to Him. Certainly no one can doubt that multitudes of men today are offering to God whatever they are pleased to bring Him without giving consideration to the express commandments of His Word.

In Genesis 4:26 we read a statement which probably indicates the inauguration of public worship. Apparently before this time the common worship of the people of God had been largely confined to families. Here, however, we read that "men began to invoke [call upon] the name of the Lord." There is some division of opinion as to the exact meaning of this verse, but if our reading is correct it is apparent that the godly seed of Adam began to gather for worship, praising the name of the Lord and offering their prayers in that name. Their worship of God caused them to be identified with the name of their God by all of the ungodly civilization around them. What a striking contrast there is between the worship of the godly seed, calling upon the name of the Lord, and the attitude of the wicked men in the land of Shinar who said, "Come, let us build for ourselves a city, and a tower whose top will reach into heaven, and let us *make for ourselves a name;* lest we be scattered abroad over the face of the whole earth" (Gen. 11:4, NASB).

Worship After the Deluge

When Noah and his family went out of the ark after the flood, we read (Gen. 8:20) that he built an altar to the Lord as a special act of worship and gratitude for the salvation of himself and his family. In connection with this act of worship we find a distinct enlargement of the sacrificial rite. This is the first mention of the building of an altar. Cain and Abel may simply have placed their offerings on a designated rock or high piece of ground. There is no mention of their offerings being burned. For generations their practice may have been followed. Noah, however, built his high place or altar. In this incident also we have the first mention in the Bible of a burnt offering. It is significant that Noah's burnt offering was made only of the "clean" animals which he had taken into the ark. There was in this act an apparent recognition of the fact that God can accept from man only that which is clean and pure. The psalmist would cry out many years later, "Who shall ascend into the hill of the Lord? or who shall stand in his holy place? He that hath clean hands and a pure heart" (Ps. 24:3, 4). We need to remember this warning of the psalmist in our own day and not attempt to offer worship to God when our hearts are full of unconfessed sin.

Returning to Noah, let us note that the patriarch served as priest for his entire redeemed family. This is the initial appearance of the priestly function in the Scriptures. It is indeed a beautiful thing that the patriarch's first concern after leaving the ark was to worship the God who had given to him and to his family such an unusual experience of His goodness and mercy. Arising out of Noah's acceptable sacrifice came a special renewal of God's covenant of redemption with a new and specific revelation of His eternal purpose (Gen. 8:21—9:17). Recognizing the basic depravity of man, God promised to spare the world from another destructive flood so that multitudes could enjoy the blessings of His grace through the coming Redeemer. What a fitting climax this was to the worship of the redeemed patriarch and his family! Every time we look upon a rainbow in the sky we should pause and worship God, thanking Him for His eternal covenant and His grace that gave it to us.

The Worship of the Hebrews Before the Exodus

In the lives of Abraham, Isaac, and Jacob, we are enabled to see something of the worship of the Hebrews before the exodus. Abraham's worship began in response to God's appearance to him and the revelation of His will with respect to Abraham's life (Gen. 12:7). Abraham has been properly identified as the man of the tent and the altar. The tent would seem to indicate the pilgrim character of his life on earth, for we are told in the Book of Hebrews that he "looked for a city which hath foundations, whose builder and maker is God" (11:10). Wherever he pitched his tent he built an altar in order that he might express his faith through worship (note Gen. 12:8; 13:17, 18; 26:25). The theological character of his worship is noteworthy. It is described as calling upon the name of the Lord (Gen. 12:8). This involves much more than may be commonly understood by such an expression. To Abraham were revealed several different names of the Lord: El-Elyon, God Most High (Gen. 14:18, 19); El-Shaddai, God Almighty (Gen. 17:1); Jehovah-El-Olam, God Everlasting (Gen. 21:33); and Jehovah-jireh, the Lord Who Provides (Gen. 22:14). These names, in addition to his understanding of the basic names Elohim and Jehovah, gave him insight into the character of God. Thus, to call upon the name of the Lord meant recognizing and believing all that is indicated in all of the various names of the Lord and worshiping Him for all the aspects of His character which these names revealed, because all are included in the one designation, the name of the Lord. Worshiping congregations in our day need a greater understanding of the significance of the name of the Lord, and what it means to pray in that name.

Of special significance in the development of Hebrew worship was God's appearance to Abraham when he was ninety-nine years old in order that He might reaffirm His covenant with Abraham and his seed. It was at this time that He established the ordinance of circumcision as a sign of the covenant, a seal of the righteousness of faith (Rom. 4:11) and the distinguishing mark of the covenant household (v. 12). This sign was to symbolize the casting off of the flesh and thus the entrance into the spiritual life of God's own children. The male who was not circumcised was to be cut off from among the people of God. Thus the uncircumcised were to be no part of the worshiping community. Throughout the history of the children of Israel they were reminded of the spiritual significance of the ordinance of circumcision and exhorted to circumcise the foreskins of their heart (Deut. 10:16). I have written elsewhere of my convictions concerning the significance of the covenant sign in our day.[1] The reader who is in-

---

[1] R. G. Rayburn, *What About Baptism?* (St. Louis: Covenant College Press, 1957).

terested can examine that argument. I shall not repeat it here.

It is also of special interest that in the scriptural record of the life of Abraham we have the first instance of tithing. This took place when Abraham encountered Melchizedek, king of Salem and priest of God Most High (Gen. 14:18-20). Abraham recognized that Melchizedek, who had come out to bless the victorious patriarch, was a priest and thus an official mediator between God and him. As a token of his gratitude for God's deliverance he gave to this great priest a tithe of the spoil taken from his enemies. It is not possible to know for sure whether Abraham had received specific instruction concerning the principle of the tithe although it seems most probable. The fact that his grandson, Jacob, after his awesome experience at Bethel made a vow to the Lord which included the giving of the tithe (Gen. 28:22) would certainly indicate that in some way God had revealed the fact that one-tenth of the income of His children belonged to Him, and that the bringing of the tithe to God was a fitting act of worship. It is a concrete means of recognizing and proclaiming that all that the believer possesses comes from the gracious hand of God. Moses made it clear in his day that "the tithe . . . is the Lord's; it is holy unto the Lord" (Lev. 27:30). Today multitudes of believers ignore the law of the tithe as though it were part of the ceremonial law done away with in Christ. However, it antedates the ceremonial law by many generations. It was mentioned by Jesus Himself (Matt. 23:23; Luke 11:42). The apostle Paul instructed believers that their principle in giving should be "that there may be equality" (II Cor. 8:14); this could only be by the tithe. The pastor's call during the service for believers to worship God "with tithes and offerings" should not be regarded as mere words. God honors faithful tithing.

We cannot leave this brief consideration of the worship of the Hebrews prior to the exodus without reference to the vision which Jacob saw at Bethel. He saw "a ladder [which] was set upon the earth with its top reaching to heaven; and behold, the angels of God were ascending and descending on it" (Gen. 28:12, NASB). When Jacob awoke, his response to this vision which he had seen as well as to the promise which God had given him was, "Surely the Lord is in this place, and I did not know it" (Gen. 28:16, NASB). In this response is indicated a very basic truth. The foundation of all true Christian worship is always the presence of God with His people. Many years after Jacob's day, when the incarnate Son of God was here on earth, He said to one of His disciples, "Truly, truly, I say to you, you shall see the heavens opened, and the angels of God ascending and descending upon the Son of Man" (John 1:51, NASB). In this very obvious reference to Jacob's vision of the ladder Jesus Christ introduced to Nathanael (and to all subsequent believers) the all-important fact that He is Himself the presence of God with His people. He is the Ladder by whom God communicates to man and through whom man communicates with God. It is only in the presence of Christ, who has promised His presence where even two or three are gathered in His name, that true Christian corporate worship takes place. As William Nicholls has pointed out, "Christ is the essence of worship, and our understanding of the Church's worship must take its starting point from Him. In Him is embodied the downward movement of God's love and grace, as He reveals Himself to man, and reconciles man to Himself; and also the upward movement of man's response, perfectly dependent upon that love, and drawing from it all the resources of strength which are needed to make that response in all circumstances of life, and even in death itself."[2]

Worship in the Mosaic Period

The decisive event in the history of Israel, which determined not only Israel's faith and practice, but also her worship, was the exodus from Egypt.[3] It was in this event that

[2]William Nicholls, *Jacob's Ladder: The Meaning of Worship* (Richmond: John Knox Press, 1958), p. 26.

[3]A. S. Herbert, *Worship in Ancient Israel* (Richmond: John Knox Press, 1959), p. 7.

God gave to His people an understanding of what it means to be redeemed. In introducing the Ten Commandments, the moral law for His people, God said, "I am the Lord your God, who brought you out of the land of Egypt, out of the house of slavery" (Exod. 20:2, NASB). That which has always distinguished both Hebrew and Christian worship from the worship of any other religions in the world is the fact that the worship of God's people has always been the worship of those who have been redeemed. This means that true biblical religion always begins with what God has done and not with what He requires of men or what men decide to bring to Him. As we have seen, the evidences of corporate worship in the Book of Genesis are at best only fragmentary. However, with the exodus the Lord undertook a new beginning with His people, revealing Himself more fully, not only in His works but also in His words through Moses His selected vessel. Having heard the cry of His chosen people, weak and suffering in their slavery because of their sin, He saved them from their bondage in Egypt and bound them to Him in the covenant. Through this experience it became clear that the God of Israel was first of all their Savior-God. He had taken the initiative in their redemption. Their worship was essentially a response of gratitude to Him. He had taken the initiative in the establishment of the covenant also and it was clear that true worship could take place only within the covenant. As we have already pointed out, the uncircumcised were not to be considered any part of the worshiping community.

The objective fact of the nation's redemption was to be observed annually in the ceremonial worship of the Passover celebration. Because God chose to reveal Himself and His character in a progressive manner, He established external ceremonial acts of worship in order that they might discharge a pedagogical function as well as be a means of the expression of gratitude and praise (Deut. 6:20-25). We shall have more to say concerning the teaching value of the ceremonies and especially the sacrifices when we consider the tabernacle and the offerings.

Worship and the Attributes of God

It was God's purpose that His people on earth should reflect His own character, that they should be a holy people, "a holy nation" (Exod. 19:6). When Moses heard the voice of God from the burning bush he was told that the place on which he was standing was holy ground. That which made it holy, of course, was the presence of the holy God. The Old Testament frequently speaks of God as "the Holy One of Israel" (see II Kings 19:22; Ps. 71:22; Isa. 1:4; 30:12; Jer. 50:29; Ezek. 39:7, etc.). He is represented often as being in the midst of His people (Exod. 33:5; Isa. 12:6; Hos. 11:9). The language of Israel's worship makes it clear that the devout Israelite thought of God as being locally present. That which the believing Hebrew dreaded the most was the prospect that God might depart from him (Ps. 89:38ff.; Ezek. 8-11). Without the Lord's presence there was no sense of security. As the children of Israel moved from the land of Egypt across the Red Sea and into the wilderness the presence of the Lord with them was manifest in the pillar of cloud by day and the pillar of fire by night (Exod. 13:22). The realization of the very presence of God with them was at once both awesome and comforting. It was also productive of a consciousness of sin and a desire for holy living. God said to them, "Ye shall be holy: for I the Lord your God am holy" (Lev. 19:2). These words are no less significant for God's people today.

While holiness is undoubtedly the most significant aspect of the character of God, if we are to fully understand the worship of Israel we must recognize that there are other attributes of God's character which had an effect on the kind of worship which was offered to Him. While it might be insisted that most of the other attributes are all encompassed in the one word, holiness, we nevertheless should consider them individually because the quality of any man's worship depends upon and is conditioned by the object of his worship. And each of the divine attributes adds to our understanding of the character of God. The psalmist in speaking of the heathen who make idols with eyes that do not see and ears that do not hear added the fact that "those who make them will become like them, everyone who trusts in them" (Ps. 115:8, NASB). In like manner those who trust in God and truly worship Him will become like Him.

The excellencies of His character are too numerous for a detailed discussion of each one of them here. We must mention, however, such significant attributes as His righteousness and His justice as well as His grace, mercy, and lovingkindness. The Hebrew words which are rendered by these terms in our modern English versions are actually very difficult to translate adequately, for each one has more than moral and ethical significance. These words include the purpose of God as He works out His own will in the world and in the lives of His own people (see Exod. 34:6, 7). The Hebrew word *hesed,* for example, is variously translated in modern versions as "lovingkindness," "mercy," "constant love," but none of these is adequate to convey the full meaning of the word, which includes the idea of God's graciousness toward a rebellious people. We must not forget that from the first the factor which determined the way that Israel worshiped was the character of the One who was the object of her worship. Understanding of the true character of God is sorely needed in the church today. Unfortunately in many churches there has been such a distorted presentation of the love of God that scores of people have been led to feel that God is indulgent with respect to sin and indifferent with respect to justice. An understanding of God as He truly is, the sovereign Lord of heaven and earth, inflexible in His holiness, righteous in all His ways, unwilling to countenance sin, even in His own children, but gracious beyond all human capacity because of the eternal sacrifice of His Son, would be reflected in the worship of His name and would thus certainly bring glory to His person.

The Tabernacle and the Sacrificial System

With Moses and the establishment of detailed external worship ordinances, God began in a special way to teach His children permanently abiding spiritual principles. Through the elaborate sacrificial system and even through the construction of the tabernacle in the wilderness, He taught them the importance of the coming Redeemer who would fully and forever satisfy the demands of perfect righteousness. By bearing in His own body the sins of men He would provide them forgiveness and eternal salvation. Through these ordinances it was possible for the devout Israelite not only to learn of God but also to express the deep devotion of his heart in acceptable worship.

As God took the initiative in calling Abraham out from the land of Ur and establishing the covenant with him and his seed forever, so He took the initiative in the confirmation of the covenant with the children of Israel at Sinai and the giving of the detailed instructions for the building of the tabernacle. He called Moses to come up to the mountain to worship and to receive His instruction for the tabernacle construction. Before Moses went up, however, he arranged for burnt offerings and peace offerings and took half of the blood of these offerings to sprinkle upon the altar. He then took the book of the covenant and read from it to the congregation, after which he sprinkled blood on the people. They affirmed their willingness to be fully obedient to the Lord. Moses responded, "Behold the blood of the covenant, which the Lord hath made with you" (Exod. 24:8). The sprinkled blood was not only the seal of the covenant but also a means of giving them impressive instruction concerning the fact that the covenant was made with them only through the shedding and sprinkling of blood and that thus God's acceptance of them was only by virtue of an atoning sacrifice. All of God's blessings under the covenant were secured only through His grace.

Today we make no blood sacrifices nor do we sprinkle any blood in our worship services. The very idea of it might seem to be somewhat revolting. Our Savior has come and has offered His blood for sinners once and for all. We must never allow ourselves to forget as we worship the living God that our salvation depends fully upon the shed blood of the Lord

Jesus Christ. As the apostle Peter put it, "You were not redeemed with perishable things like silver or gold from your
futile way of life inherited from your forefathers, but with
precious blood, as of a lamb unblemished and spotless, the
blood of Christ" (I Peter 1:18, 19, NASB). With such a price
having been paid, our worship should always be offered with
the consciousness of the redeeming blood and with gratitude
for its powerful efficacy. Our services should never be without explicit and meaningful reminders of the eternal sacrifice
of Christ.

Whatever other business occupied Moses on the mount
and whatever other disclosures were made to him during his
forty days there, that which chiefly occupied him was the receiving of directions concerning the tabernacle. Again it
must be noted that it was God who took the initiative in the
building of this house of worship. "Let them make me a
sanctuary; that I may dwell among them, according to all
that I show thee, after the pattern of the tabernacle" (Exod.
25:8, 9). Again and again we are reminded in the Scriptures
that our worship and service of God are simply a response to
His grace and goodness. How careful we should be to make
the proper response.

It is worthy of notice also that the sanctuary which was to
be built was to be constructed of materials which were the
voluntary offerings of people whose hearts were devoted to
the Lord (Exod. 25:2). The almighty God was pleased to
dwell among His people in a boarded and curtained tent if it
was erected for Him by those who cherished a desire to enjoy
and perpetuate His presence among them.

The tabernacle itself may be studied from several different
viewpoints. (1) It is occasionally referred to in Scripture as a
type of temporary abode. It was just this for the children of
Israel in the desert as they journeyed to Canaan, and thus it
is a fitting figure of the pilgrimage of the saints of God as
they pass through the earth on their way to their heavenly
home. (2) In a particular sense it prefigured the human body
of the Lord Jesus Christ during His sojourn upon earth (see
John 1:14, where the word *dwelt* in the KJV is properly ren-

dered "tabernacled"), and it is also a figure of the frail body of every believer in his earthly pilgrimage (II Peter 1:13, 14). (3) It is clearly "a pattern of things in the heavens" (Heb. 9:21-23).

The scope of this present work does not permit a detailed study of the tabernacle. A number of very competent scholars have produced comprehensive analyses of this structure and all its parts. Unfortunately there have also been many Bible teachers who have given rein to fertile fancies as they examined the symbolism of the tabernacle and have produced extravagant and improper views of the significance of its parts. The only safe guide to the interpretation of the symbolism of this remarkable structure is direct scriptural warrant. This includes both the explicit statements of the Old and New Testaments and also the inferences which naturally grow out of them.

We are concerned here specifically with the lessons that may be learned from this structure concerning the worship of God. It was erected according to God's own directions for the worship of His name in the wilderness. Perhaps the first thing that should be mentioned is the principle of proper proportion with which God guided the construction of the tabernacle. This principle shows up in the proportion which appears in the plan of the structure even to its smallest parts. For example, in the tabernacle all of the basic architectural dimensions were in multiples of ten, the simplest, earliest, and most scientific number system. (Even today the decimal system supersedes all others.) The practical lesson seems to be that the entire structure with all the details of its construction and furnishings was to be a lesson for the people of God in the importance of order, which is "heaven's first law." The economy and regularity as well as the convenience of the entire edifice were apparently designed to instruct the chosen people that their God, the Creator, Preserver, and Judge of the entire universe, was honored by proper and harmonious arrangement of all their lives, and especially by their worship of Him.

Without doubt the colors found in the tabernacle are of

consequence, as are also the various materials used in construction as well as the forms or shapes of the objects in and around the tabernacle, but a detailed examination of these is beyond the scope of our present study. Of course, some features such as the arrangement of the drapery, the embellishments of the candelabrum, the jewels, and the decoration of the priestly robes were mainly ornamental. In this connection it has been well said that "the aesthetic is never neglected by the divine Architect, nor was it sacrificed to utility in the somewhat severe style of the Tabernacle any more than it is in nature where birds and flowers and graceful forms mingle in delightful harmony with the athletic forces and the rugged aspects of earnest existence. True science and chaste art are the legitimate twin offspring of genuine piety."[4]

Consideration must now be given to the principal articles of furniture in the tabernacle, for it is especially from them and their arrangement that we learn much about God's provision of the proper means of approach to Him on the part of His people. It should be noted that in giving Moses instruction for the building of the tabernacle (Exod. 25-27) God began with a description of the ark of the covenant including the mercy seat with its spread-winged cherubims on the two ends. He then proceeded to instructions for the table of showbread, the golden candlestick, the curtains, and the veil. The last major article of the furnishings to be described initially was the brazen altar of burnt offering, which was to sit in the court outside the tabernacle proper.

It is no accident that in these first directions given to Moses the Holy Spirit omitted the description of the altar of incense in the Holy Place as well as the laver in the courtyard. The altar of incense was included in the second listing of the furnishings (Exod. 35:15) and was mentioned in all subsequent detailed accounts of the tabernacle appointments. The explanation of this would seem to be that God

---

[4]James Strong, *The Tabernacle of Israel* (Grand Rapids: Baker Book House, 1952), pp. 90-91.

purposed first to describe the way in which He would manifest Himself to man, and after that the mode of man's approach to Him. Man in his sinfulness would not dare to approach God, but God could approach man and meet him as a repentant sinner. Justice and judgment could only condemn the sinner, but mercy and truth, which were equally part of the character of God, could bring Him to show grace and provide salvation for sinners. God must first be seen as the Lord of heaven and earth seated upon the throne of His glory. This was represented by the ark of the covenant. The Shekinah which hovered over the mercy seat was intended merely to mark the divine presence in some physical and visible manner. The entire tabernacle and its precincts clearly displayed for the children of Israel the residence of Jehovah their God in the style of an oriental king. The successive screens of the tent of meeting kept out all unqualified visitors, and the furnishings with their glittering gold spoke clearly of the royal character of the King who was in residence among His people. We shall see in succeeding chapters that the presence of Jesus Christ our King in the midst of His people today is the prime consideration of the believer in appraising experiences of corporate worship.

The ark of the covenant occupied the most significant position in the tabernacle. It was Jehovah's throne of judgment and justice (Ps. 89:14). It spoke to the children of Israel of God's gracious covenant with them and of His purpose to have a sanctuary or dwelling place among them. The word "ark" in Hebrew is a different word when used for the ark of the covenant from the word used for Noah's ark and the ark in which the infant Moses was placed. The idea behind the words, however, is very similar. An ark preserved Noah and his family together with all orders of animals as they passed through the waters of judgment in the great flood. An ark later preserved the infant Moses from the wrath of Pharaoh. The ark of the covenant (Num. 10:33) was to show that God would preserve His covenant even in the midst of a sinful and rebellious people. God could never break His covenant. That covenant abides today and it should be featured in our worship of God.

Within the ark the second tables of God's holy law were deposited. The first tables had been broken into pieces by Moses when he came down from Sinai and found the people dancing in idolatry. This breaking of the tables demonstrated the failure of sinful man to attain unto the righteousness demanded by a holy God. Man's best efforts would fail, but God could never break His covenant. His moral law must be preserved in all of its divine perfection. Even as he dwelt among His people He would establish His throne and govern His nation according to the perfect standards of His own righteousness as they were set forth in the Ten Commandments. He could never violate that standard to the slightest degree. The position of the tables of stone underneath the mercy seat, however, shows us that while God's law is inviolable it is not a ground of salvation for fallen man who has already broken the law and can never keep it unaided by the Holy Spirit. The sinner's only hope is found in the blood-stained mercy seat. The typical character of the stone tablets as they relate to life in the church today and to the individual believer who seeks to worship God is beautifully set forth in both the Old Testament (e.g., Prov. 3:3; 7:3; Jer. 17:1; 31:33) and the New Testament (e.g., II Cor. 3:3, 7; Heb. 8:10; 10:16). The moral law must ever be present in the consciousness of the worshiping congregation.

The table of showbread in the Holy Place next to the Holy of Holies speaks to us of God's manifestation of Himself to man in Christ as the Bread of Life. Showbread literally means "presence bread" because the twelve loaves pointed symbolically to Christ the never-failing source of spiritual sustenance and refreshment for His people. He is the One who is verily the food and drink of His people, supplying them all needed nourishment for spiritual life and growth. They must first understand that God has made this provision for them before they will ever be able to appropriate it properly in their worship. Of course, it is the Holy Spirit who takes the things of God and shows them to believers as they worship. The light and power of the Holy Spirit are clearly manifest in the golden candlestick which is found near the table of showbread in the Holy Place.

It is in the large court outside the tabernacle proper that we come upon those furnishings which set forth the method by which sinful man approaches a perfectly holy God. We note that there was only one door of access to this courtyard, even as there is only one Door by which men may find their way into the saving presence of God (John 10:9). The inner part of the large court of the tabernacle was accessible only to the priests and Levites, for they were the God-appointed mediators between Jehovah and His people. The repentant sinner could bring his sacrifical offering to the brazen altar, but that was as far as he could go. The priests took over as soon as the animal was killed.

When God delivered His people out of the bondage of Egypt and brought them "on eagles' wings" unto Himself at Mount Sinai, He renewed the covenant that He had made with their fathers and called the nation to be a separated people. They were to be peculiarly "a kingdom of priests" (Exod. 19:6). This meant that the whole nation would consist of nothing but priests. Every Israelite was to possess and exercise the duties and the privileges of the priesthood. It was almost immediately apparent, however, that the people of Israel were in no condition to enter into this priestly vocation. The function of priests is to draw near unto the Lord and to hold immediate and personal intercourse with Him (Num. 16:5). But, when the Lord descended at Sinai and proclaimed with thunder and lightning from the smoking mountain the ten great words of His covenant law, the people hurried away in terror. They cried to Moses, "Speak thou with us, and we will hear: but let not God speak with us lest we die" (Exod. 20:19). These are the words by which they renounced the high privileges of the priesthood. Their consciousness of sin made them sure that it was not safe for them to enter upon the privileges which the priesthood gave them. They needed a mediator. Initially Moses became their mediator. Later, his brother, Aaron, was called to that office and God set apart his family as a permanent priesthood for the nation.

Today the Aaronic priesthood no longer exists, for the Lord Jesus Christ has become the mediator of the new covenant which was established in His blood. Jesus Christ is our

great High Priest "who is set on the right hand of the throne
of the Majesty in the heavens; a minister of the sanctuary
and of the true tabernacle, which the Lord pitched, and not
man" (Heb. 8:1, 2). Moreover, because God sees all true believers in His Son He has given to them the special privileges
and ministries of priests. All of them belong to a royal
priesthood (I Peter 2:9; Rev. 1:6). Each one of them is per-
mitted not only into the outer court of forgiveness and
cleansing from sin, but also into the very presence of God to
offer up pure worship to His holy name. Alas, far too many
believers today understand little of their responsibilities and
privileges as priest. Very few actually are consciously discharging their priestly function of intercession during the intercessory prayers of their corporate worship services.

Within the outer court stood first the brazen altar of burnt
offering, which represents the meeting place between a holy
God and a guilty sinner. It was certainly evident to the devout Israelite that "without shedding of blood is no remission" for sin (Heb. 9:22). The brazen altar was the place
where all the blood of atonement was shed. Sin was there
dealt with in accordance with the righteous judgment of God
upon it. That this altar prefigured Christ's meeting of the fire
of divine judgment on the cross is too obvious to need special
comment. But it must be remembered that it is only the soul
who has accepted by faith that work of Christ in quenching
the fire of divine wrath who has found his own heart kindled
with the desire to worship his Redeemer. He not only has the
desire to worship, however. He also has been made eligible at
the brazen altar of Calvary to stand in the presence of the
Holy One and to offer his worship. Without this fervent desire to worship and the attendant sense of eligibility to enter
the presence of the holy God it is not any wonder that many
who gather with believers in their worship services today find
themselves bored and restless.

Beyond the brazen altar, midway between it and the tabernacle proper, stood the laver (Exod. 30:18). This was the
only other conspicuous piece of apparatus for the service of
God in the outer court. It provided a convenient place for the

priests to wash their hands and feet before entering into the Holy Place. Here there was not repeated blood sacrifice, but simply a washing to preserve the fitness of the priests for the continuing worship and service of the sanctuary. This process of washing was of necessity repeated, according to Exodus 30:20, 21, every time the priests entered the Holy Place or officiated at the altar. It speaks to us today of the fact that there can be no acceptable worship offered to God apart from personal holiness (I John 1:6). It certainly should remind us of the importance of sincere and open confession of sin fervently offered even as we begin our corporate worship of God. One cause of the failure of so much of the priestly intercession of believers today may be their neglecting that activity so clearly foreshadowed by the laver.

Mention must now be made of the altar of incense which, as has been noted, was not listed in the first directions recorded by the Holy Spirit for the furnishings of the tabernacle. No flesh was ever sacrificed on this altar, although the atoning blood was taken from the brazen altar of burnt offering and brought into the Holy Place whenever expiation was made for the priests themselves or for the priestly nation. The blood was administered to only the horns of the altar of incense. The imposition of hands on and the slaughtering of the animals, however, belonged exclusively to the outer courtyard.

The incense offering on this altar was to be renewed and kindled every morning and every evening. It was a symbol, not of the work of God, except in His provision for it, but of the prayers of the saints as they exercised their priestly prerogatives. The offerings of the Holy Place represent the fruits of sanctification in the lives of those who, having previously appropriated by faith the vicarious atonement, need only to apply continually the virtue of the shed blood to their personal lives as they offer their worship to God.

The Sacrifices

The sacrifices, whether they were animal or vegetable, were burned in whole or in part upon the altar of burnt offering. The purpose of the burning was that from the sacrifice Jehovah might derive satisfaction. He would smell the vapor of the burning as the sacrificial gift was purified by fire and would find satisfaction and honor in it. The offerings burnt upon the altar were intended for Him personally and He accepted them with pleasure and in turn blessed the offerer (Exod. 20:24). That which was most important about the offering, however, was not the gift itself but the gift as the expression of the self-surrender of the worshiper. This was what was well-pleasing to God. It was the absolutely essential element of sacrifice. The prophets had to remind the children of Israel continually that sacrificial offerings without the surrender and obedience of the offerer were an offense to the Lord (see Isa. 1:11; Jer. 6:15, 20; Hos. 4:14, 19; Amos 4:4-6, etc.). Going through the motions of worship without a heart that is surrendered to the Lord is still an abomination to Him.

When the offering was an animal sacrifice, not only was the burning of the sacrifice essential, but also the sprinkling of the blood upon the altar before the sacrifice was consumed. The design of this regulation is expressed in Leviticus 17:11, "For the life of the flesh is in the blood: and I have given it to you upon the altar to make an atonement for your souls: for it is the blood that maketh an atonement for the soul." As J. H. Kurtz has said, "It is very apparent that the two acts—the sprinkling of the blood upon the altar, and the burning of the sacrifice upon the altar—were essentially and necessarily connected. The sprinkling of the blood, or expiation, was the means; the burning, or dedication to Jehovah, the end. In order that the second should be a 'savour of satisfaction to the Lord,' it was necessary that the first should precede it; the first, therefore, was the basis or prerequisite of the second."[5] Such joys as the knowledge that the Lord has been pleased with the believer's sacrifice and also the delight of personal fellowship with Him (as in the sacrificial meal) could not possibly be attained in any other way than by

---

[5]J. H. Kurtz, *Sacrificial Worship of the Old Testament* (Edinburgh: T. & T. Clark, 1863), p. 57.

means of expiation. This certainly gives to expiation an incomparable importance.

Oh, that worshiping congregations in evangelical churches today might understand more clearly that in their worship every offering given to the Lord, if it is to be pleasing to Him, must be a token of self-surrender intended for God alone and offered freely to Him only because of the efficacy of the blood of His Son our Savior which was freely offered for the sins of His people.

The altar sacrifices of the Old Testament were closely related to prayer, but they must be distinguished from it. While it is true that sacrifice and prayer are indispensable to one another, sacrifice is something different from and something more than prayer. One might say that prayer expresses longings for the blessings of salvation. Sacrifice did not express those longings, but was (and is for the believer today) essentially the expression of an objective assurance of salvation. Truly only the one who has turned from his sins in repentance and put his trust in the Lord can render to God any acceptable sacrifice, even the sacrifice of praise.

The Typical Offerings

Before we conclude our discussion of the Old Testament sacrifices we must give at least brief consideration to the typical aspect of the various offerings as they were set forth in the Book of Leviticus. This book was essentially the worship manual for the Old Testament saints, but it teaches us much which will enrich our worship today. It is especially important that believers understand the typical significance of these offerings, for they point to Jesus Christ "who his own self bare our sins in his own body on the tree, that we, being dead to sins, should live unto righteousness; by whose stripes ye were healed" (I Peter 2:24). It is, of course, true that the children of Israel who brought their offerings to the tabernacle and later to the temple, according to the instructions which the Lord gave to Moses, understood little if any of the typical significance. This was due to their spiritual dullness and lack of faith (Luke 24:25, 26). It seems clear, however, that they did know that the offerings pointed to a coming Redeemer. It is only in the light of the New Testament revelation with its full picture of the person and work of Christ that we can see the deep significance of that which was typical in the offerings. Since the types in Leviticus do clearly speak of the marvelous and highly diversified aspects of the work of Christ on our behalf, we can find in them elements which bear directly upon our worship of Him. With an understanding of these features of the offerings we shall be able to worship Him in a more acceptable manner, for we shall be able to glorify Him more fully through a deeper comprehension of His grace.

In the Levitical offerings not only do we see the Christ who has redeemed men from the bondage of sin, but we also see in type the One who has brought believers into a blessed place of fellowship and worship and keeps them in this place, restoring them when they fall. If the fullness of Jesus Christ were less multifarious and the riches of His work for sinners were less varied, it would be much easier to represent Him and His work in single types or figures. However, although He is only one person and He offered Himself for the sins of men only once for all time and eternity, the representation of the manifold aspects of His work requires many distinct figures. This is one reason why God gave to the people of Israel so many different offerings, each of which was typical of Christ and His work for sinners. God wanted them, and us, to see the many relations of the person and work of Christ to the lives of believing saints.

The Burnt Offering

Let us consider first the burnt offering, the instructions for which are given in the first chapter of Leviticus. Notice that the offering was to be "of a sweet savour unto the Lord" (vv. 9, 13, 17). The sweet-savor offerings included the meal offering and the peace offering; all of them were offered on the brazen altar which stood in the court of the tabernacle near to the door. In the sweet-savor offerings Jesus Christ is seen not so much as the sin-bearer, although that aspect of His ministry is always present when blood is shed and the offerer identifies himself with the offering by the laying of his hands on the head of the victim. The emphasis in the burnt offering is upon the offering up to the Lord that which is a sweet savor unto Him. It is necessary therefore in regard to the Antitype to see Jesus Christ as the sinlessly perfect One offering Himself to God for us, not as our sin-bearer, but, as the apostle Paul put it, as the One who "also hath loved us, and hath given himself for us an offering and a sacrifice to God for a sweet smelling savour" (Eph. 5:2). The Son gave to God that which pleased Him and satisfied Him forever. Everything that Christ Jesus did while He was here on earth was well-pleasing to His Father (Matt. 17:5). Now as we worship God we must remember that He delights in the perfections of His Son. The burnt offering was the first of the offerings which God ordained. Surely God is pleased when we offer up to Him our praise not only for Christ's having been delivered for our offenses, but also for the perfections of His life.

> Fairest Lord Jesus, Ruler of all nature,
> O Thou of God and man the Son!
> Thee will I cherish, Thee will I honor,
> Thou, my soul's Glory, Joy, and Crown.
>
> Fair are the meadows, fairer still the woodlands,
> Robed in the blooming garb of spring:
> Jesus is fairer, Jesus is purer,
> Who makes the woeful heart to sing.

The burnt offering was also an offering by which the offerer found acceptance with God (Lev. 1:4). There could never be any acceptance of man in his innate sinfulness. The man of faith put his hand on the head of the animal of the burnt offering. Both God and he were then satisfied because both of them accepted the offering. Man accepted it as adequate for himself. God accepted it as an adequate atonement (Lev. 1:4). The burnt offering differs from the sin offering in that the burnt offering is a satisfaction of God's holy requirement while the sin offering satisfies offended justice.

Both of these our Savior satisfied. He was flawlessly perfect in His own character, and His atonement perfectly met the just penalty for all believers.

The burnt offering differs from the meal offering in that in the burnt offering a life was offered while in the meal offering only corn, oil, and frankincense were offered. Our Savior gave His life for us. He did not offer up some portion of His creation. Man's duty to God is to yield his whole life, body and soul, unto God (Rom. 12:1). This is his spiritual worship. The burnt offering further differs from the meal offering as well as from the peace offering in that in these latter two offerings only a part of the offering was burned with fire while the burnt offering was entirely burned on the altar. How clearly this points to the great Antitype, our Savior Jesus Christ. All He was, all He did, all He ever said or thought, was offered up to His Father. He Himself said, "I do always those things that please him" (John 8:29). If we are to worship God in Christ, all of our thoughts, our feelings, our affections, and our actions must continually be offered up to God. Is not this the first and great commandment?

The Meal Offering

The second offering which God provided the children of Israel for their worship of Him was the meal offering (meat offering, KJV). Like the burnt offering it was an offering of a sweet savor unto the Lord. We have already discussed the significance of this aspect of the offering. However, the materials of the meal offering differed substantially from those of the burnt offering. There was no giving of life. In the Levitical offerings a meal offering was a gift to God of the daily food of the people. Corn or wheat flour, oil, and frankincense were the substances offered. The corn or wheat flour and oil of the offering were the fruit of the plants and the trees which God had given to man for food (Gen. 1:29). Thus they symbolize man's own rightful claim in God's creation. As the burnt offering speaks of the fulfillment of man's duty to God, the first table of the law, the meal offering speaks of the fulfillment of his duty to his fellow man, the second table of the law. Christ, who was the perfect sacrifice, offered Himself not only to fulfill all righteousness for the glory of God but also to meet the needs of sinful man. Thus the meal offering became a necessary concomitant of the burnt offering. That is why in the Book of Numbers the meal offering is always spoken of as connected with and even belonging to the burnt offering (Num. 28:31; 29:6). As Cain's offering of the fruit of the vine was unacceptable to God, so any meal offering without the burnt offering would be unacceptable. In corporate worship today we must not presume to bring to God offerings which are the fruit of our own labors, our service to our fellow men, unless we have first worshiped Him for the perfect burnt offering of His Son, our Savior. Far too many have substituted the social gospel of good works to men for the primary concern of God, which is the glorification of His Son. When one has made the proper response of faith to the gospel of salvation through the death of Christ, good works will always follow.

It should be pointed out that in contrast to the burnt offering the meal offering was not entirely burned. A handful was burned, being only for God, but the rest was eaten by the priests (Lev. 2:2, 3). The frankincense was not mixed with the flour but added to the handful that was burned. Christ, although He faithfully performed His duty to man, offered Himself most holy unto the Lord. He is also very specially the spiritual food of man, offered to God *for* us, but given *to* us as priests to feed upon daily. In every worship service where Christ is honored and His Word is proclaimed the believers have the privilege of feeding on Him.

The Peace Offering

The third offering given to Moses for the nation of Israel was the peace offering. It was a sweet-savor offering like the previous offerings we have considered; in this particular it is not distinguished from them. It differs from all the other typical offerings, however, in that not only the offerer but also the priest and God Himself fed upon the offering (Lev. 3:9-11; 7:15-34). What a beautiful picture it is—God, offerer, and priest all feeding upon the same offering and finding joy and satisfaction in it! The one who made the offering feasted upon the offering, a portion of which must first have been offered to God (God's portion had to be fully consumed upon the altar). Thus the offerer was himself given a satisfying participation which he did not enjoy in the burnt offering or the meal offering.

We must always remember that Christ as the Antitype is not only the offering, but He is also the offerer. He offers Himself for us. Whatever He does He does *for* us. Yes, instead of us. Actually He does it *as* us, so that what is true of Him is actually true of us who are in Him (Eph. 1:6). "As he is, so are we in this world" (I John 4:17). If Christ is satisfied with the offering, then the believer must be also. Far too many believers, however, never realized this aspect of the peace offering; there can be no lasting peace apart from the apprehension of this important truth. Christ found His satisfaction, His "meat," in doing the will of His Father and finishing His work (John 4:34). The finishing of that work took Him with joy (Heb. 12:2) to the cross of Calvary where He was satisfied with the travail of His soul (Isa. 53:11). How very important it is that worshiping believers today apprehend the truth that is foreshadowed in the peace offering. They must realize and remember that nothing is more satisfying to the believing mind than that offering which has perfectly satisfied God in Christ. Our own efforts will never satisfy us. We cannot feast upon the works which we have done, but we can take liberally of the sweetness that is found in Christ and there find daily delight. This is the way of peace. Having found peace let us offer ourselves to God in spiritual sacrifices "acceptable to God by Jesus Christ" (I Peter 2:5).

The Sin Offering

We come now to the non-sweet-savor offerings, the first of which is the sin offering (Lev. 4:1—5:13). In the non-sweet-savor offerings we see one aspect of the sacrifice in type which is different from anything in the first three offerings we have considered. In them we have not been faced directly with sin. In them was offered that which was sweet to God. But in the sin offering and in the trespass offering we are faced with the reality of sin and with God's judgment upon it. It is not sweet to God. Judgment brings Him no pleasure.

It is in the sin offering of Christ that most of us today find our greatest comfort. Because we are sinners and recognize that we deserve the judgment of God we can heartily rejoice in the knowledge that our sin has been fully judged in another and that because of His bearing our judgment we do not need to tremble in fear of the terrible consequences of our sin. Most believers are much more able to apprehend the truth of Christ as our sin-bearer than they are to appreciate Him as the burnt offering or the meal offering. For this reason although the non-sweet-savor offerings are last in the order of their institution by God they are undoubtedly first in the order of their appropriation and application by men. Long before most believers understand the glorious perfections of Christ's work in offering Himself as a sweet-smelling savor to God they already understand that He bore their sins on the cross of Calvary.

The sin offering is distinguished from the other offerings in several ways. As we have already noted, it was not a sweet-savor offering even though it was to be without spot or blemish. In this offering we see in type Jesus Christ sacrificing Himself, not as something perfect and sweet to be offered up to God, but rather as bearing the awful weight of the sin of mankind. He is the substitute for us. He who knew no sin became sin for us (II Cor. 5:21). He was made a curse for us (Gal. 3:13). This is why the offering is not a sweet savor unto God. It represents an aspect of the work of Christ in which the Father took no delight. However, we must not forget that the sin offering needed to be without spot or blemish just as much as did the burnt offering. It foreshadowed the fact that only the perfect Son of God who was absolutely free from any stain of sin Himself could take away the sin of men.

Another characteristic feature of the sin offering is the fact that it was burned without the camp (Lev. 4:12). This distinguishes it from all the other offerings, for they were without exception burned on the brazen altar in the tabernacle court. A part of the sin offering, the fat, was burned on the altar, perhaps to show that the offering was perfect and the offerer was accepted. But in order that all present might go back to their homes with deep conviction of the heinousness of sin, even when it has been forgiven, the body of the victim was carried forth outside the camp. In this connection it would be impossible to forget that "Jesus also, that he might sanctify the people with his own blood, suffered without the gate" (Heb. 13:12). Our Savior was condemned to die and cast out of the city of Jerusalem as a common criminal, unfit to have a place in the city of God. What He suffered when He bore our sins we cannot even imagine because such suffering as He endured is beyond the scope of human experience. But it was His agony and anguish which purchased our redemption. When He took our sins upon Himself He had to suffer what we should have had to suffer ourselves if we had been judged in our own persons. This is why, in giving the instructions for the sin offering, God included the anointed priest as one who needed the offering, for he also sinned "according to the sin of the people" (Lev. 4:3, 4). Believers today have been made priests unto God and we discharge our priestly functions when we gather for worship, but we must never forget that our ministry in this office calls for personal holiness. When we sin, we must immediately avail ourselves of the propitiation for our sins provided by our great advocate, who is also our sin-bearer (I John 2:1, 2).

Before we discuss the last offering an important distinction must be made. It must be pointed out that the sin offering was for sin and not just for trespasses. That is, the sin offering was for sin as it exists in the nature of every man. The trespass offerings were for the individual trespasses which are the fruit of our sinful nature. In establishing the sin offering God did not mention any individual acts of sin. Guilty sinners were to confess their sin, even though their specific sins may have been committed in ignorance. How unfortunate it is that many believers today do not understand that Christ died not only to forgive them for their individual acts of sins (trespasses), but also to make full and final atonement for the sin that is in them. Their worship of God will be greatly enriched when this truth is fully comprehended.

The Trespass Offering

The last offering to be considered is the trespass offering, which, while closely linked to the sin offering, differs from it decidedly in certain particulars. Both are non-sweet-savor offerings because both have to do not with offering up that which is pleasing to God but rather that which provides expiation for sin. Christ is seen here in type (as He is seen in the sin offering) as the great substitute who suffers in place of His people, taking all of their sins upon Himself.

We have already mentioned that this offering, in contrast to the sin offering, was an offering for trespasses, not for indwelling sin. Trespasses included particular sins against God as well as those against one's fellow men (Lev. 5:14—6:7). In every case wrong was done and another was injured, although, of course, often it was only God who bore the injury.

It is of solemn significance also that the trespass may have been committed in ignorance. It nevertheless came under the judgment of God and made necessary the trespass offering, because it is not the measure of light possessed by a man which is the standard by which his sins are determined. Rather it is the eternal truth of God. If a man's conscience or his light were the standard, there would exist a different rule for each man. Good and evil would depend not upon God's revealed law but upon man's understanding of it. This is not the case, however, for God judges evil as evil wherever it is found. Our ignorance and blindness do not change the eternal truth of God. Yet in His grace and goodness God has provided a way of forgiveness for our trespasses even when they are committed unknowingly.

The trespass offering was always a ram without blemish. It was a fitting reminder to the children of Israel of God's substitution of the ram when Abraham prepared to make an offering of his son Isaac. Along with the bloody offering of the ram, the value of the trespass, according to the priest's estimation of it, was paid in the shekels of the sanctuary to the injured party. Then a fifth part more was added in shekels, and the entire amount was paid by the one who had committed the trespass to the one against whom it had been committed. This provision was entirely absent in the sin offering. There is a clear reason for this. No estimate could be made by a priest of the offense of our evil natures in their rebellion against God. A perfect victim, our Lord Jesus Christ, who offered an infinite sacrifice, was the only one who could bear the penalty for our sin.

In our individual trespasses it is not unusual for our particular acts of sin to cause injury to others. Here the problem is not only what we are—that is, sinners by nature—but also what we have done in wrong deeds against someone else. The death of a substitute, paying the penalty of all of our sins, would satisfy the demands of justice, but would not repair the injury which had been inflicted. Therefore restitution must be made and the wrong fully repaid.

In the congregation of worshiping saints we unite in the Lord's Prayer and ask God to "forgive us our trespasses [debts] as we forgive those who trespass against us [our debtors]." When we do so, we must remember that while Christ has fully satisfied the Father's just penalty for our trespasses, if we are sincerely repentant and truly desire forgiveness, we must seek to make restitution to any whom we may have injured by our sin.

Although we have given only a brief summary of the offerings instituted by God at Mount Sinai, it should be clear that the principles involved in the worship of His name today are not substantially different from those which He made clear to His people in the wilderness.

Worship in the Temple

Many years after the tabernacle was constructed and the Levitical offerings introduced in the wilderness, when David became the second king of Israel, it was his desire to build a temple for God which would be a permanent resting place for the ark of the covenant and a permanent dwelling place for the Lord among His people. God did not permit David to build the temple, but He promised that Solomon, David's son, would have the honor of building the house for the name of the Lord. In the fourth year of his reign Solomon began the construction of the temple. Because of the immense number of workmen he employed, it took only seven-and-a-half years to complete the splendid edifice. The temple building was not large by modern standards, but the magnificence of it made it one of the wonders of the ancient world. The whole interior was overlaid with gold, so that neither the wood nor the stone used in the construction could be seen. Nothing met the eye inside the temple but pure gold!

The formal inauguration of this great place of worship did not take place until eleven months after it was completed so that the ceremony could be held in a jubilee year a few days before the Feast of Tabernacles. The dedication ceremony itself was an amazing event with the king leading a magnificent march toward the new temple along a route where a large number of priests were stationed at various points to offer up an immense number of sacrifices. The ark of the covenant and the old tabernacle were also brought along in the solemn procession by a number of priests, after which the Levites carried along the vessels and ornaments of the old tabernacle to be placed in the new house of the Lord. After the ark of the covenant had been placed in the Holy of Holies and the priests who carried it in had come out again, the glory of the Lord filled the house of the Lord. It was then that King Solomon turned to the great congregation and blessed them. Then he knelt before the Lord and poured out his great prayer of dedication. That prayer is worthy of the careful study of all believers and especially of the ministers who lead the prayers of the congregation of the Lord's people.

The dedication of Solomon's temple was not a ceremony established by law. It was done in accord with that reverence which should always be associated with buildings which are set apart especially for divine worship. God does not inhabit our church buildings today as He did the tabernacle in the wilderness and the great temple of Solomon. Nevertheless, it is most appropriate that even a very humble structure erected for the distinctive purpose of serving as a place of Christian worship should be dedicated to the Lord in a fitting ceremony.

The worship of the Lord's people during the reign of David was organized upon a grand scale. It became even more magnificent after Solomon's temple was completed. Great choirs trained under professional musicians provided sublime music for the awe-inspiring services of worship. It was only in the splendor of the ceremony that the worship of the temple was different from that of the tabernacle. The same sacrifices, offerings, and feasts were observed. The emphasis upon worship through music, both instrumental and vocal, seems to be the only added element. God introduced this emphasis largely through the poetic and musical gifts which He had given to His servant King David. We do not know how David's music sounded, but his inspired Psalms are still an integral part of our services of worship. We should be as concerned as David was to make our songs truly praise the name of God (Ps. 69:30).

3

Corporate Worship
in the New Testament

As we turn to the consideration of corporate worship in the New Testament, it must be pointed out at the outset that what we know of the worship practices of the earliest Christians is quite limited. The New Testament gives us only the barest glimpses into the services of worship conducted by the apostles. We have no suggestions of the order of the services which are mentioned in the Scriptures and we have no real description of the liturgy used. In recent years, as we shall see, it has been quite popular for students of the New Testament to find liturgy in many passages of Acts, the Epistles, and especially Revelation, but in most cases reliable evidence of liturgy is simply not in the text. Let us, however, briefly examine what the Scriptures do tell us about the background and development of distinctly Christian worship. There is much in the New Testament which is important for our consideration in connection with our worship today.

Jewish Worship and Christian Worship

Christian worship has its origins in the worship of the temple and the synagogue. The first Christians, who were Jews, did not inaugurate an entirely new kind of worship. Jesus and His disciples worshiped in both the temple and the synagogue. After the ascension of Jesus, the Christian community continued many of the observances of both. It has been said that "distinctively Christian worship bears the same sort of relation to Jewish worship as the distinctively Christian writings do to the Jewish Scriptures."[1] The orthodox Christian sees the Scriptures of the New Testament not as contradictory to, but rather continuous with the Old Testament Scriptures. The Bible is the complete written revelation of God. It is a composite whole. That which the Old Testament reveals in germ is in the New Testament fully expounded. That which the Old Testament reveals in detail is assumed in the New Testament. The Creator and covenant-keeping God of the Old Testament is seen in the New Testament as fully revealing Himself and His love for man in the person and work of His Son Jesus Christ, whose death on the cross of Calvary is anticipated in every Old Testament sacrifice.

As the New Testament writings were built upon a foundation of Old Testament words, so the worship of the Christians of New Testament times was built upon the foundation of Old Testament worship. That there is a distinct continuity between Israel's worship and our own Christian worship forms much of the argument of the Epistle to the Hebrews. Christian worship, then, was continuous with the worship of the devout believing Israelite, yet because of the completion of the redemptive plan in the death and resurrection of Christ, it stands in some points in marked contrast to the worship of the devout Jew. So while we can say that Christian worship was born within the context of the temple and the synagogue, we must remember that from the very first it had its distinctively Christian aspects. While there were in the

[1]C. F. D. Moule, *Worship in the New Testament* (Richmond: John Knox Press, 1964), p. 9.

pattern of synagogue worship, for example, elements which could properly be retained by the Jews who became Christians, their most decisive concern was for recognition of Jesus Christ as the Son of God and the only Savior of men. Proper worship would reflect all that He is, all that He has done, and all that He is doing.

All elements of the synagogue worship which did not allow for this confession of the incarnate Christ and proper worship of Him were immediately eliminated. For example, we find no trace of the use of the *Shema* in any early Christian worship services. The *Shema,* with which the synagogue service began, was a confession of faith in the one God of Israel. It was not a Trinitarian confession, for the most devout Jews had only a faint understanding of the doctrine of the Trinity. The *Shema* emphasized the formal acknowledgment of God by outward signs, while Christ emphasized the attitude of the heart, warning of the danger of mere formality and outward signs. The prayers of the synagogue emphasized the external aspects of the expected kingdom of God, while Christ had announced the truth that the kingdom of God is within the believer. While the kingdom does have certain external aspects to be realized in the future, it must first be recognized as a spiritual kingdom in which each born-again believer participates. It is clear then that while there is a direct connection between Jewish worship and Christian worship the liturgy of the latter was purged of those elements which were inconsistent with the fuller revelation of God found in Jesus Christ.

With the new understanding of spiritual truth made possible by the gift of the Holy Spirit together with the deeper understanding of the Third Person of the Trinity Himself, and with the reality of a new relationship to God through the living Christ possessing their hearts, believers began to worship in a new and more meaningful manner. Their corporate worship was the expression of their conviction that the worship of God was the most important activity of life. Because of their deeper insight into the character of God as He had revealed Himself in His Son Jesus Christ, they knew that elaborate ritual and external trappings meant little. It was the attitude of the heart which mattered. The prime purpose of the liturgy for them, then, was to give proper and adequate opportunity for corporate expression of truly spiritual worship.

Efforts to Find Liturgy in the New Testament

As a result of the present-day repudiation of the apostolic origin and thus the full verbal inspiration of the New Testament Scriptures, every possible effort is being made by liberal scholars to show that the Scriptures are the product of the Christian community of the second, third, or even later centuries. They are not the writings of the individuals whose names they bear, but rather the "deposit of community life," it is said. To enhance this argument it is quite fashionable for eager students of the New Testament who have embraced this presupposition to find liturgy scattered everywhere throughout the New Testament. Moreover, they don't find liturgy only, but doctrinal formulations as well. Many of those doctrines which the orthodox Christian accepts as having come to the apostles directly from the Lord or after His ascension by the inspiration of the Holy Spirit are seen instead as having arisen spontaneously in the Christian community. For example, Gerhard Delling says concerning the doctrine of the Holy Spirit, "Now it becomes clear, in a most essential relationship, how belief in the Spirit came to be of such decisive meaning for primitive Christian piety; it derived *from worship.*"[2] This would mean that Christian doctrine and Christian liturgy were not derived from the Scriptures but rather that the Scriptures were derived from Christian convictions and practices. This idea we must reject most emphatically.

Additional impetus to the effort to identify liturgical elements in the New Testament Scriptures has come from those who are absorbed in the liturgical movement of our day,

---

[2]Gerhard Delling, *Worship in the New Testament* (Philadelphia: Westminster Press, 1962), p. 5.

which is often referred to as a liturgical renewal. While we must agree that a renewal of Christian worship is needed today and that a careful study of the worship of the primitive church will help us to determine what liturgical elements seem not only to have apostolic authority but also to be best suited to our needs, we must exercise great care in our examination of the New Testament record that we do not, as one author has put it, "detect the reverberations of liturgy in the New Testament even where no liturgical note was originally struck."[3]

Our Lord's Example

We could not begin even a brief study of worship in the New Testament without giving careful consideration to our Lord's own example in worship. It is clear that He worshiped in the temple. Luke tells us that He was brought there as an infant for presentation as a child of the covenant (Luke 2:21-24) and that as a youth of twelve years He was back in the temple again (Luke 2:41ff.), a possible indication of study in the temple school. During His public ministry He frequented the temple. John tells us in his Gospel (7:2ff.) that Jesus was present for the Feast of Tabernacles, and again (10:22) for the Feast of Dedication. When He came back the final time for the Passover, it was to be put to death by His enemies. We must also take note of His great zeal for the purity of the temple. At least twice during His public ministry He exercised great fervor in cleansing the temple of the moneychangers and those who had defiled it for personal gain. It would be impossible to miss the obvious truth demonstrated so forcibly by the Savior that the worship of God must be pure and undefiled and that there must be no ulterior motives in our going to His house to worship.

While there is no evidence in the Gospel accounts that Jesus either did or did not offer sacrifices in the temple, we do know that He clearly endorsed the principle of sacrifice. It is

---

[3]Moule, *Worship in the New Testament,* p. 7.

also clear that when He offered Himself once and for all as the perfect sacrifice for the sins of the elect, the function of the temple ceased, being fulfilled by the death of Jesus Christ Himself. During His earthly ministry He had instructed His critics that they must learn what the prophecy of Hosea 6:6 meant, "I will have mercy and not sacrifice: for I am not come to call the righteous, but sinners to repentance" (Matt. 9:13; 12:7). His disciples likewise needed to learn that the temple was indeed only a type or foreshadowing of the Lord's own body. Jesus called His earthly body the temple of God (John 2:19), and this it was because His body of flesh and bones was the dwelling place of the living God. It was in that body that the eternal and perfect sacrifice for the sins of men was made, and once this sacrifice had been offered to God there would be no further need for the temple. When He died, the veil of the temple was rent in twain (Matt. 27:51), symbolizing the end of temple worship with its Holy of Holies and its sacrifice. The perfect cleansing from all sin and the perfect entrance into the holy presence of God had been purchased and provided for all true believers. Jesus Christ proclaimed Himself as the new focal point in Christian worship (John 2:19; 4:21-23).

Not only is Jesus Christ the focal point of true worship, but in His body, which is the church and which He calls the temple of God (I Cor. 3:16), is the place of corporate worship today. He indicated this with His simple statement, "Where two or three are gathered together in my name, there am I in the midst of them" (Matt. 18:20). It is most important that believers today understand how fully and completely the worship of the temple is fulfilled in true Christian worship. All the temple provided the devout believer of Old Testament times, the believer finds in Jesus Christ today.

Because Christian worship is also closely related to synagogue worship, we must also take note of our Lord's example in this matter. We are told by Luke (4:16) that He regularly attended the synagogue on the Sabbath day, and that He sometimes participated in the service itself, expounding the Scriptures. In each Gospel it is evident that He made it a practice to use the synagogues for His teaching ministry (Matt. 4:23; Mark 1:21; Luke 6:6; John 6:59; 18:20). Some of His most significant encounters with His enemies took place in the synagogues (cf. Matt. 12:9ff.).

Synagogue worship was far less elaborate than that of the temple. It contained no sacrificial element. It consisted largely of prayer and the reading and exposition of the Old Testament Scriptures. There probably also was some chanting of the Psalms. Yet, it became apparent early in His ministry that Jesus did not fit fully into the framework of the synagogue worship, for His exegesis of the Scriptures was completely different from that of the scribes of His day. The scribes bent the Scriptures to fit the traditional interpretation established in the Torah. Jesus proclaimed something that only a devout handful of believers had anticipated, the decisive irruption of God into the affairs of men to provide eternal salvation by the offering of Himself for the sins of men, an action so decisive that its very proclamation served to interrupt the synagogue service and to antagonize those who heard Him there on one occasion. Jesus wanted man to understand that he cannot expect to win forgiveness by the shedding of the blood of animals, but it is bestowed upon him by the grace of God because of what He Himself has done. Righteousness is the gift of God and cannot be earned or merited. Further, Jesus did not need to overthrow the worship of the temple or the synagogue by violence. Those who truly believe in Him and who therefore are members of His body already live in Him, live by Him, and find Him the object of their worship and the source of true fulfillment and joy in this their highest activity.

Worship in the Apostolic Age

Moving from our consideration of worship as we see it exemplified in the person of our Lord, let us consider the character of worship in the Apostolic Age following the resurrection and ascension of Christ. The New Testament throws considerable light on the practices of the apostolic church, which most believers accept as normative for the Christian church today. It is quite clear that early in the apostolic period the apostles and the Jewish Christians continued to worship in the temple in Jerusalem. In fact, we read in Acts 2:46 that they went daily to the temple. Luke mentions that they "were continually in the temple" (Luke 24:53). Even the apostle Paul went into the temple to pray (Acts 22:17), and on his very last visit to Jerusalem he sponsored four Jewish men who had taken upon themselves a Jewish vow and went with them into the temple. Paul, and probably the other apostles as well, gave observance to the Jewish feasts and holy days (Acts 20:6, 16; I Cor. 16:8). This suggests the *possible* origin of the "Christian Year," observed in many churches today, even some Reformed churches. Such observances of holy days as were inconsistent with the freedom of the Christian life, however, Paul emphatically denounced (see Gal. 4:10ff.; Col. 2:16).

While the first Christians continued to worship for a time in the temple, it must here be observed that the fundamental basis of their worship was what God had accomplished in His Son Jesus Christ. Thus while they found themselves using the Old Testament Scriptures in worship, they recognized that Christ was Himself the One to whom the Old Testament pointed and that He had fulfilled much of those Scriptures and given to them a transcendent meaning. Early Christian worship was thus continuous with the Jewish worship but it was from the first absolutely distinctive. Jesus of Nazareth was worshiped as God manifest in the flesh, as the perfect sin-bearer, and as the author of life.

As there was continued worship in the temple during the transition period of the early Apostolic Age, so there was also constant contact with the synagogue. Stephen disputed with certain leaders of the synagogue who opposed the gospel (Acts 6:9); and, wherever possible, Paul customarily began his missionary work in the Jewish synagogues (Acts 9:20; 13:5, 14; 17:1, 2, 10). Apollos also preached in the synagogues (Acts 18:26), and Priscilla and Aquila apparently went there to hear him.

Of course, the Christians' expulsion from the synagogue was inevitable. This was evident even during the time of Jesus' own public ministry. The rulers of the Jews had agreed that "if any man did confess that he [Jesus] was Christ, he should be put out of the synagogue" (John 9:22). The man born blind who was healed by Christ did make a clear confession and indeed they cast him out. Jesus made it clear in His parable in the tenth chapter of John's Gospel that this casting out was actually a leading out by the great Shepherd of the sheep. The apostle Paul was impelled to separate himself from the synagogue in Corinth after the Jews there opposed him and blasphemed (Acts 18). He entered into the house of Justus, a believer, next door to the synagogue, and there continued his preaching and teaching. It can hardly be doubted, however, in the light of all the evidence, that the worship of the synagogue had a profound effect upon the worship of the early Christian church. The relationship which existed between the synagogue and the early Christians was so close that the synagogue worship could not fail to be an important factor in influencing the form of public worship for the believers.

We have seen that the early Christians maintained a relationship with the temple in Jerusalem for some years—perhaps even until its destruction in A.D. 70, but the liturgy or what we should perhaps call the order of worship in the Christian churches appears not to have been influenced at all by the worship of the temple but rather by that of the synagogue. The connections which the medieval commentators sought to point out between the ritual of the books of Exodus, Leviticus, and Numbers and that of the Christian church cannot be taken seriously. They are the result of the imagination of the writers and have no basis in historical fact. The synagogue worship, on the other hand, involved no blood sacrifices, no oblations of the inanimate produce of the harvest, no offerings of firstfruits, and no incense. Various attempts have been made to show that in the sacraments Christian worship has preserved the worship of the temple and in the preaching of the Word has preserved the nonsacrificial, nonsacramental worship of the synagogue. But such efforts are an oversimplification of both the Old Testament worship and that of the Christian Era. Generalization can be misleading. It is best to simply note the fact that Christian worship arose in a Jewish setting and to note what elements show the distinctive influence of the Jewish worship of Christ's own day.

Elements in Worship

There were four significant elements in synagogue worship. I have already referred briefly to them, but let me mention them again. First, there was the reading of the Scriptures and the other sacred books of the Jews. Second, there were the chants upon texts from the Psalter. A third element of the worship was prayer, which may have occupied the most prominent place in the service, for there can be no doubt that the devout Jews gathered themselves together for common prayer, even as did Lydia and the other women who gathered with her by the riverside at Philippi (Acts 16:13). The fourth part of the service, which occupied a less essential place and may often have been omitted, was the homily, usually upon a subject suggested by the reading from the Scripture. It is easy to see that all four of these elements were adopted immediately by the Christian church. In addition certain liturgical elements have their parallel in Christian worship today. For example, we are told that the synagogue "service began with an invitation to prayer given as a proclamation in the words, 'Bless ye the Lord who is to be blessed.' To this the people replied, 'Blessed be the Lord who is to be blessed forever.' This was followed by the confession of faith that from the first word became known as the Shema (Deut. 6:4-9, to which later was added Deut. 11:13-21 and Num. 15:37-41)."[4] These elements are indeed very similar to our call to worship and the use of the Apostles' Creed. The synagogue service

---

[4]H. L. Drumright in *Wycliffe Bible Encyclopedia* (Chicago: Moody Press, 1975), p. 1641.

closed with a benediction, as do Christian services universally today. At the close of the prayers in the synagogue the congregation responded with "Amen," and when benedictions of more than one verse were given from the Scriptures the congregation responded with an "Amen" after each verse.

However, we must see that if the Christian church took over entirely the basic elements of synagogue worship, it added to those elements at least one distinctly Christian element, the sacramental, which originated in the upper room when Christ instituted the Lord's Supper with His disciples. The details concerning this sacred meal are given to us in the Synoptic Gospels and also in the First Corinthian Epistle (ch. 11), in which the apostle Paul takes up some problems which have grown out of the observance of the sacrament. From this epistle we learn that originally the celebration of the Lord's Supper was preceded by an ordinary meal partaken of in common by the believers. This is what was referred to as the *agape,* or love feast. However, even in Paul's day this custom allowed for the introduction of serious problems. Because of these problems and the inconvenience of providing for such a feast under the severe persecutions to which the Christians were subjected, the liturgical *agape* disappeared within about one hundred years after the founding of the Christian church, although a form of the love feast was observed in some areas for perhaps five centuries.

Justin Martyr, who lived from approximately A.D. 100 to 165, and is therefore among the earliest of the fathers of the church outside the apostles themselves, described the early worship services of the Christians as follows:

> On the day of the Sun [Sunday] all who live in towns or in the country gather together to one place, and the memoirs of the apostles or the writings of the prophets are read as long as time permits. Then when the reader has ceased the president verbally instructs and exhorts to the imitation of the good examples cited. Then all rise together and prayers are offered. At length . . . prayer being ended, bread and wine and water are brought, and the president offers prayer and thanksgivings to the best of his ability, and the people assent by saying

Amen: and the distribution is made to each one of his share of the elements which have been blessed, and to those who are not present it is sent by the ministry of the deacons.

It is easy to see from this brief description that those elements of the synagogue service which we have mentioned (with the exception of the chanting of Psalms) are all present and that in addition there was the weekly observance of the Lord's Supper. It is argued by many that in New Testament times there was no corporate worship without the sacrament. Such testimonies as we have just read from Justin Martyr would certainly seem to indicate that observance of the sacrament was frequent and probably weekly. However, there is no way to establish from the New Testament the teaching that the sacramental element should always be present in Christian worship.

It is also evident, both from the New Testament itself and from the subapostolic evidence which is available to us, that the early church had no fixed ritual for its worship services. Acts 20:7-11 indicates that preaching preceded the Lord's Supper on some occasions. Acts 20:36 suggests that the churches founded by the apostle Paul may have been accustomed to preaching followed by prayer. While the general procedures followed in the order of worship may have been and probably were almost identical everywhere because they so closely paralleled the synagogue service, there was evidently not sufficient importance attached to the particular forms used so that there would be any special sanction which would fix some of them permanently in the liturgy. As L. Duchesne has said, "It was not in accordance with the practice of early days to attach to things of this nature that importance which would sanction and fix them."[5] Local diversities apparently were introduced into the services of worship so that by the third century the rituals used in Rome differed substantially from those of Antioch or Alexandria.

Now we must turn to examine the New Testament itself to

---

[5]L. Duchesne, *Christian Worship: Its Origin and Evolution* (London: S.P.C.K., n.d.), p. 54.

see what light it sheds upon the form and content of corporate worship. Let us begin with the first description of the assemblies of the believers following Pentecost and the establishment of the Christian church as a distinct organization. It is found in Acts 2:42-47. We read:

> And they continued stedfastly in the apostles' doctrine and fellowship, and in breaking of bread, and in prayers. And fear came upon every soul: and many wonders and signs were done by the apostles. And all that believed were together, and had all things common; and sold their possessions and goods, and parted them to all men, as every man had need. And they, continuing daily with one accord in the temple, and breaking bread from house to house, did eat their meat with gladness and singleness of heart, praising God, and having favour with all the people. And the Lord added to the church daily such as should be saved.

Here we see the earliest evidence of the elements of worship in the first Christian community. Note that they included (1) the apostles' teaching, (2) fellowship, (3) breaking of bread, (4) prayer, and (5) praise. Of course, it would be impossible to determine from this brief account just where these elements appeared in the services. In fact, as we shall see, it is quite impossible to recognize from the New Testament sources, even the letters of Paul, which give us the most information, any fixed forms or any particular order of primitive Christian worship.

Let us briefly examine the elements which we find in Acts 2. The first is the apostles' teaching. It can be said without fear of contradiction that Christian worship from the earliest times has been characterized by the fact that the Word of God is central. Doctrine is the very soul of the church. This passage refers to the doctrine of the apostles, and certainly that expression by itself would mean New Testament truth as well as apostolic instruction from the Old Testament Scriptures. The apostles had learned from the Lord what the Old Testament meant and how it was to be interpreted. Delling maintains that "there does not appear to be any justification for supposing that in the forms of service peculiar to Jewish Christianity readings from the Old Testament took place:

there is no indication in the New Testament that they did."[6]
While we agree that there is no specific evidence in the New
Testament that the Old Testament Scriptures were read and
expounded in the early Christian services, in the light of what
we have already seen concerning the close relationship which
the Christians sustained to the synagogue, and also in the
light of the constant references which the letters of the apostles make to the Old Testament Scriptures, it would seem certain that readings and expositions from the Old Testament
were common in these early services. Justin Martyr's
reference to readings from the prophets would also substan-
tiate this assertion. In the New Testament epistles, the Gentile Christians as well as the Jewish Christians were assumed
to have a familiarity with the Old Testament Scriptures.
They could hardly have had this familiarity unless these
Scriptures were read to them in their services. In the Book of
Romans, for example, Paul bases much of his argument
about the principle of righteousness coming through faith on
illustrations which he has drawn from the Old Testament.
The Roman church was largely Gentile. Individuals did not
have their own copies of the Scriptures. What they knew of
the Old Testament would have come from hearing those
Scriptures read. The logical place for us to assume that they
heard them would be in the services of common worship.
Perhaps the most conclusive indication that the Old Testament Scriptures were read to the people in their services
along with the New Testament documents then available is
Paul's clear statement in Romans 15:4, "For whatsoever
things were written aforetime were written for our learning,
that we through patience and comfort of the scriptures might
have hope." That the apostles used the Old Testament copi-
ously suggests strongly that reading and exposition of the
Old Testament formed a large segment of what is called "the
apostles' doctrine." Paul, of course, attached very real importance to the reading aloud of his own letters in the Christian services (see Col. 4:16; I Thess. 5:27).

---

[6]Delling, *Worship in the New Testament,* p. 92.

The next element in the early worship was fellowship. The Greek word *koinonia* is now widely used in English. Some would insist that the use of this word in Acts 2:42 is an anticipatory reference to the joint possession of goods by the early Christians. Undoubtedly the sharing of goods must have consisted in a large measure in the sharing of food, which may have been the practice at the communal meals which preceded the observance of the sacrament. The distribution of the necessities of life to the indigent was certainly a mark of true fellowship. Perhaps there are those who would insist that while fellowship is important in the life of the body of believers, it has little to do with their worship. However, I would insist that fellowship is a particularly important element in corporate worship, and especially in the observance of the sacraments if one is to experience all the fullness of true Christian worship. There is no substitute to the Christian for the realization of the spiritual bond which unites him with other believers and with the Lord Jesus Christ. It is a lack of a sense of true fellowship with other believers that mars the worship experiences of many today. It is especially easy for this to be lacking in large churches where many worshipers sit among total strangers. The Christian faith is first an individual matter, but it never remains that. Jesus Christ first brings a soul to Himself, but then He always unites that soul to other believers in His body, the church. The church itself is first a spiritual organism, but then its outward form must give expression to its corporate life. The unattached Christian is an impossibility. The Lord's special presence in worship is promised only for those occasions when at least two or three are gathered together. Thus fellowship in worship must be expressed and experienced.

There are various interpretations of *koinonia,* the word for fellowship here. Some feel that it is a reference to the Lord's Supper, but the word is never used of the communion service in this way without some additional words which would identify it as referring to the sacrament. John Calvin believes it refers to the believers' mutual association and those things which give witness to brotherly fellowship. He rejects the idea that it refers to the communion, believing instead that the expression "breaking of bread" refers to that sacrament. The warmth of sweet fellowship is one important safeguard against spiritual coldness. Perhaps Christians today should restore the greeting of one another with a holy kiss, which was a practice of apostolic times. It might give us a sweeter sense of fellowship.

The next element is breaking of bread. A large number of commentators including Calvin feel that this is a clear reference to the Lord's Supper. Personally I agree. There are a number, however, who feel that it is a reference to the *agape* or love feast, while some insist that it indicates simply the fact that the Christians ate their meals together. There is no reason to believe that every meal eaten together with other Christians carried the significance of the particular sacramental meal inaugurated in the upper room. That meal was for the earliest Christians a covenant rite by which the believers identified themselves as God's true Israel (Gal. 6:16) under the new covenant which Christ had sealed with His own blood. One cannot state dogmatically that the breaking of bread in Acts 2:42 refers to their sacramental observance, for there is a possibility that Luke is speaking only of the customary and special fellowship meal here. It is obvious from what Paul tells us in I Corinthians 11 that there was some confusion of such meals with the Lord's Supper, at least in the Corinthian church. This ultimately led to the complete segregation of the sacramental observance of the breaking of bread and sharing of the cup from the real or fellowship meal. However, I believe that Luke, the historian, was recording those marks which would identify the church in the eyes of those outside the church; certainly participation in the sacrament was one of those marks. In this observance they were testifying to the redemptive work of Christ as well as to their anticipation of His coming again. They were also feasting spiritually on Jesus Christ as they partook of the communion elements. If the believers who were so near to the death and resurrection of their Savior needed the blessing of frequent observance of the Lord's Supper, how much more do we today!

The fourth element in the worship of the early church was prayers. It is interesting to note that the original here actually says "the prayers." Some commentators feel that the use of the article implies that the Christians were using in public certain stated prayers such as the Jews used in the temple. These prayers, of course, became new when offered in the name of Jesus Christ. Whether this is true or not we cannot tell, but the important thing is that the church cherished the opportunity for direct communication with God and never failed to offer up petitions to Him when gathered together to worship Him. Paul in his First Epistle to Timothy (2:1) seems to place prayers as of first importance in the gathering together of the church and he includes in his exhortation several different kinds of prayer. From what he says in his instruction to the Corinthian Christians (I Cor. 14:16), we can tell that just as the devout Jews responded to prayers in the synagogue with an "Amen," so the Christians followed this practice in the primitive church. I shall have something more to say about this practice when I discuss the matter of our worship today. But for the moment let me say I have wondered many times why such a practice as this, which has such solid scriptural authority, has ceased to be observed in the Reformed churches of this country, especially when they insist that the Scriptures are their only guide in worship.

The fifth and last element mentioned in the passage in Acts 2 which we have been considering is praise. It is not mentioned in sequence with the other items in verse 42, but is added in verse 47 as a part of the daily activity of the people. It was, then, not limited to their corporate worship gatherings. However, there is certainly a clear inference that this element was a part of their prayers and also found expression in singing, for the Lord's people have always found that one of their most meaningful methods of expressing their praise is the lifting of their hearts and voices together in sacred song.

That singing was a major part of the worship services of the earliest Christian churches cannot be denied. Paul wrote to the Ephesian Christians that they were to speak to one another in psalms, hymns, and spiritual songs. This would suggest an assembly of believers in corporate worship; since they were to be "singing and making melody in [their] heart to the Lord" (Eph. 5:19), the burden of their songs was certainly praise. Paul wrote similarly to the Colossians (Col. 3:16) that they were to teach and admonish one another with "psalms and hymns and spiritual songs, singing with thankfulness in [their] hearts to God" (NASB). The Corinthian church was also a singing church, for the apostle spoke of the fact that when they came together it was customary for each one of them to be prepared to suggest a psalm for singing (I Cor. 14:26). Paul also spoke of the importance not only of singing with the mind but also of singing with the spirit.

Most commentators believe that Paul was quoting a Christian hymn that was in common use in his day when in writing to Timothy (I Tim. 3:16) he spoke in poetical language of the common confession of the mystery of godliness:

> He who was revealed in the flesh,
> Was vindicated in the Spirit,
> Beheld by angels,
> Proclaimed among the nations,
> Believed on in the world,
> Taken up in glory. (NASB)

Of course, it is possible that this was a creedal statement in poetry which was used in the liturgy of the early churches, but it seems much more probable that it was a widely-used hymn.

Perhaps a brief word needs to be said here concerning those of our Reformed brethren who believe that only psalms should be used in singing the praise of God in the church today, and that they should be sung without instrumental accompaniment of any kind. This teaching is based upon the well-known regulative principle which is stated in the Westminster Confession of Faith, Chapter 21, "The acceptable way of worshiping the true God is instituted by Himself, and so limited by His own revealed will, that He may not be worshiped according to the imaginations and devices of men, or the suggestions of Satan under any visible representation, or any other way not prescribed in the holy Scripture." In Section 5 of this same Chapter 21 of the Confession, which is a description of acceptable worship, there is included the phrase, "singing of psalms with grace in the heart," but no mention is made of hymns and spiritual songs. This omission does not mean that we should sing the Old Testament psalms only. The Confession uses the word in a wider sense to refer to hymns sung to God.

When we turn to the Word of God, we find that it would be difficult to establish on any sound exegetical basis that "psalms, hymns and spiritual songs" in Ephesians and Colossians refers to the inspired psalms of the Old Testament only. This is the argument of our Covenanter brethren, based upon the fact that the Hebrew words for hymn and song do appear in the titles of the Psalms, and further that the reference to "spiritual songs" means that they must be inspired by the Holy Spirit. We do not have space for a detailed answer to this argument. Suffice it to say that the very fact that three types of song are mentioned rather than one alone is significant. If the Holy Spirit had intended that we sing psalms exclusively, He would have made this very clear by using only the one word. Morever, the argument that the Hebrew words appear in the titles of the Psalms is inconclusive; scholars do not generally argue that these titles are divinely inspired, but even if one allowed for their inspiration, it is impossible to find any threefold classification of the Psalms from the usage of these three words in the titles. And the argument that the word *spiritual* before songs means that they must be divinely inspired songs cannot be sustained, for the word *spiritual* is used in the New Testament in connection with men who are not divinely inspired of the Holy Spirit (e.g., I Cor. 14:37; Gal. 6:1) and in Ephesians 6:12 it is used to refer to spiritual wickedness. Let me add also the fact that the root meaning of the word *psalm,* both in the Hebrew and in the Greek, is a "song with instrumental accompaniment," although this fact would not be a conclusive argument by itself.

Before we leave the subject of worship in the New Testament we must make reference to some of the other elements of public worship which are present in the New Testament record. It is clear that preaching had a prominent part in the assemblies of the believers in apostolic times. We have already referred to the fact that the apostles' doctrine occupied a prominent place in the assemblies of the believers. Undoubtedly this doctrine was communicated by what we understand as preaching today. Paul's commandment to Timothy in I Timothy 4:13 seems clearly to urge upon him careful attention to the public reading and preaching of the Scriptures. In his second epistle he reminds Timothy (II Tim. 3:16, NASB) that the whole of Scripture is divinely inspired and therefore "profitable for teaching, for reproof, for correction, for training in righteousness." The apostles as well as other believers went everywhere throughout the known world of their day doing evangelistic preaching. There are a number of evangelistic sermons recorded in the Book of Acts, but it is apparent that there was also preaching for the Christians when they gathered together for worship and for the celebration of the Lord's Supper. One example will suffice. When Paul was in Troas on the Lord's Day (Acts 20:6ff.), the believers gathered together to observe the sacrament and Paul preached such a long sermon that Eutychus, sitting on a window sill, fell asleep. He tumbled from the third floor and was picked up dead. Paul restored him to life by miraculous power. There is no evidence that such an event lessened the interest of the early Christians in hearing the Word of God expounded by the apostle Paul.

Another element of worship which is included in the New Testament is the giving of offerings to the Lord. That the offerings were made in public is indicated in Acts 5, where we read that Ananias "sold a piece of property, and kept back some of the price for himself . . . and bringing a portion of it, he laid it at the apostles' feet" (vv. 1, 2, NASB). This was a hypocritical pretense which the apostle Peter called lying to the Holy Spirit. You are familiar with the sad consequences. Paul had much to say to the Corinthians about the matter of offerings. He encouraged them to lay aside their gifts to the Lord's work regularly upon the first day of the week (I Cor.

16:1, 2). In his second epistle to them he spoke of their liberality (9:13) as a service which not only supplied the needs of other believers, but overflowed in praise to God. Giving was a form of Christian sacrifice well-pleasing to God. Paul himself received the offerings of the churches for the poor saints in Jerusalem as well as gifts which were gathered and sent to sustain him in his own ministry of the gospel.

I must mention one other matter, lest I be accused of deliberately overlooking an element in early worship which is clearly indicated in one letter of the apostle Paul (I Corinthians). This is the matter of speaking in tongues. Unfortunately the scope of the present discussion does not permit me to go into the matter of tongues-speaking in any detail at all. It is my personal conviction that the Scriptures clearly indicate that when the early Christians spoke in tongues they spoke in a language which was known to someone in the congregation who could interpret what they said to the assembled believers. The New Testament Scriptures were not yet complete and available to the people of God; there was apparently some need for this particular special manifestation of the power of the Holy Spirit. Special signs were still needed at this time to validate the Christian message. It is clear that tongues appeared in some services. Unquestionably the Holy Spirit did give this gift to some. However, it was for a sign, not to believers but to unbelievers who were in the congregation.

Unfortunately today the so-called gift of tongues is being used in many places as a sign of believers' baptism in the Holy Spirit. I would insist most emphatically that it is not! It has produced in many places the same kind of problems that it produced in the Corinthian church. The Corinthians gave much more attention to the gift of tongues than to any other because it was more showy; it caused amazement in those who heard it demonstrated. There is something in human nature that delights in being able to cause wonderment in other people. It seems sad indeed that in our day, when there is such a crying need for the knowledge of God, there are many intent on seeking some kind of an ecstatic experience which

would convince them that they are possessed of a supernatural power. God bestows no gift upon His church unless
there is some use for it. Certainly tongues were of use in the
early church. It is regrettable that there is so much misguided
zeal for tongues in the church today. Certainly Paul gave
very strict regulations for their use in any public worship service. Had the gift of tongues been something that all should
seek as a manifestation of sanctification, the Scriptures
would certainly have said so. None of the other apostles even
mention the gift of tongues as they urge the Christians to live
holy lives, and Paul certainly indicated to the Corinthians
that the gift of tongues was inferior to other gifts which were
exercised in the church.

The Sacraments in the New Testament

We cannot bring this brief discussion of corporate worship
in the New Testament to a close without some mention of the
sacraments as they appear in the New Testament, for the sacraments are certainly an integral part of the common worship of the church. The subject of the sacraments has so
many ramifications that we will be able only to touch on
some of the main features of baptism and the Lord's Supper
as they appear in the New Testament. We are primarily concerned with the principles of sacramental worship as they are
given in the New Testament Scriptures, particularly in the
epistles of Paul.

It is clear from Paul's discussion (in I Corinthians) of the
problem of meat offered to idols that the apostle recognized
the fact that under certain circumstances the material elements used in sacramental worship were the means by which
believers partook of specific spiritual blessings. "Is not the
cup of blessing which we bless a sharing in the blood of
Christ? Is not the bread which we break a sharing in the body
of Christ?" (I Cor. 10:16, NASB). He even agreed that in
partaking of meat which had been offered to idols there was
a distinct possibility of becoming "sharers in demons"
(I Cor. 10:20, NASB)—this in spite of the fact that he had

agreed that an idol is nothing in itself. Thus Paul argued that although the material element, meat, undergoes no transformation, the particular use which is made of it does affect our spiritual relationship either with the Lord or with demonic powers.

The New Testament contains no definition of a sacrament. But there is in both sacraments a divine mystery. Paul refers to the high mystery of the spiritual conjunction between believers and Jesus Christ in connection with the observance of the Lord's Supper. "Because there is one loaf, we, who are many, are one body, for we all partake of the one loaf" (I Cor. 10:17, NIV). The mystery of the union of two in one in the relationship of Christ and the church is referred to in Ephesians 5:32. So the union of the sacrament and the thing which is signified by it must be of the same nature, mystical and spiritual. The partaking of the bread and the cup in Christian worship when received by faith does then effect an actual participation in the whole Christ whose life was offered as a sacrifice for sin. The devout participant in the communion is thus united with Christ and with other true believers in a real though mystical way. This conjunction was so real to the apostle Paul that he indicated in I Corinthians 11:29, 30 that unworthy participation in the sacrament—that is, eating and drinking the elements without spiritual discernment—brings illness and even death. As Moule has said, "For St. Paul the Lord's Supper was no mere recalling of a memory from the past, nor only a looking forward to the future but a potent means of present contact with the risen Lord."[7]

Our Lord set forth the same truth in His discourse recorded in John 6. Having assured the multitude that He was dealing with spiritual realities in such statements as "the bread of God is that which comes down out of heaven, and gives life to the world. . . . I am the bread of life; he who comes to Me shall not hunger, and he who believes in Me shall never thirst" (vv. 33, 35, NASB), He proceeded to

---

[7]Moule, *Worship in the New Testament,* p. 36.

warn them, "Unless you eat the flesh of the Son of Man and drink His blood, you have no life in yourselves. He who eats My flesh and drinks My blood has eternal life; and I will raise him up on the last day. For My flesh is true food, and My blood is true drink. He who eats My flesh and drinks My blood abides in Me, and I in him" (vv. 53-56, NASB). Then lest He be misunderstood the Savior averred that "the flesh profits nothing: the words that I have spoken to you are spirit and are life" (v. 63, NASB). These words assure us all that salvation is something more than just learning about Christ and striving to follow His teachings and His example. It is actually partaking of Him and becoming united with Him in a vital way so that His life becomes our life. The reality of this union is most vividly and forcefully renewed for us in the sacrament of holy communion.

The New Testament clearly sets forth the sacrament of baptism as the initiatory rite of the Christian church. We have mentioned the Lord's Supper first because communion is observed more frequently as a part of corporate worship. Actually throughout the New Testament baptism is mentioned far more often than is communion. However, it is not usually found as a part of a service of common worship, although in some instances, such as the baptism of Lydia and her household in Philippi, it came at the close of a service of prayer and preaching.

Matthew 28:19 gives us the command of Jesus Christ to perform baptism as the way of entry into the church. It is this authorization which establishes it as a sacrament. Throughout the Acts and the Epistles baptism is recognized as the ordinance of admission into the fellowship of the house of God, although actual descriptions of baptisms are very brief. Since I have already written a book in which the meaning of baptism, the mode of administration, and the proper subjects are discussed, I will not treat these matters again here.[8] Suffice it to say that baptism, like the communion, was a

---

[8]The reader is referred to the author's volume *What About Baptism?* (St. Louis: Covenant College Press, 1957).

covenant rite. It identified the baptized individual as a member of the covenant household, the true Israel of God. The water which symbolized the work of the Holy Spirit was itself without cleansing power, but when administered by faith and to faith it truly set the recipient apart as belonging to the family of God, although in the case of infants it did not indicate that they had been regenerated. It anticipated the work of regeneration as the faith of the covenant parents was manifest in the works of obedient nurture of their children.

4

The Nature and Manner of True Worship

We turn now to a consideration of what is involved in worship which is acceptable to God. That each Sunday a congregation should worship in a manner which will glorify God is of supreme importance because the spiritual integrity of the corporate worship of the church will determine the vitality of the church's life. The church is faced with the increasing secularization of society today, and there are strong pressures toward the secularization of the church's worship. If resistance to these pressures is to be successful, the people of God must exercise theological discrimination and be able to discern which worship practices fulfill God's requirements and which do not. It is not enough that the motives of our hearts in gathering for a service of worship should be right. Indeed, there must be a very sincere intention to offer up appropriate worship to God. But God has revealed Himself to us, and He has given us certain clear principles which must guide our minds as well as our hearts.

Basic to our discussion of the subject before us is our
Lord's statement to the woman of Sychar referred to in
Chapter 1, "They that worship him must worship him in
spirit and in truth" (John 4:24). Before we discuss in detail
what it means to worship in spirit and in truth, we must first
take note of one fundamental principle which also arises out
of the conversation of our Lord and the Samaritan woman.
This is the fact that the object of our worship, or what we
worship, is all-important. The Savior said to the woman at
the well concerning her worship and the worship of the Samaritans, "Ye worship ye know not what: we know what we
worship: for salvation is of the Jews" (John 4:22). It is obvious that the Lord was including Himself as the proper object of worship, for He Himself is the salvation of His people. It is through the Second Person of the Trinity, Jesus
Christ, the Son, and only through Him, that man can worship God. Christ Himself said, "No man cometh unto the
Father, but by [through] me" (John 14:6). But, of course,
there was more to His statement. The Christian knows that
there is only one true and living God, and that this one God
exists in three distinct persons, the Father, the Son, and the
Holy Spirit. The mystery of the Trinity is not something that
can be fully and satisfactorily explained or understood. It is
accepted on faith, because it is clearly taught in the Scriptures.

The Evil One, whom we call Satan, or the devil, desires to
be as God, and he seeks to be the object of the worship of
men, even as he sought the worship of Jesus (Matt. 4:9; Luke
4:7). All non-Christian worship is an expression of Satan's
attempt to draw away worshipers from the one true God and
to bring them to worship him. The apostle Paul makes this
clear with reference to the worship of idols, as he deals with
those in the Corinthian church who were troubled about eating meat offered to idols. "What say I then? that the idol is
any thing, or that which is offered in sacrifice to idols is any
thing? But I say, that the things which the Gentiles sacrifice,
they sacrifice to devils [demons], and not to God: and I
would not that ye should have fellowship with devils

[demons]'' (I Cor. 10:20, 21; see also II Cor. 6:14-18; II Thess. 2:3, 4; Rev. 13:4, 8, 12f.). In the Scriptures it is clear that God cannot be worshiped except as the Triune God. The denial of the doctrine of the Trinity renders the worship of the living God impossible. All those who reject the Triune God of the Bible and worship another god, perhaps one they have created in their own imaginations, are falling prey to the subtle efforts of Satan to seek worshipers for himself. The worshipers of all unitarian sects, as well as the worship of all churches belonging to the historic Protestant denominations which have turned away from orthodoxy to unitarian theology, is unacceptable to God. So also is the worship of any churches that deny the personality of the Holy Spirit, or who reject the blood atonement of the Lord Jesus Christ. The Bible makes clear the fact that ''without shedding of blood is no remission'' (Heb. 9:22), and worship will not be received by a righteous God from unforgiven sinners. Isaiah 1:10-20 makes precisely that point.

It would not serve the purpose of this present work to mention, much less to discuss, all of the various aberrations of doctrine which would render worship unacceptable to the one true God. At the risk of being misunderstood, however, I must say that some of those who have expended the greatest effort toward liturgical reform have been misguided because their reforms (or what might better be called their changes) indicate that they are more sensitive to contemporary cultural influences than they are to eternal theological truth. Acceptable worship must be directed to the God of the Bible, the one, true, and living God.

Worship in Spirit

We give consideration now to the meaning of our Lord's statement that ''they that worship him must worship him in spirit . . .'' (John 4:24). There is more than one thought conveyed by this expression ''in spirit.''

1. Worship must be in the Holy Spirit. Although there is no definite article in the text, it seems quite obvious to most

commentators that this is what "in spirit" means. Paul identifies the true worshipers, whom he calls the true "circumcision" (in contrast to those who simply mutilate the flesh), as those "who worship in the Spirit of God" (Phil. 3:3, NASB). This is a fundamental requirement in all Christian worship. It must be stated most emphatically that it is the work of the Holy Spirit which makes worship truly Christian. His ministry is inseparably related to the Lord Jesus Christ. It is His ministry not only to teach the truth concerning Christ to believers (John 16:13), but also to glorify Christ (John 16:14), which is certainly the supreme objective of all Christian worship.

The ancient church from as early as the second century addressed the prayer of invocation called the *epiklesis* to the Holy Spirit. This is the invocation to the name of the Lord by which the early Christians were identified—"those who call upon the name of the Lord" (see Acts 9:14, 21; I Cor. 1:2, etc.). In addressing this prayer to the Holy Spirit either at the opening of the service or before the celebration of the Lord's Supper there was a recognition of the fact that although the presence of Christ in worship is something upon which believers can rely, on the basis of His promise, nevertheless the church is not the dispenser of His presence, nor is any priest or minister. God is free and sovereign. Those who worship Him must recognize that He is not at their disposal. This does not mean that they cannot trust the Lord, that He might fail to keep His promise, or forget to be among them. It simply means that the Holy Spirit is the One who in His sovereign activity makes the presence of the Lord actual in the experience of the faithful worshipers. As J. J. von Allmen has well said, "Christian worship is open to the free and sovereign action of its Lord; it does not seek to manipulate it. In this sense it is the antithesis of magic."[1] Because the Holy Spirit is free and sovereign in His activity in the church, it is impossible for men to establish any regulations by which

---

[1] J. J. von Allmen, *Worship: Its Theology and Practice* (New York: Oxford University Press, 1965), p. 29.

any particular manifestation of the presence and/or power of the Spirit may be guaranteed. We do have in the Scriptures, however, clear teaching concerning the Holy Spirit's person and work which makes it possible to know what man's responsibilities in worship are, if he expects to experience the guidance and the power of the Holy Spirit in his worship.

If the Holy Spirit is to glorify the Lord Jesus Christ in the hearts of men and women gathered in the church for worship, He must not be quenched or grieved by sin in the lives of individuals, nor by the corporate sin of the congregation in failing to properly discharge its duties or to discipline its members. There are theologians who make a distinction between "quenching" the Spirit (I Thess. 5:19) and "grieving" the Spirit (Eph. 4:30). It would seem, however, that such a distinction is somewhat artificial. The apostle Paul, who is the author of both expressions, as he gave instructions concerning the living of the Christian life, was simply making clear in slightly different ways the importance of complete yieldedness to the Holy Spirit on the part of the people of God. If this is important in the everyday life of the Christian, it certainly is also important when he comes to worship in the congregation of the saints.

We can both grieve and quench the Holy Spirit by unconfessed sin in our lives, no matter what the particular nature of the sin may be. It is for this reason that the corporate confession of sin belongs in the very beginning of a service of worship. The confession of sin as an integral part of the order of worship has been eliminated in many evangelical churches of our day. Perhaps the general smugness of our time has made it unpopular, although I have heard some rather strange excuses for having omitted it. To begin a service of worship of the living God without a recognition and admission of our utter unworthiness to approach Him because of our sin is to be quite unprepared to appropriate the majestic presence of Christ and to render to God the glory due unto His name. The true believer's initial step in his salvation was genuine repentance for his sin. Only when he

possessed a truly repentant heart was he prepared by the
Holy Spirit to believe on the Lord Jesus Christ and receive
His saving grace. That same Holy Spirit who originally regenerated the believer (John 3:5, 6) continues to make him
conscious of the daily sins which are an offense to God (John
16:8). The Christian needs to continually remind himself of
his sin and to openly confess it (I John 1:9), even in the assembly of believers (James 5:16), for this is the means God
has provided for the forgiveness and cleansing so necessary
before worship is acceptable to God. "If I regard iniquity in
my heart, the Lord will not hear me" (Ps. 66:18), but "the
Lord is nigh unto all them that are of a broken heart; and
saveth such as be of a contrite spirit" (Ps. 34:18). Some time
ago I watched a television movie in which a well-born and
charming Anglican lady objected to her rector concerning
the use of the General Confession. "I am not a miserable of-
fender," she insisted most emphatically; but clearly the fact
that she insisted that she was not was in itself the definite
proof that she was. How thankful we should be for the ministry of the Holy Spirit in making us aware of our sins so that
they can be honestly confessed as we come to worship.

The convicting ministry of the Holy Spirit is, however,
only a small part of His activity in services of worship where
the people are yielded to Him. He is the One who gives liberty in the service (II Cor. 3:17). He also gives a sense of the
unity of the Spirit to each faithful believer when he worships
with his fellow Christians, a feeling which is not present in
any gatherings outside the church. He enables the singing to
be truly worshipful (I Cor. 14:15). (Singing is not worshipful
when people sing unthinkingly, as they so often do, very
familiar words to well-known tunes.) He directs and enables
as the congregation prays together (I Cor. 14:15; Eph. 6:18),
and His special prayer ministry is realized in intercession for
the saints according to the will of God (Rom. 8:26). When a
Spirit-filled minister stands in the pulpit to preach the Word
of God, it is the Holy Spirit who gives him utterance (Acts
2:4), and through this ministry of the Word the Holy Spirit
speaks to the churches (cf. Rev. 2:7, 11, 17, 29; 3:6, 13, 22).

When the Spirit speaks through His faithful ministers the people are enabled by Him to understand even the "deep things of God" (I Cor. 2:10). It is also the Holy Spirit who enables the believers who have heard the Word in the church to obey it (I Peter 1:22) as they go forth into the world.

Apart from the operation of the Holy Spirit Christian worship would be merely a human act, like heathen worship. It would be human effort to please God and merit His favor. Because of the Holy Spirit, however, Christian worship is actually a work of God in and through the believing community gathered unto Him. He glorifies His own name among the people in the midst of whom He dwells. Worship in the Spirit will always be accompanied by rejoicing. The exuberant joy which is spoken of in connection with the worship of the early church (Acts 2:46) and with the worship of heaven (Jude 24; Rev. 19:7) is not the result of human effort. It is the product of the Holy Spirit. Moreover, there is in the activity of the Holy Spirit an anticipation of the eschatological expectation which belongs to the church. It was expressed by Ezekiel as God tabernacling with His own: "I will be their God, and they shall be my people" (Ezek. 37:27). It is always especially evident in the observance of the sacrament of the Lord's Supper when the congregation remembers the death of the Lord Jesus "until He comes."

2. Worship must be spiritual activity in contrast to activity which is purely intellectual or physical. It is, of course, the whole human personality which is involved in Christian worship. This includes a person's thinking, feeling, and willing. However, to make the worship of God to be exclusively rationalizing or emotionalizing or moralizing is to limit in an unfortunate way the range of man's communication with God. There is a skepticism abroad which denies man's capacity to reach and touch reality apart from the material universe, but the witness of seers, saints, and sages through the centuries of history to the reality of spiritual communication with God stands perfectly sure. There is also an unbelieving rationalism which demands the satisfaction of the intellect in all religious activity, including faith. But the Scriptures make

it clear that men are not converted by logical argument. Faith in God's Word, produced by the Holy Spirit, is essential for conversion. It is also necessary for worship. While theistic proofs cannot by themselves convince the unbelieving, they do serve for confirmation of the faith by intelligibly relating the religious experiences of man to his rational, moral, and social interests and needs. This enriches his worship. Regenerated man is possessed of a spiritual life (I Cor. 2:15). The unregenerate are spiritually dead (Eph. 2:1). When a man repents and believes the gospel, the Holy Spirit gives him the gift of eternal life (John 6:63). He is born again. From this time on he has spiritual capacities (I Cor. 2:15), one of which is the ability to communicate with God in worship and to learn from Him spiritual truths which cannot be known apart from the ministry of the Holy Spirit (I Cor. 2:11, 12).

It is the spiritual activity of regenerated man as he communicates with God by faith which is to be differentiated from the reasonings of the mind or the actions of the body which are characteristic of all men everywhere whether they are regenerate or not. Jesus Himself made it clear that the activity of the Holy Spirit cannot be fully explained any more than we can explain where the wind comes from or where it is going when we hear it blowing (John 3:8).

The Christian must ever remember that he lives in a universe which is inhabited by dark, rebellious spiritual powers that are arrayed against the true and living God. These powers are under the command of Satan himself, who is called "the prince of the power of the air" (Eph. 2:2). However, the believer knows that the power of the indwelling Spirit of God within him is greater than the power of all the satanic forces (I John 4:4). He is thus enabled to use his spiritual resources and through the exercise of his spiritual privileges to defeat the efforts of evil powers and to worship God sincerely and acceptably.

As we have pointed out in an earlier chapter, it is easy to confuse that which is purely emotional with that which is spiritual. True spiritual worship, however, never leaves one emotionally exhausted nor does it bring on a nervous headache. Spiritual worship is produced through faith in a known

God and leaves one with a sense of peace. Remember also that while we worship God "in the beauty of holiness," we are never to confuse the aesthetic response to beauty with a spiritual response to the God who is beautiful Himself (Isa. 33:17), who has created the beauty of this world, and who blesses us with all spiritual blessings in Christ Jesus. Of course, this certainly does not mean that we should eliminate beauty from our worship. In the Old Testament, while no effort was spared to beautify the worship of God, He still required a spiritual response from His people. What needs to be understood today is that worship if it is truly spiritual must be beautiful. The aesthetic endowment, like the moral and rational qualities of man, is a truly spiritual endowment. This needs to be recognized in all worship which is an offering to God. It is so easy to degrade our worship with ugliness, bareness, and frippery. Our worship should reflect our understanding that "strength and beauty are in his sanctuary" (Ps. 96:6). An important rule to be observed in giving beauty to our worship is this: Anything which makes it easier for us to worship spiritually should be encouraged while anything that draws attention to itself rather than to God should be eliminated from our corporate worship services.

Perhaps a word needs to be included here concerning the physical movements of the body which are associated with worship, but may not in themselves have anything to do with spiritual worship. To bow one's head while another person prays in a worship service is not necessarily an act of worship. It may be an act of conformity to the customs of the people who make up the worshiping congregation. It is only to make spiritual worship easier or more meaningful that physical actions are of any real value in worship. Going through any physical motions apart from the lifting of one's spirit to God or the humbling of one's spirit before God is without significance.

Worship in Truth

Our Lord said that our worship must not only be "in spirit," but also "they that worship him must worship . . . in truth." We must now examine this phrase to see what it means.

1. Our worship must be in and through Jesus Christ. Just as the first phrase in the Lord's declaration, "in spirit," has been seen to refer to the Third Person of the Trinity, so this phrase obviously has reference to the Second Person, the eternal Son of God. Our Lord identified Himself on another occasion as the Truth (John 14:6). His humility, of course, would have caused Him to place Himself last in His statement about worship. As we have already seen, the character of Christian worship must correspond to God's revelation of Himself, which is essentially trinitarian. Christian worship, therefore, must always be carried on within the framework of the doctrine of the Trinity. Professor Hoon is correct when he says,

> While both worship and theological reflection upon its nature are carried on "through Jesus Christ our Lord," they are also to be carried on "in the name of the Father, and of the Son, and of the Holy Spirit." . . . The Trinity constitutes a basic morphology which cannot be violated if liturgical theology is to be Christian. As we explore the triune character of Christian revelation as basic for thought, however, we still must understand that here, as elsewhere, the integrating reality is Jesus Christ . . . so the decisive center of liturgical theology lies not in the Trinity in general but in Jesus Christ in particular.[2]

Let us remember that when we say that we offer all acceptable worship to God in and through Jesus Christ we must understand that this means Jesus Christ in all the fullness of His being and His work. We must see Him as the incarnate Son of God, as both the man Jesus and God's Anointed One, the Christ. In our worship we must always remember that the Eternal Word became a man in order that He might deliver man from the bondage of sin and accomplish on the cross all that was necessary to save believing man, the elect, from all the guilt and corruption of his sin and from death itself. In

---

[2]Paul W. Hoon, *The Integrity of Worship* (Nashville: Abingdon Press, 1971), p. 115.

our brief look at the worship of the Old Testament we were reminded of the fact that every Old Testament sacrifice pointed forward to the sacrifice of Christ.

It must not be overlooked—in fact, it must be constantly stressed—that since by the sacrifice of Himself the Lord Jesus Christ offered the one absolutely sufficient sacrifice for sin, which is the basis of all Christian hope, the corporate worship of the Christian church will always have that salvation event as its firm foundation. The sacrifice of Calvary cannot be repeated as the priest of the Roman cultus would attempt to repeat it day after day. It was offered "once for all" (Heb. 10:10). Jesus Christ "offered one sacrifice for sins forever" (Heb. 10:12). The idea of attempting to repeat this sacrifice is abhorrent to God and to all men who understand the price which was paid by the Savior when He died for the sins of men. The sacrifice of Christ then not only makes all priestly offerings of sacrifice an affront to God and a presumptuous invasion of the holy prerogatives of the God-man, but it also renders superfluous all acts of sacrifice which are offered to God as a means of achieving credit in His sight. If man could attain merit in the eyes of God by his own efforts, the value of the sacrifice of Christ would be greatly lessened. Christ alone made the one effectual and eternal offering for sin when He offered up His life on Calvary. Everything that is done in corporate worship, every part of the service, grows out of this dynamic event. The preaching of the gospel is the proclamation of this event. The prayers of the congregation are offered through the merit of it. The celebration of the Lord's Supper is the remembrance of it. Even the Lord's Day on which believers gather for their worship together is a part of the triumphant climax of the redemption event in Christ's resurrection from the dead. The apostle Paul was not minimizing the crucial importance of Christ's sacrifice to true and acceptable corporate worship when he urged upon the Roman Christians that they (and all of us) should present (or yield) their "bodies a living sacrifice, holy, acceptable unto God" (Rom. 12:1). He called this their "reasonable service," or perhaps a better translation would be their "spiritual service of worship" (NASB). He was simply making clear the fact that any form of worship which might pretend to contain an element of sacrifice was meaningless, in the light of Christ's death upon the cross, apart from the worshiper's having yielded his own life, body and soul, in obedience to the Lord.

The eschatological event which is the final climax to the salvation provided by the Son of God, His second coming, must also be kept before the worshiping congregation if Jesus Christ is to be honored and appropriately worshiped in the liturgy. This does not call for an undue emphasis on prophecy, but it demands careful consideration of the necessity of a liturgy which is theologically complete. While the second coming of Christ is always clearly presented in the institution of the Lord's Supper, one should not allow those occasions to be the only times when the blessed hope of the Lord's return is mentioned in the services of worship.

2. Worship "in truth" means to worship God in a manner thoroughly consistent with His revelation of Himself in the Scriptures. God has made known His will; He expects His children to be knowledgeable about what He has said, to believe His Word, and to be obedient unto it. Christian worship is always based upon a strong theological foundation. We have previously pointed out that in order for worship to be acceptable to God it must be offered to the Triune God in strict accord with what the Bible tells us about each person in the Godhead. In addition to this, man must offer to God only that which is acceptable to Him. God can have nothing to do with that which is false; He cannot accept what He has said is unacceptable to Him.

For example, we cannot offer to Him something to make up for, or, in other words, to atone for, our sins. Penance is a Roman Catholic institution by which penitent sinners are assigned certain tasks, perhaps repetition of the "Hail, Mary" or the Lord's Prayer. This is to counterbalance the sins which they have committed. While no Protestant churches practice the assigning of penance, there are a good many Protestants who practice something akin to it by attempting to make up for their sins. I remember very well an officer in my regiment when I was on active duty in the Korean War who said to me one Sunday morning after a service which I had conducted, "Chaplain, I haven't been a very good boy this week, so I thought I ought to come to the church service." His attitude demonstrated that he expected God to receive his attendance at a service of worship as at least in some measure making up for the sinful indulgences of the previous days. Such an offering is totally unacceptable to God. We must keep in mind Christ's all-sufficient atonement for sin if we are to understand what the psalmist, David, said after confessing his own horrible sin. "Thou desirest not sacrifice; else would I give it: thou delightest not in burnt offering. The sacrifices of God are a broken spirit: a broken and a contrite heart, O God, thou wilt not despise" (Ps. 51:16, 17). His prayer was, "Hide thy face from my sins, and blot out all mine iniquities. Create in me a clean heart, O God; and renew a right spirit within me" (vv. 9, 10). In view of Christ's sacrifice what the believer needs when he sins is a truly repentant heart; he cannot atone for the evil. It does not honor God for us to come to Him as though He had not done what He has done, or as though His promises were undependable.

3. Worship "in truth" must be worship offered in a thoroughly truthful way; therefore, there can be in true Christian worship no pretense or insincerity. We can expect God to receive glory to Himself only from that worship which is based upon genuine faith in Him and absolute confidence in His Word. A number of times in recent months I have had men tell me after a Sunday morning worship service that they really did not believe the Bible was thoroughly trustworthy, and they could not personally accept as valid much of what was done in the service, but they thought it was good for them to attend anyway. One wonders how many who have never put their personal trust in the Lord and who seriously doubt His Word still may attempt to worship Him. Their worship would not qualify as being offered "in truth."

We must never forget that truth is reality. In every approach of men to God, whether it be as individuals or in groups, there must be absolute reality. If in any part of our worship service there is a suggestion of unreality, of sentimentality, of insincerity, if there are words spoken or sung without the worshiper's thinking about what he is saying or singing, or if one participates simply to make an impression or for the gratification of one's ego, then the validity and integrity of worship are lost. Christianity demands truth.

The Question of Order

We have already seen that every Christian should have a strong sense of belonging to a community of believers, of being a member of a society which has a corporate life, the most important and characteristic activity of which is the public worship of God. The fact that Christians worship in groups makes certain demands upon them. A group is more than a crowd of individuals. In a true church gathered for worship there is a unity of the believers with a self-consciousness of its own. Corporate or group action always requires a certain form. An individual who worships alone may act in his own way, but when an aggregate of individuals comes to be what is called a congregation or community of believers they must have form and order in their worship. In the church this is called ritual or liturgy. There are those today who express strong objections to all ritual in the worship of God. Let me say very candidly that such an objection is simply foolishness, for once a group comes together to worship, inevitably there must be some ritual. The question is really not whether there will be ritual, or what we refer to as liturgy. The only question is whether there will be good or bad ritual, a liturgy that is helpful and meaningful or one that is not. I have discovered that in churches where there is a strong insistence that they are nonliturgical there is often a very strict liturgy. The order of service does not vary one whit from Sunday to Sunday. No one would dare suggest that the service should begin in any other way than it always does.

Since there are order and structure in the human body, and order and structure in the universe, it is not at all strange that God has decreed that in the church everything should be done purposefully and in order (I Cor. 14:40). The church is the body of Christ. All of us recognize that every Christian worship service is composed of a number of different items, hymns, prayers, and the like. How are these to be arranged? All too often one gets the impression that they might have been shuffled like a deck of cards and arranged the way they happened to fall. At other times they appear to have been arranged according to the particular convenience or inclination of the pastor who prepared the service. Often they seem to have stayed in an arrangement fixed many years before and continued because the more elderly members of the congregation felt comfortable with the familiar order and resisted any suggestion of a change.

The question arises quite naturally, is there a correct order for a worship service which should always be followed? The Anglican and American Episcopal and Reformed Episcopal churches with their Books of Common Prayer would probably argue for an affirmative answer to this question, for they have a prescribed order which has been the same for many years for both their Morning and Evening Prayer. These allow for only slight variations of the order, all of which are themselves prescribed. It is not my purpose to argue the right or wrong of a fixed liturgy. I have received great blessing in worship in Anglican churches, as I have from worship in congregations without a prescribed order of worship. To insist on a fixed order of worship, however, seems to me to go beyond the liberty which I believe the Holy Spirit gives us in Christian worship. This conviction is strengthened by the fact that the New Testament contains no instructions whatsoever concerning the order of service. In fact, there are but the barest hints as to what order of worship there was in the churches established by the apostles. To say, however, that I believe a fixed order of worship is unnecessary is certainly not to say there is no structure upon which to properly build a worship service. That Christian worship certainly does have a definite structure seems clearly indicated in the Scriptures. This appears preeminently in the fact that biblical worship is dialogue.

Worship as Dialogue

There are two basic principles which should be observed by all those whose responsibility it is to establish the order for any individual worship service. These same two principles should always be taught to the members of the worshiping congregation so that they will understand why the order is arranged as it is and will appreciate the significance of the various parts in their places. If they understand they will certainly be able to worship more intelligently. The first of these principles is that worship should be looked upon as a dialogue between God and His people. God speaks to them and they answer Him. God speaks again and they reply. The pattern of a dialogue is found again and again in the Scriptures, particularly in the Old Testament where much detail is given concerning the worship of the Lord's people and where there are numerous instances of God's speaking directly to His people.

One of the best examples of the dialogue pattern, and the one which seems to be the starting point for many theologians in their study of worship, is found in the account of Isaiah's vision of God recorded in the sixth chapter of his prophecy. The first two verses contain a description of the throne of God in the heavenly temple:

> In the year that king Uzziah died I saw also the Lord sitting upon a throne, high and lifted up, and his train filled the temple. Above it stood the seraphims: each one had six wings; with twain he covered his face, and with twain he covered his feet, and with twain he did fly.

No attempt is made by the prophet to describe the form of God Himself, although it is immediately apparent that the central figure of worship is God and not the worshiper. The seraphim, those fiery angelic beings whose task it is to serve the Lord and who therefore stand in His presence awaiting their orders, are described in some detail. Their very posture is full of meaning. In the presence of the One who is the very perfection of holiness they use only two of their wings to fly at His bidding and to carry out His will. Four of their six wings are used to cover themselves because they are in His holy presence. We can learn much from this. We far too often presume upon God's goodness and come to Him with no recognition of our own unworthiness. The seraphim begin the dialogue as they speak for God Himself. Their words are both an ascription of praise and a call to worship.

> And one cried unto another, and said, Holy, holy, holy, is the Lord of hosts: the whole earth is full of his glory. (v. 3)

The next verse indicates that it was the Lord Himself who spoke through the seraphim. The perfections of His power are indicated in the shaking of the foundations of the threshold. The Shekinah glory, as well as the incomprehensible fullness of His being, is suggested by the statement that the house (temple) was filled with smoke.

> And the posts of the door moved at the voice of him that cried, and the house was filled with smoke. (v. 4)

The first response of the prophet in the dialogue follows. It is a confession.

> Then said I, Woe is me! For I am undone; because I am a man of unclean lips, and I dwell in the midst of a people of unclean lips: for mine eyes have seen the King, the Lord of hosts. (v. 5)

The dialogue continues as God acts and speaks again through the seraph who flies to the prophet, bringing a burning coal from the altar, laying it upon his mouth, and pronouncing absolution.

> Then flew one of the seraphims unto me, having a live coal in his hand, which he had taken with the tongs from off the altar: And he laid it upon my mouth, and said, Lo, this hath touched thy lips; and thine iniquity is taken away, and thy sin purged. (vv. 6, 7)

The Lord continues the divine side of the dialogue with a direct call to service.

> Also I heard the voice of the Lord, saying, Whom shall I send, and who will go for us? (v. 8a)

The prophet responds with the offering of himself.

> Then said I, Here am I; send me. (v. 8b)

Finally God explains the amazingly difficult task to which Isaiah has been called, and what the results of his labors will be.

> And he said, Go, and tell this people, Hear ye indeed, but understand not; and see ye indeed, but perceive not. Make the heart of this people fat, and make their ears heavy, and shut their eyes; lest they see with their eyes, and hear with their ears, and understand with their heart, and convert, and be healed. (v. 9, 10)

The prophet has a final question.

> Then said I, Lord, how long? (v. 11a)

And God a final response,

> And he answered, Until the cities be wasted without inhabitant, and the houses without man . . . and the Lord have removed men far away, and there be a great forsaking in the midst of the land. (v. 11b, 12)

Certainly this dialogue is a pattern of what should take place in every worship service, with the exception of the prophet's last question and the Lord's response. We do not always have these two details. Unfortunately in many of our services it is unclear just who is speaking to whom. It often appears that the choir is responding to the minister while the congregation observes and listens.

Another noteworthy example of dialogue is found in Jeremiah 1:4-8. We will not look at it in detail, but you will find that it is the account of the call of Jeremiah. God speaks first, and the prophet answers with a confession of his inability. God speaks again, reassuring the prophet with the promise of His presence.

That a dialogue should take place does not mean that one or the other of the participants is talking all the time. Communication often takes place in silence. There is an uplifting of the heart to God which is actually best rendered in silence. There is in stillness an opportunity for the developing of a deeper acquaintance with God. I am convinced that in most of our evangelical churches today there is too much talking. Visiting with one's friends is a pleasant occupation, but it certainly is no help in preparing for communion with God. Often one hears a service opened with the familiar introit of the choir which is based upon Habakkuk 2:20,

> The Lord is in his holy temple;
> Let all the earth keep silence before him.

But the service proceeds without a moment of silence. We must learn not only to sing to God when we worship Him, but also to be silent before Him. There are times that the voice of God can be heard only if His people are hushed in His presence.

We must also realize in connection with the divine-human dialogue that while the Word of God may be and is communicated through words, it is actually far more than words. God has said, "So shall my word be that goes forth from my mouth; it shall not return to me empty, but it shall accomplish that which I purpose, and prosper in the thing for which I sent it" (Isa. 55:11, RSV). God works in His Word. It is active and dynamic. It accomplishes His purposes. Similarly man may work in his response to God, so that we need not say that his response is limited to words. Obeying the Word is just as much a response as are any words that he speaks. God Himself is active also in the response of man as He is in all true worship. We have already noted that the Holy Spirit works not only in empowering the message of God as it goes forth from the lips of the preacher, but also in enabling the members of the worshiping congregation to make the proper response to it.

Perhaps the best illustration which we have of the dialogue between God and man in worship is found in the Genesis story of Jacob's dream at Bethel (Gen. 28:10-22). In his vision the patriarch saw a ladder reaching from earth to heaven. On the ladder the angels of God were moving in both directions, upward to heaven and downward to earth. This represents the two-way communication which takes place between God and man. The Lord, standing above the ladder, was the first to speak. He always takes the initiative in worship. He promised to make Jacob and his descendants the heirs to His special covenant promises given to Abraham. He further promised to be with him wherever he wandered and to bring him back into the land of his fathers. Jacob's response to these words came when he awoke. It was not only a verbal response in which he expressed his reverential fear; it was also a response of action, for he took a stone, the very stone which was his pillow, poured oil upon it, and made a solemn vow. If the Lord would keep the promises made to him, Jacob vowed that the Lord would be his God; Bethel, the place of the vision, would be designated a house of God; and of all his substance the patriarch would give to God a tithe. As Stephen Winward has said in his valuable discussion of this event, "Here is revelation and response, message and prayer, divine promise and human vow, the sentiment of awe and sacramental act, symbol and sanctuary. Divine revelation, seen and heard, vision and message, elicits a response in which emotion, word, and action are combined."[3]

Many other instances of dialogue could be pointed out from the Old Testament. Jacob's experience was that of an individual worshiper, as were the visions of Isaiah and Jeremiah. Jacob's ladder was undoubtedly the figure behind the Lord's statement to the apostle Nathanael that he would see heaven open, and the angels of God ascending and descending upon the Son of man (John 1:51). Christ was making it clear that communication with God was to be obtained only through His own person. This teaches us an important lesson about both individual and corporate worship.

There are, of course, ample illustrations in the Scriptures of the corporate response of the children of God to the Word

---

[3]Stephen F. Winward, *The Reformation of Our Worship* (Richmond: John Knox Press, 1965), p. 16.

of God. A striking example is found in the experience of people of Israel when God renewed the covenant with them at Mount Sinai. Having redeemed His people from their bondage in Egypt, the Lord (again taking the initiative) called the leaders of the people to worship Him on the mountain. He then took Moses aside alone in order that He might deliver to him His holy ordinances and through him ratify the covenant with His people. Moses came down from the mountain and recounted to the assembled congregation the words of the Lord. There was an immediate response from the people, "All the words which the Lord has spoken we will do" (Exod. 24:3, NASB). Having received this response from the people to God's revelation of His will, "Moses wrote all the words of the Lord, and rose up early in the morning, and builded an altar under the hill, and twelve pillars, according to the twelve tribes of Israel. And he sent young men of the children of Israel, which offered burnt offerings, and sacrificed peace offerings of oxen unto the Lord. . . . And he took the book of the covenant, and read in the audience of the people: and they said, All that the Lord hath said will we do, and be obedient" (Exod. 24:4-7). Here again we see clearly God's Word to a redeemed people, and man's answer. There are a sacred book, a faithful preacher, an assembly of God's people, a sacrament, and a divine covenant. Finally there is a human commitment. These are the basic elements in the worship of God's people in any age.

When we turn to the New Testament we find that dialogue continues. God has spoken to the world in His Son (see Heb. 1:1, 2). True believers respond to Him by the yielding of their bodies as "a living and holy sacrifice, acceptable to God, which is [their] spiritual service of worship" (Rom. 12:1, NASB). It is particularly interesting to see something of the dialogue of revelation and response in the account of what transpired on the day of Pentecost, the birthday of the church in its New Testament form. Here God again took the initiative when the believers were gathered together. The Holy Spirit appeared with a mighty noise and with tongues like fire resting upon the apostles, who began to speak in languages which were not their own. At the sound of the Holy Spirit's coming there was a response from a multitude of Jews who were from other nations but were living in Jerusalem. They gathered together and responded to the miracle of the tongues of the apostles with a question, "How is it that we each hear them in our own language to which we were born?" (Acts 2:8, NASB). Then Peter, speaking for God, preached his great sermon, expounding the Word of God and explaining the gospel of salvation. The response of the assembled multitude came clearly, "Brethren, what shall we do?" (v. 37). God's instructions through His servant were, "Repent, and be baptized every one of you in the name of Jesus Christ, for the remission of sins, and ye shall receive the gift of the Holy Ghost" (v. 38). This particular dialogue concludes with a response which certainly must have been accompanied by spoken profession. Those who "gladly received the word were baptized: and the same day there were added unto them about three thousand souls" (v. 41).

From Revelation 19 it is clear that dialogue continues in the worship of heaven. The apostle John in his vision heard the sound of a multitude of redeemed people with the twenty-four elders and the four living creatures worshiping God. Then a voice came out of the throne, saying, "Praise our God, all ye his servants . . ." (Rev. 19:5). The response came with thundering power, "Alleluia, for the Lord God omnipotent reigneth" (v. 6). Then God's messenger, an angelic being, spoke with instructions to the apostle to write down the vision. He replied by falling down to worship, but the angel forbade this and called upon him to worship God (vv. 9, 10).

Undoubtedly a clear understanding of the principle of dialogue in worship will greatly assist the minister in his preparation and conduct of worship services. It will also substantially aid the individual worshipers to unite with their fellow believers in meaningful worship. In the history of the Christian church there have been many periods when the worship deteriorated to such a degree that the sense of dialogue completely disappeared. The church members of the early centuries of Christianity were actively involved in every service. This is clear from the descriptions of those services which we have from the early church fathers. During the Middle Ages unfortunately the Roman Church so distorted the dialogue that those who gathered in the churches lost any sense of personal response to a loving and forgiving God. The Scriptures were no longer read in the language of the people. Only on the rarest of occasions did the priest address a sermon to them. The worshipers became mere spectators to the mystical and awesome activity of the priest, who was himself the sole worshiper as he stood before the altar with his back to the congregation. For the people the important thing was simply to observe the sacred rite. How could there be any response when the people did not hear the Word of God?

As a result of the Reformation the active participation of the people in worship was to a great extent restored. Martin Luther not only gave to the people the Bible in their own language so that God could speak to them clearly, but he also gave them beautiful hymns in the vernacular with which they could unitedly respond to the grace of God in praise and adoration. Luther and Calvin, as well as the lesser Reformers, returned to the people their active participation in the worship of God.

In the centuries following the Reformation there was again a very serious distortion of the dialogue in public worship, a distortion which has continued down to our own day. With the strong Calvinistic emphasis on the sovereignty of God which came out of a large segment of the Reformation, with the prominence given to His work as the basis of every worthwhile act of man, there was a marked tendency to lay an excessive stress on the downward, divine side of the dialogue and to neglect the upward human response. The Puritans, great as they were in their theological discernment and in their zeal for personal purity of life, so emphasized the awesome holiness of God and His requirement of righteous living on the part of His people, that the assembly of the believers became little more than an opportunity to hear the Word of God read and preached. Only metrical versions of the Psalms were allowed to be sung in the worship services so that even the singing which was done was entirely God's Word to His people. The long prayers of the pastors were to be listened to, for they contained much of instruction and edification for the people. Any sense of corporate response to a loving God of infinite compassion and mercy was largely lost and again the people became spectators. Of course, it must be admitted that there were significant exceptions to this general rule, but for the Puritans and their successors the response of the children of God was to come in the daily living of the Christian life, not in the service of worship. They considered the sacrament of the Lord's Supper highly important, but it was observed only infrequently, and even in the communion the emphasis was upon the Word of God, not upon the response of the people.

Among the Anglicans and American Episcopalians the dialogue was somewhat distorted from the opposite side. The emphasis was placed too much upon the corporate activity of the people and not enough upon the Word of God. It is certainly true that Archbishop Cranmer in the compiling of the Book of Common Prayer made provision for the Scriptures to be read at both Morning and Evening Prayer, but there was very little emphasis upon preaching. The sermons were often little more than brief homilies. In neither the Morning nor Evening Prayer was a sermon indicated as part of the liturgy. The emphasis, somewhat borrowed from the Roman Church, was placed upon what was transpiring on the altar during the communion services. The liturgy was all-important because it afforded the proper means for corporate worship, including confession, adoration, thanksgiving, praise, and intercession. By this means the church as a body offered itself to God, yet without giving much attention to the demands made upon the believer by his holy God as they are recorded in the written Scriptures. It must be admitted, however, that one of the reasons that the liturgy of the Episcopal Church has had such strong appeal to young people who have been reared in the more evangelical Protestant churches and who have become discouraged in an attempt to find meaning in the services of their own churches is that the liturgy of the Book of Common Prayer gives them an opportunity to experience personal participation in the corporate response of a congregation of believers offering up meaningful worship to God.

As I have already pointed out, in the majority of the evangelical churches of our day there has been little or no instruction in worship. Believers do not generally understand the significance and special meaning of corporate worship. They do not understand that a group of sincere worshipers in a church is not simply an aggregate of the individuals that compose the congregation, but that something important is added, something both spiritually and psychologically valuable, which is not present in other groups. Americans have developed a spectator mentality. From early childhood they have seated themselves comfortably in front of their television sets to watch for hours the cartoons (while they were young), the dramas, the movies, or the sports events which are taking place on the picture tube before them. When they leave their homes it is to be entertained as spectators at the movies, at concerts, or at the sports stadium. Is it any wonder that when they attend a church service they carry their spectator attitude with them? They have learned to be enthusiastic for that which is highly entertaining and that which gives them an emotional thrill. Should it be a source of surprise that what they expect and desire most from their church services is a kind of personal enjoyment arising out of an entertaining program or an uplifting sermon?

Sadly enough, many modern churches where the Bible is honored as the Word of God are catering to this desire for entertainment so prevalent in our modern society, perhaps without fully realizing what they are doing. Using the latest of the current musical patterns, with rhythms much more appropriate on the stage or in a dance hall, singers well-trained in Hollywood techniques will pour forth sentimental songs which leave the members of an audience gasping with pleasure in their personal enjoyment of the music and with genuine appreciation of the skill of the performers. There is, however, no corporate worship involved. In lieu of applause the one conducting the service may appeal to the congregation for a loud unison "Amen," but this is not an expression of praise to God; it is an indication of sincere appreciation for the ability and personality of the musicians. It must be admitted that all of us enjoy good Christian entertainment, and there are times when it is appropriate. There is nothing intrinsically evil in a somewhat sentimental Christian song, as long as it stays within the boundaries of truth. Such songs, however, have no place in the assembly of believers gathered together to render acceptable worship to God.

Not long ago I attended a church of my own denomination. In the middle of the Sunday morning service a flutist of considerable skill rose without any introduction to play a solo. On the bulletin it was listed as "Ministry of Music." The young lady played a difficult classical composition with admirable technique. When she took her seat and the service continued, I doubt if anyone in the audience besides myself wondered what the "ministry" of that solo actually was, whether it was supposed to be God speaking to us through the beauty of His holiness. I am reasonably sure that the reaction of almost everyone in the congregation was simply enjoyment of the music. I could have enjoyed it greatly in a concert or recital, but a church service is not a musical recital.

The desire for personal enjoyment in the services of the church is evident with respect to the preaching as well as the musical parts of the service. We have all heard comments like this: "Dr. Smith is such a comforting preacher, and he has such a wonderful voice! I always feel better after listening to him." I could not number the times that individuals have shaken hands with me at the close of a service in which I had preached as clearly and as forcefully as possible some of the specific demands of the Word of God with respect to Christian living only to have them say, "I certainly enjoyed your sermon!" Now I would be the first to admit that there are often many truths in a biblical sermon which a devout believer can genuinely enjoy hearing, but sermons are not preached for enjoyment. The value of worship should not be judged by its effect, soothing or otherwise, on the worshiper. The fact that so many Christians gauge their personal estimate of the worth of a worship service on the basis of personal enjoyment indicates that they do not really comprehend what is involved in corporate Christian worship.

Subjective or Objective Worship?

This brings us to a brief discussion of the essential nature of true worship from the standpoint of the individual worshiper. Should a service of Christian worship subjectively focus a man's attention upon himself and his world? Or should his worship be directed exclusively Godward? Should the sermon simply objectively expound the Scriptures, or should it be aimed at a subjective response on the part of the worshiper? The answer to these questions is certainly very important for every pastor who is engaged weekly in the preparation of worship services. It is very easy to be misled if one reads exclusively the writings of certain liturgical theologians who have specialized in studies of this matter in recent years. On the other hand, it is possible to become greatly confused if one reads widely, because there are exactly opposite viewpoints expressed by those who have been interested in promoting liturgical reform. Some insist that worship which is objective, that is, which is addressed to God, is far better than subjective worship, which is addressed to the needs of men. Others would insist that worship is truly genuine only when it is worship which helps people.

Perhaps much of the problem stems from the fact that the terms *subjective* and *objective* are not by any means uniformly understood or used by those who discuss them in relationship to worship. Those who write on the subject use these terms with quite a wide variety of meanings. Sometimes they insist that what is called liturgical worship is objective while the more free or evangelical worship is subjective. Others would say that the Calvinist who emphasizes the sovereignty of God and designs his worship services to emphasize the expounding of the infallible Scriptures is objective, while the one who stresses the need of a response of faith in the worshiper is being subjective. There are those who insist that worship is proper and objective if it repudiates any appeal to the emotions, and improper and subjective if there is any engagement of emotion. Some would ridicule anyone who considers worship in terms of "receiving a blessing," and still others belittle objectivity as they understand it because it ignores the fundamental realities of human need.

The limitations of this book make impossible a detailed discussion of the problem of objectivity versus subjectivity in worship. That would involve a complete book itself, for the subject can be approached from many angles. There are a few things which must be said, however, or the practical results which I hope will attend the reading of this book will not be forthcoming. To begin with let me point out that it is not an easy matter to separate objectivity and subjectivity in worship, and great care must be exercised so that we do not stress one to the exclusion of the other. Those who would insist that in objective worship we give while in subjective worship we get ignore the clear fact that normally the subjective experience of the worshiper is intensified to the degree that he is truly involved in the giving of himself in the worship of God.

It is fundamental that we recognize that all true Christian worship must be theocentric. It is objective in the sense that the primary motion and focus of worship are Godward. This is why I would insist that if one goes to a worship service essentially for what he can "get out of it," he has missed the most vital concern that a true worshiper should have, that God be praised and glorified. At the same time I consider it obvious that the worshiper who seeks with all his heart to magnify and adore God and to listen reverently to His Word will be the one who goes away from the service with the deepest sense of personal blessing. We must remind ourselves that worship is giving to God the glory and honor due to His name, and that those who sincerely seek the honor of God will in turn always be honored by Him. God never ignores the needs of His children. He seeks our worship; at the same time He knows that we are completely dependent upon Him for the riches of His grace and goodness which alone sustain and satisfy us as we live the Christian life in this world.

I have pointed out before that it is the presence of Jesus Christ Himself in corporate worship which makes it what it is. Then let us remember that while Jesus lived all of His earthly life for the glory of God His Father and not to please Himself, at the same time He was here in this world not "to be served, but to serve, and to give His life a ransom for many" (Mark 10:45, NASB). It is therefore quite certain that if Jesus is Himself active in our services of worship, He will always minister to the needs of His faithful worshipers. Professor Hoon has well said, "The most essential nature God bears toward His creatures is that He is that life on which they depend, and the most essential nature of His grace is that it desires to be drawn on in its fulness. . . . The God of Christian faith is always a God who is glorified exactly in the sense, and to the degree, that His grace in all its fulness is importuned by man in his humanity and need."[4]

The faithful preacher who proclaims the Word of God will always be directing that Word to the needs of men, for that is how God Himself has focused His message in the Scriptures. Sometimes the proclamation of the Word results in deep conviction of sin. It often produces true conversion, for it is only through the Word that men are born again. Often the ministry of the Word edifies and instructs. Again it comforts and encourages. It also calls men to obedience and empowers them to obey. All of these may be considered subjective responses of men, but they are evidences of the working of God by His Holy Spirit in a service prepared supremely for the glory of God. It must always be kept in mind that the results which are sought in the response of worshipers in the divine-human dialogue of the service are secondary, not primary. Unless this is kept in mind there is the sad possibility

---

[4]Hoon, *Integrity of Worship*, p. 209.

that man will come to worship with no other desire than to satisfy his self-interest. If he has the impression that the only worthwhile service of worship is one in which he has a deep emotional experience, he may suffer the spiritually deadening malady of worshiping his experience instead of worshiping God.

To summarize, if the primary emphasis of our worship is the magnification of God, and the movement of the service is Godward, we can expect that there will be notable subjective results in the lives of the worshipers.

Worship as Offering

Let us turn now to a consideration of the second principle to be observed in our worship. It arises out of the objective aspect of our worship, which is always primary. It is the principle that worship must be regarded as offering. From the very beginning of the history of mankind those who desired to worship God brought an offering to Him. In our brief look at worship in the Old Testament period we saw that in the first recorded act of worship by Cain and Abel, the sons of Adam and Eve, each of them brought an offering unto the Lord. It is significant, of course, that Abel's offering was a sacrifice offered by faith while Cain's was an offering of the fruit of the ground. For our present purposes, it is important to note that the worship of God began with offering. Throughout the history of the Hebrews God's people erected altars and made offerings upon them to their God. Whether it was during the lives of the great patriarchs, who were in effect the high priests before the Egyptian bondage, or in front of the tabernacle in the wilderness, or within the courts of the temple in Jerusalem, to worship God was to bring an offering. The psalmist gave the invitation clearly, "Give unto the Lord the glory due unto his name: bring an offering, and come into his courts" (Ps. 96:8). This is perhaps the simplest statement in the Scriptures as to what is involved in the worship of God. Worship is not to be considered chiefly as getting from God; worship is giving. Worship is offering. If there is anything that evangelical Protestants need to understand today, it is this fact.

The great majority of the offerings of the Old Testament were sacrifices. Since Jesus Christ, the Son of God, offered Himself as the perfect sacrifice for the sins of men, there is no longer any need for blood sacrifices. The Roman Catholic teaching that the mass is a repetition of the sacrifice of Christ on the cross has been thoroughly repudiated by evangelical Protestants, but this very reaction against the erroneous teaching concerning the reoffering of the sacrifice of Christ has resulted in the false assumption that there is no longer any sacrificial element whatever in Christian worship. But this is to miss the clear teaching of the New Testament.

Because the sacrifice of Christ is the basis of all Christian faith and hope, if we are to be faithful to Him that sacrifice must always be prominent in our services of worship. It is a mistake to think of Christ's sacrifice as involving only His death on Calvary. It involves His resurrection from the dead and His ascension into heaven itself with the blood of the eternal covenant as well as His present intercession for the believer (see Heb. 13:20, 21). All this is included in His offering of Himself for sinners. Nothing can ever be added to that sacrifice; it is impossible for any other sacrifice for sin ever to be offered to the God of all righteousness.

It is clear, nevertheless, that Christians are to continue to sacrifice to the Lord as a part of their worship of Him. One of the most precious doctrines of the Reformation is the truth of the priesthood of all believers. The apostle Peter said, "Ye are a chosen generation, a royal priesthood, an holy nation, a peculiar people" (I Peter 2:9). Alas, far too many believers today have little or no consciousness that they belong to a holy priesthood with priestly functions. One of those priestly functions is indicated by Peter. "Coming to Him as to a living stone, rejected by men, but choice and precious in the sight of God, you also, as living stones, are built up as a spiritual house for a holy priesthood, to offer up spiritual sacrifices acceptable to God through Jesus Christ" (I Peter 2:4, 5, NASB). Here it is evident that those belonging to the Christian priesthood are to be exercising that priesthood in the offering up of spiritual sacrifices. These are in no sense to replace or to increase the efficacy of the one offering of Christ. Rather they are made possible by that one eternal sacrifice and are to be offered as a response to and in perfect union with that sacrifice.

What are the spiritual sacrifices which the apostle Peter tells us that believers offer to God? Let us look at what the Scriptures tell us about them.

First, the writer of the Epistle to the Hebrews tells us that we are to offer the sacrifice of praise. "Through Him, then let us continually offer up a sacrifice of praise to God, that is, the fruit of the lips that give thanks to His name" (Heb. 13:15, NASB). This does not mean that the mere singing of songs or the recitation of prayers with our lips in the services of worship constitutes acceptable sacrifice. The "fruit of the lips" must be the response of the spirit to the unfathomable grace of God in Jesus Christ. As we sing in the services of worship, let us remember that our songs are to be sung to the Lord, even though they also serve to edify and admonish other believers as well as ourselves. "Let the word of Christ dwell in you richly in all wisdom; teaching and admonishing one another in psalms and hymns and spiritual songs, singing with grace in your hearts *to the* Lord" (Col. 3:16). This is spiritual sacrifice.

A second spiritual sacrifice the Christian is to offer is the doing of good works. "Do not neglect doing good . . . for with such sacrifices God is pleased" (Heb. 13:16, NASB). Not all the good deeds of men are acceptable to God. That man who presumes to offer to God his own good works instead of placing his full trust and confidence in the sacrifice of Christ is offering an insult to God and incurring His wrath. The apostle Paul spoke of the sad condition of his own countrymen, the Jews, who in "going about to establish their own righteousness [had] not submitted themselves unto the righteousness of God" (Rom. 10:3). He warned such men that "wrath is come upon them" (I Thess. 2:16). However, the true believers were reminded by the same apostle that they were to "be careful to maintain good works" (Titus 3:8). These are the works that are a spiritual sacrifice. What is included? Any deed which is done because of the love of God and the desire to honor Him is a spiritual sacrifice acceptable to God.

A third spiritual sacrifice, mentioned in the same verse with doing good, is sharing (Heb. 13:16, NASB). This is the spiritual sacrifice of which Paul was the beneficiary when he wrote to the Philippians, "I have all, and abound: I am full, having received of Epaphroditus the things which were sent from you, an odour of a sweet smell, a sacrifice acceptable, well pleasing to God" (Phil. 4:18). Whenever the believer in sheer thanksgiving to God shares his material substance with those who are engaged in the ministry of the Word, or when he gladly places a generous check in the offering plate to support the work of his church, he is making an acceptable offering to the Lord. The receiving of an offering in a service of Christian worship should never be looked upon as a necessary interruption of the worship service, required for the maintenance of the church. It definitely belongs in the service; it should never be relegated to a box in the narthex of the church. During one of my pastorates, while I was still quite young, I yielded to the request of some of my elders to have the offering eliminated from the services and a small chest placed in the vestibule of the church where the worshipers could place their offerings as they came in or as they departed. This was a serious mistake. With some of the members of the church it produced a false sense of superior spirituality. The most unfortunate aspect, however, was that the sense of making an offering to God was completely gone. Worship is not exclusively offering, but the sincere offering of our money to God is worship. In the service the presentation of the offering should be impressive; it should be clearly evident that this is a response of the entire congregation to the goodness of God.

Paul spoke of his evangelistic work as an offering to God. The Gentile converts of his ministry were offered up to God as a spiritual sacrifice (Rom. 15:16). Because of the intense

opposition of evil men to the missionary work he was doing
he was prepared for martyrdom as his supreme and final offering to God (Phil. 2:17).

Finally, all true Christians are called upon to offer their
bodies continually unto the Lord for the living of pure and
holy lives before Him. "I urge you therefore, brethren, by
the mercies of God, to present your bodies a living and holy
sacrifice, acceptable to God, which is your spiritual service
of worship" (Rom. 12:1, NASB). In offering our bodies
as living sacrifices we are united with Jesus Christ "who
through the eternal Spirit offered himself without spot to
God" (Heb. 9:14). At some point in every corporate worship
service individual believers should make this climactic dedication of their entire personality to God. This may come in a
hymn following the sermon. It may at other times come as
part of the response following the confession of sin and the
declaration of pardon. When the communion is being observed it is very appropriate as a part of the communion service. Included in such an offering is the willingness to do His
will no matter what the cost, to love the brethren with pure
Christian love, and to seek in all aspects of life to demonstrate the reality of the living Christ dwelling within. No
sacrifice which man can offer to God can be a substitute for
self-sacrifice and self-offering.

I could not bring this discussion of worship as offering to a
conclusion without mentioning the sacrament of holy communion as offering. It has been pointed out that in no sense
can the observance of the Lord's Supper be considered a re-
enactment of the sacrifice of the cross or a reoffering of the
Lord's body and blood. Yet the sacrament may rightly be
considered as a sacrifice of praise and thanksgiving for the
saving grace of God in Christ and for the multiplied blessings
which come to us from being able spiritually to feed continually upon the Bread of Life Himself and to be constantly
cleansed by the efficacy of His shed blood from the stain of
our daily sins. The sacrifice of Christ, offered once for all, is
effective in the believer's life perpetually. The celebration of
the sacrament, then, must be a very special time, not only of

genuine thanksgiving but also of personal offering of the believers themselves fully and gratefully to the Lord.

Stephen Winward eloquently summarizes what I have said with respect to worship as offering. "The bridegroom does not merely give the ring itself to the bride; it is a sign and token of his loyal-love and commitment. In genuine worship, psalms and hymns, prayers and gifts are the signs and tokens of self-oblation. No man has truly worshiped unless he has given himself to God. This sacrifice, this oblation, must be made in life and conduct, in work and service, for the Christian liturgy does not end with the benediction. In order that it may be made in life as a whole, it should also be made in the context of worship."[5]

---

[5]Winward, *Reformation of Our Worship*, p. 50.

5

General Considerations Concerning the Order of Worship

Whenever a group of the Lord's people gathers together to worship Him, whether it be in a church building or in another place of meeting, and to one is assigned the task of preparing an order of service and then leading the corporate worship, he is indeed given a very serious responsibility. If he does his job well, the believers who have come together will go away with a deep sense of peace and spiritual refreshment. If he does not, they may feel empty and unsatisfied. It is of utmost importance that the leader be spiritually prepared and psychologically attuned to the needs of those whose worship he will lead. Andrew Blackwood has called worship "the finest of the fine arts." He says, "If preaching is a fine art, as many of us believe, public worship should be finer, as the whole should be better than any of its parts."[1] If

---

[1]Andrew Blackwood, *The Fine Art of Public Worship* (Nashville: Cokesbury Press, 1939), p. 8.

this be true, and I personally believe that it is, then the minister who prepares and conducts the service of a worshiping congregation week after week needs to become a master of the art of leading the worship of the people of God. Let me assure you that such mastery will not come easily. The preparation of the other parts of a truly meaningful worship service and placing them in the proper order will often take almost as long as the preparation of the sermon. Whenever I say this to seminary students, they often express incredulity. Later, after some months of experience in the pastorate, they tell me that they have discovered that I was right.

It certainly is true that every member of a congregation of the Lord's people gathered for worship has an individual responsibility to take part fully in the common worship and thus contribute to the corporate experience. The mastery of the art of participation in corporate worship on the part of individual worshipers is vital to their spiritual growth and well-being. It is nonetheless true that the one whose lot it is to formulate the order of worship and then lead the praises and prayers of the people has a most significant responsibility. There is always the temptation for a minister, when he becomes dissatisfied with his worship services, to introduce some novelty or to tinker with the order of service just for the sake of change. This is not the solution. Each one who has the privilege of leading worship must study the subject carefully and must make sure that he is giving sufficient time to the preparation of each service of worship so that it will be not only theologically accurate but also psychologically correct and intellectually satisfying.

There are many ministers today whose only preparation for the worship service on Sunday morning, apart from the preparing of the sermon, consists in changing the hymn numbers on their regular order and deciding which Psalter selection shall be read responsively so that the bulletin can be printed or mimeographed well in advance. It is not surprising that when pastors conduct worship services prepared in this way the services convey to the worshipers little sense of unity and of the proper movement and meaning of each of their component parts. Ministers who function in this manner are simply carrying through an order established firmly by custom. They have given little or no thought to the reason for the order of the service, as for example, why a hymn always follows a particular prayer or the offering is received at a specific place each Sunday. If the movement of the service has little meaning for the minister who leads, it will certainly have less for those who make up his congregation. It would be quite a rare thing today to find members of evangelical churches with a free liturgy who could provide a rationale for the series of things which make up the worship services to which they are accustomed. This to me points up the tragedy of the neglect of the all-important subject of worship in our churches today. It demonstrates a woeful ignorance of all the biblical, theological, historical, and psychological factors that contribute to an authentic service of Christian worship.

There are churches, many of them today, where pastor and people would be indignant if they were accused of being liturgical. Yet they have a liturgy which is more rigid than that of the Anglican Book of Common Prayer. In many churches which I have attended, the service every Sunday morning begins in exactly the same way, with the singing of the doxology, and proceeds according to a pattern which is never changed. If one were to suggest the omission of the doxology from the service or even a variant way of beginning the worship, he would run into rigid opposition. Now the word *liturgy* comes from a Greek word which simply means "the work or service of the people." So a church's liturgy is just the order of the service which the people follow. As Donald Macleod has so well said, "The issue . . . is not, nor can it be, a matter of a liturgical versus a non-liturgical service. The problem has been bad liturgy—shapeless and formless."[2] Thus we must be concerned about finding a way to reform and improve the worship in our churches.

---

[2] Donald Macleod, *Presbyterian Worship* (Richmond: John Knox Press, 1965), p. 11.

The Heritage of Our Liturgy

As we search for the proper means of shaping our liturgy, our order of worship for the people of God, we need to give serious attention to our Christian heritage and to carefully examine the practices of the church down through its history. The fact that a particular practice is old does not necessarily mean that it is good. Those of us who share the Reformed faith and rejoice in the deep theological insights which were passed down to us by the Reformers certainly ought to be concerned about learning all that we can from them about the matter of corporate worship. Our Protestant heritage of doctrine and tradition from the apostolic church through the Reformation down to the present day has been enriched by many small streams flowing into it. To ignore this heritage is to miss much that would aid us in making the Sunday morning hour of worship more meaningful to all who come to worship.

It is an interesting fact that, while a large number of evangelical Protestants today identify themselves as Calvinists, and they consider that the word of John Calvin concerning a doctrinal matter would be second in importance only to the inspired words of Scripture, if a minister were to introduce into the worship services of his Calvinistic congregation some of the liturgical practices instituted by John Calvin in the churches of Geneva, he would probably be accused of going liberal or at least would be stigmatized as having gone "high church" or ritualistic. For example, Calvin was opposed to allowing ministers to pray extemporaneously. He composed written prayers for the use of the pastors associated with him.

Many of those evangelicals whose doctrinal position is Arminian probably do not realize that John Wesley did not break with the Church of England because of any objections he had to the liturgy. Through their great hymns he and his brother Charles contributed much to the enrichment of the musical worship of the established church as well as to that of evangelical Christian churches throughout the world. Let me make it clear that I am not advocating a return to the practices of any former day. However, I am deeply concerned that we all learn all that we can from the great Christians of the past as well as from those living today about ways and means of enriching our worship services and making them more meaningful to all of the participants. Every element of the worship service should be examined carefully. We can learn much of great interest and of enriching value by examining the historical significance of some of the forms in use in modern worship services. It will greatly increase the appreciation of worshipers if they understand that they are participating in a brief litany, such as the Sursum Corda, which comes from the very ancient church, or that they are following a form for the confession of their sins which was used by John Calvin or John Knox. I have known believers to be both surprised and blessed to find that a hymn they were singing had been written during the very early centuries of the church and had been used by believers for many hundreds of years.

There are those who would insist that one who shows concern about careful preparation of the order of worship as well as his leadership of the service is being unspiritual and formalistic and is occupying himself with superficial decorations instead of essentials. They would insist on simply following what they would call "the leading of the Holy Spirit." But we must remember that it was concerning the conduct of the worship service at Corinth that the inspired apostle Paul wrote, "Let all things be done decently and in order" (1 Cor. 14:40). It is certainly wrong then for us to use the work of the Holy Spirit as an excuse for refusing to think seriously about our worship services and to plan carefully for every part of them, preparing the order of worship under the guidance of the Word of God and the ministry of the Holy Spirit. It is not intellectually honest for us to make an emotional appeal to the Holy Spirit instead of taking the time for the careful, prayerful thought and planning which preparing worship services demands. If corporate worship is to bring glory to God and also bless the worshipers as it should, its component parts should be fully understood so that none will be omitted and so that each will contribute to the unity and meaning and relevance of the whole.

Instruction in Worship

I am well aware that in attempting to suggest the instruction that should be given to worshipers and the methods of establishing proper orders of worship I am going to propose things to which some readers will take exception. It is my earnest hope, however, that each one will give serious consideration to the scriptural and psychological reasons behind the suggestions which are made and make sure that his objections are based upon equally sound reasons and not just upon personal taste or the desire to maintain a familiar routine. I have already indicated my opinion that instruction concerning the all-important activity of worship has been sadly neglected in most of our evangelical churches. It has also been seriously neglected in Bible schools, Christian colleges, and theological seminaries. This is perhaps the reason why most evangelical Christians today evaluate their worship experiences almost entirely on the basis of the sermons to which they have listened.

Let me, in the light of the need for instruction, suggest some basic matters which every faithful pastor needs to make sure that the members of his congregation understand. I have already mentioned the fact that every true worshiper must personally know God through faith in His Son Jesus Christ, for it is the Triune God whom he worships. To be a true worshiper he must be a believing member of the covenant household. I have also mentioned that the presence of the risen Savior, the Lord Jesus Christ, according to His promise, is the single most significant factor which should draw the believer irresistibly to the common worship of the church. If Christians truly understand this they will not make their decision as to whether they will attend a worship service on the basis of which minister is occupying the pulpit. Rather they will realize that they cannot afford to be absent when their living Lord visits His people and fellowships with them as they worship in His name.

A very good place to begin in giving church members instruction in worship is a study of the early assemblies of Christians as they are recorded for us in the New Testament. In these will be found important lessons. We will examine only one of them and that briefly. The first Sunday service of the Christian church as we know it was held on the evening of the first Easter, the day of resurrection. The disciples were assembled behind closed doors, but the risen Savior whom some of them had seen earlier in the day, suddenly appeared in their midst, exactly where He had promised to be when His own were assembled in His name. What follows indicates what takes place when Jesus meets with His own.

"Then were the disciples glad, when they saw the Lord" (John 20:20b). True gladness will always be characteristic of those who sincerely assemble in the name of the Lord and by faith recognize His presence among them.

"Then said Jesus to them . . ." (vv. 19, 21). Those who come together in the house of the Lord to honor their Savior will always hear Him speak to them, no matter how inadequate the sermon of the minister may be. I well remember hearing my father tell of an experience he had while serving as a Sunday school missionary in a rather wild western mining camp for a few months before he entered theological seminary. After he had delivered a Sunday morning sermon to the best of his ability at that time, he was standing at the door of the schoolhouse (which served as the church building) and was greeting the worshipers as they left the service. A godly Christian woman who was a faithful attendant at all of his services shook his hand and said, "Mr. Rayburn, I have never heard a sermon so poor that I couldn't get something good out of it for my own spiritual needs." My father would have been the first to admit that the sermon wasn't good that morning, but it was evident that one worshiper had come properly prepared to worship God and to hear His Word.

"Peace be unto you" (v. 21a). The worshiper who has experienced the Lord's presence and who has heard Him speak and has responded with an obedient attitude will always leave the service with a deep and abiding sense of peace.

Jesus continued and said, "As my Father hath sent me, even so send I you" (v. 21b). While this statement contains much which is not particularly relevant to our discussion, I do believe that there is an indication here that the true worshiper will go away from any properly conducted worship service with a renewed sense of his mission in the world, and with an understanding of something specific which is required of him in obedience to the Lord.

"And when he had said this, he breathed on them, and saith unto them, Receive ye the Holy Ghost!" (v. 22). A sense of the renewal of the power of the Holy Spirit should always characterize the experience of one who has been refreshed in personal communion with and worship of God through His Son the Lord Jesus Christ.

The first appearance of the risen Lord with His own makes clear by example the fact that the true worshiper should come away from a worship service with a sense of joy and peace, with the knowledge that God has spoken to him, with a clearer understanding of his responsibilities in the world, and with renewed assurance of the enabling presence and power of the Holy Spirit. Apart from such general matters, however, rather more specific instruction will be necessary to insure that the congregation will take its rightful place in the several parts of common worship.

The nature and significance of corporate worship and the importance of each member of the congregation accepting his own responsibility for contributing to the common worship experience have already been stressed, as has the matter of overcoming the "spectator syndrome." Instruction must also be included concerning some of the general elements of the order of worship. We will examine each of the constituent elements of the order of worship in turn.

Prayer

Let us speak first about prayer in the service, for every worship service will always include prayer. The Anglicans call their Sunday services "Morning Prayer" and "Evening Prayer." Most Christians need instruction about their individual participation in all of the prayers that are offered. Too many are accustomed to listening quietly and reverently to the prayers but without any sense of personally uniting in and offering up the prayers themselves. As a matter of fact it is very difficult even for one who is well instructed in worship and conscious of his responsibility in common worship to keep his mind upon the prayer being offered by the pastor and to pray with him. There are a number of contributing factors to the failure of so many individual worshipers to properly share in the congregational prayers. Many pastors have a bad habit of making long prayers in the pulpit. These tax the powers of concentration of even the most well-disciplined members of the assembly. I recall very vividly the famous warning which was repeated to a seminary class by one of my godly professors. He said, "Young men, long prayers are for the closet, and short prayers are for the pulpit, and the devil will always seek to get you to practice the opposite." He reminded us of the ease with which we excused ourselves from even brief prayers at the close of the day. We were sure that the Lord would understand how tired we were. Yet when we stood in the pulpit it would be easy to pray on and on. I have passed this advice on to another generation of seminary students, and I trust they have remembered it.

Some prayers are often designated "pastoral prayer" in the church bulletin; this very name suggests that it is the prayer of the pastor and not of the congregation. Prayer should have a proper designation such as "Prayer of Thanksgiving," or "Prayer of Intercession." Often prayers are offered by the pastor in such flowery language that many of the people in the congregation find it difficult to identify with the elaborate expressions used and therefore do not try to make the prayers their own. Of course, one of the contributing factors to the problem is the fact that rarely are new converts provided any instruction about what they should do when the pastor is praying. Even many of those who grew up in the church have never received any real instruction in how to take part in the pastor's prayer, or in the audible prayer of anyone who is praying in a gathering of Christians. Pastors rarely suggest to their congregations that they are expected to participate in the prayers that are offered. Some pastors apparently have the idea that by some sort of spiritual osmosis the members of their churches will assimilate the fact that they are expected to pray with the pastor when he prays, using his words as their words. The simple request, "Let us pray," as a minister begins his prayer is not sufficient to convey to many individuals the idea that they are to be active in offering up the prayer of the pastor in unison with him.

Of course, a pastor cannot begin every prayer with words of instruction concerning proper congregational participation. If, however, there is adequate instruction apart from the worship services themselves, and if in brief rubrics introducing especially the prayers of intercession the pastor asks the congregation to join with him as he prays, and if his prayers are brief enough and properly phrased to give the individual worshiper a proper sense of sharing in the petitions, congregations will learn to take part and will greatly appreciate the privilege.

The "Amen"

Our discussion of prayer in the services of worship would not be complete without a consideration of what I believe is one of the very best ways of making sure that all members of a congregation have a proper sense of participation in the offering up of prayer to God. This is to encourage the proper corporate conclusion to every prayer in the services of the church with a unison "Amen." I fully realize that I am suggesting something with which most evangelical congregations in this country are not familiar and against which there would undoubtedly be much opposition. In this matter, however, I believe that we can learn much from our devout Episcopalian brethren. When the quiet but distinct murmur of scores of "Amens" arises after each prayer in an Anglican or Episcopalian service, one senses in a meaningful way that he is participating with others in the offering up of specific praises and petitions to God on high, and he experiences the communion of the saints in a very significant way.

Basic to a consideration of this matter, however, is not the practice of another church or denomination but what the Scriptures have to say on the subject. The Westminster Confession of Faith, which is the historic creed of Presbyterians, and is held in high honor in many other denominations, has a clear statement that "the acceptable way of worshiping the true God is instituted by Himself and so limited by His own revealed will that He may not be worshiped according to the imaginations and devices of men or the suggestions of Satan, under any visible representation or any other way not prescribed in the Holy Scriptures." Yet strangely enough, those churches which hold firmly to this confession and require their ministers to take a solemn vow upholding it have completely neglected the offering of the "Amen," which is so clearly given full scriptural authority.

Again and again in the Bible, after the leader of a worshiping congregation offered a prayer to God the congregation made that prayer its own with a distinct "Amen." Consider, for example, the response of the congregation when King David, after bringing the ark of the covenant into the city of Jerusalem and offering a festival sacrifice and a psalm of thanksgiving, concluded with the familiar words, "Blessed be the Lord God of Israel for ever and ever." Then we read, "And all the people said, Amen, and praised the Lord" (I Chron. 16:36).

Before the people of Israel went into the land of Canaan, Moses instructed them to respond with an "Amen" to even the curses of the Lord delivered by the Levites (see Deut. 27:14-26). The psalmist used the "Amen" and called for its use by worshipers as well (see Ps. 72:19; 89:52; 106:48). Moreover, it was not only an Old Testament practice for the congregation to respond to prayer with the "Amen." That it was the customary conclusion of the corporate prayers in the churches established by the apostles is clear from Paul's warning to the Corinthian church that their prayers and

singing should not be done in an unknown language. Otherwise, "how shall he that occupieth the room [place] of the
unlearned [ungifted] say Amen at thy giving of thanks, seeing he understandeth not what thou sayest?" (I Cor. 14:16).

"Amen" is a great word. It seems to have been provided
by God for the special use of His people. It is untranslatable
and universal like "Hallelujah," which is an extremely
meaningful expression to every Christian. "Amen" is a word
that speaks of a continuity of Christian fellowship. It was
used by saints of the Old Testament and it appears frequently
in the New Testament. We find from a study of the history of
the postapostolic church that it was the custom for the whole
church to utter this word aloud in order to express cordial assent to everything that had been uttered in prayer. Saint
Jerome tells us that at times the sound of the Amen "seemed
like a crack of thunder."

Many evangelical Christians today feel uncomfortable in
the services of those churches where there is often a shouted
"Amen" from individual members of the congregation when
they heartily approve what the minister has said. Some pastors even encourage these loud tokens of endorsement for
what they have said. This is not what I am suggesting. In the
churches where the shouting of "Amen" is encouraged as an
evidence of agreement with what the minister has said, one
rarely hears the "Amen" in the scriptural use as a unison
congregational response at the end of prayer. I believe that
this word, which indicates a hearty agreement with the praise
and petitions of a prayer that has been offered, is something
which, if used by the congregation at the close of prayers,
will greatly enhance the sense of common worship in their assemblies. Martin Luther once said, "As your Amen is, so has
your prayer been." Charles Simeon says that the word
"denotes the full concurrence of the soul in all that has been
uttered." The faithful use of it in corporate worship ought to
enhance the worship of the Lord's people.

Unfortunately multitudes of believers have come to regard
the word *Amen* as the minister's way of indicating that he
has finished with his prayer. This is not what the word is to

indicate at all. It would be best if the minister leading the corporate worship did not use the word when he finished his prayers but let the congregation use it to indicate their hearty agreement with and fellowship in the offering up of the praise and petitions of his prayer. I realize that to get many evangelical congregations into the habit of offering a corporate "Amen" at the end of the pastor's prayers in a worship service would require much patience and continued reminders from the pulpit. However, from the experience we have had in a small church where my family worships regularly I can say that the observance of this practice has been a means of giving new significance to corporate prayer.

Let me suggest that if you desire to introduce this scriptural practice to your congregation ask the choir to lead in the offering of the spoken "Amen." In many of our churches the choir does sing an "Amen" following a prayer, but it is not the choir alone which should thus indicate its hearty concurrence in the prayers of the service. I have no objections to choral "Amens" as such, but it is regrettable that they have become a substitute for the "Amens" of the entire congregation. The choir can make a substantial contribution to corporate worship by leading the congregation in a spoken "Amen," in this way helping them to understand that each individual is to participate fully in the prayers which are uttered.

Music in Worship

In addition to teaching believers concerning their part in the prayers of a corporate worship service any satisfactory instruction in worship will always include at least a basic introduction to the relationship of music and worship as well as some suggestions for determining the most appropriate music to use in worship. Some familiarity with hymnology is also important for anyone who wishes to participate fully in the offering of musical praise to God, since hymn singing is such an important part of common worship in all churches.

Since the very earliest times music has been the handmaiden of religion. Music has from ancient days rendered an incomparable service to public worship in the sanctuary. Of all the fine arts music is most admirably suited to express the deepest feelings of the heart, those feelings which find satisfaction only in divine worship. There are some essential characteristics of music which make it the best qualified of the arts to express religious devotion. One of these characteristics is that when we compare it to the other arts there is much greater lack of permanence in its productions. The architect and the sculptor, for example, produce works of art which endure. But the architect and the sculptor themselves die. Their churches and statues remain. Music, however, produces no such permanent objects. The musician works with sound, and this disappears almost as soon as it appears. It must be renewed from time to time. It is this very feature which makes it especially appropriate for Christian public worship, for certainly worship is not like the building of a beautiful cathedral. It cannot be done once for all. It must be renewed continually. The score that the composer writes down does not constitute the music; the performer produces the music according to the written symbols on the page. Similarly there may be fixed forms for our worship written on a page, but these do not themselves constitute worship. The forms merely provide the possibility of worship. The living act of worship takes place when the words on the page throb with the deep devotion of our souls and this is expressed to God.

This brings us to another reason why music occupies the important place that it does in the public worship of the church. Music is that art which more than any of the others appeals most directly to the emotions of a man. Music not only impresses the feelings, but likewise expresses them. It not only acts upon them from without but serves as an outlet to them from within. The realm of feeling is the domain of the musician. The poet and the painter also appeal to the emotions, but not so directly as the musician. We must remember, however, that the fact that music appeals to the feelings does not mean that worship is simply a matter of emotion. Not at all. Worship includes much more than feelings. It includes the activity of reason. A strong doctrinal commitment is its foundation. Without correct belief, as we have already emphasized, there can be no worship in truth. But worship is not simply the assent of reason to truth in doctrine. It is the expression of the deep devotion of the heart based upon faith in the self-revelation of God and His work of redemption. Consequently, if the feelings are not brought into play and the heart thrilled with the grace and goodness of God and with the opportunity to express adoration and thanksgiving, then no true worship has taken place. If, then, music can touch the heart and aid in kindling the deep emotions which underlie true worship, it does indeed occupy a most important place in our worship.

It must be pointed out that the very capacity of music to touch the emotions also poses a threat to true worship, for if our response to God is purely emotional it is not true worship. A worship service in which our feelings are not engaged would certainly fail of its object. At the same time, while we recognize the value of feeling we must be alive to the great danger of shallow emotionalism. Unfortunately there are many professing Christians today for whom worship is almost entirely a matter of the senses. Their yardstick is sentiment. Consciously or unconsciously they measure their worship experiences by the emotional impressions that they have received. One can tell this from the reactions he hears at the close of the worship services in many churches. "I didn't care for the anthem the choir sang this morning; I wish they wouldn't do so much Bach." "I wish the organist would pep the music up a little." "Didn't Angela sing beautifully?" We could go on and on. It is worshipers of this kind who are responsible for the vast amount of sentimental music which is being heard in many evangelical churches of our day. Let us consider what has been one of the most popular of all these sentimental songs, "In the Garden." The words are:

> I come to the garden alone,
> While the dew is still on the roses,
> And the voice I hear, falling on my ear,
> The Son of God discloses.

Refrain:
And He walks with me, and He talks with me,
And He tells me I am His own;
And the joy we share as we tarry there,
None other has ever known.

He speaks, and the sound of His voice
Is so sweet the birds hush their singing,
And the melody that He gave to me,
Within my heart is ringing.

When sentimentalists sing such a song, they feel a great surge of emotion. They do not stop to think that they have been singing about an imaginary experience which is sentimentally appealing but does not deal with truth or reality. Believers today never have entered a garden alone in the early morning hours and heard an audible voice which they were able to identify as that of Jesus Christ, the Son of God. The poet who originated these lines apparently had in mind the experience of Mary Magdalene at the tomb of the Savior on the first Easter morning, but her experience was unique. None of the twelve apostles shared it. Nor is it shared by believers today, however much this sentimental song may appeal to them. The saddest part of this song, however, is the unbounded pride of the repeated refrain: the singer boasts that in sharing a fellowship with the Savior he experiences a joy which no one else has ever known! I have often wondered how large crowds of people singing this song could fail to recognize the glaring contradiction: each one of them individually professes to share with the Lord a sweetness of communion that none of the others has ever experienced. This shows how far maudlin sentimentality will carry us.

It is a mistake to imagine that music which makes the kind of appeal that the song quoted above does is worthy of admission into our services. Feeling is after all a very variable criterion. Although there are some feelings which lie deeper than thought and which words cannot adequately express, and they are stirred by music that seems to penetrate to the very inmost recesses of the heart, there are others that are shallow and sensual, that flow at the merest tickling of the ears. There is plenty of this kind of cheap music available, and it is regrettable that it so often finds a place in the services of worship of our churches.

Although "In the Garden" belongs to another generation and may no longer be popular in evangelical churches, I would point out that the gospel songs and choruses which are currently popular and are being sung in church services, and on television and radio, are not any better. One can determine even from the titles that the spiritual experiences which the songs describe are not those which are set forth in the New Testament. Here, for example, are three current titles picked at random from a list of popular favorites: "I Want to Stroll over Heaven with You," "I Could Hardly See the Road for the Tears," and "There's Something About That Name." In connection with the last of these we need to remember that the name of Jesus speaks of all that He is as both God and man and all that He has done for sinners. It is at this name that every knee in heaven and earth shall bow. There is not just "something" about it which is worthy of sentimental song.

Consider also the song "Kum Ba Yah," which one hears again and again in youth groups, adult retreats, and even in church services. I have heard stanza after stanza added extemporaneously by song leaders. Many times these added stanzas were no more meaningful than some of the original lines like "Someone's praying, Lord, Kum Ba Yah." Of course, I recognize that the strange words which give the song its title and are repeated again and again are taken from one of the African tribal languages, and are purported to mean "Come by me." But what does "Come by me" actually mean? Such words may have significant and varied meanings for some who sing them, but they do not express a scriptural concept, nor is their meaning explicit in the minds of most of those who like to sing them, as I have learned from questioning enthusiastic devotees of this song. Actually most will admit that what they like is the lilt of the music with its continual repetition.

There certainly is a place for lighter songs, especially for young people who greatly enjoy them. I would not want to suggest that in youth groups, retreats, and conferences such songs should be eliminated and only great hymns sung. There is a legitimate appeal in lighter music. I am concerned, however, that when we try to express the great realities of our Savior, His love, and His salvation, we not encourage songs which focus on the artificial or purely imaginary. Some of the best of the choruses young people sing and enjoy are the words of Scripture set to appealing tunes. Other excellent ones comprise scriptural truths expressed in youthful idiom. These are fine.

When believers worship God they should sing of things that are true. Yet how easy it is to set a falsehood to an appealing melody with an attractive rhythm and get a congregation of sincere Christians to sing it enthusiastically again and again. I was guilty of this very thing myself in my younger days when I had not given serious thought to the importance of pure worship of God. Let me give you an example of what I mean by singing a falsehood. All over the country in evangelical churches of many denominations for a whole generation children and adults alike have sung a gospel chorus, the first two lines of which are: "Every day with Jesus is sweeter than the day before. Every day with Jesus I love Him more and more." Now there never has lived a saint upon the earth who could sing these lines honestly, for this is not the experience of the true believer. If we were to sing, "Every day with Jesus ought to be sweeter than the day before," we would perhaps be much closer to the truth. But all true Christians have days when their experience is not sweeter than the previous day, and I know of no Christian who could with truthfulness say that he loves Jesus more every day than he did the day before. There are dark and difficult days in the lives of every Christian. Our Lord asserted that "in the world ye shall have tribulation" (John 16:33). The apostle Peter warned us to "think it not strange concerning the fiery trial which is to try you, as though some strange thing happened unto you" (I Peter 4:12). Is it any wonder that young people turn away in disgust from the Christian life when they discover that multitudes of Christians are singing songs which are not true?

In this connection it is important that I should mention the poor quality of many of the gospel songs used in the services of evangelical churches today. I want first to make it clear that I am not opposed to gospel songs as such. There are a number of fine ones which I enjoy singing at the proper times and places, but even many good gospel songs are not suitable for a service designed for the worship of almighty God. Some are overly didactic; others are purely hortatory. Most of them are extremely subjective, couched in the first person singular and emphasizing the experience of the believer and often going beyond what has actually taken place in the life of the individual who is singing. Only a few are addressed to God, and rarely does one find in them an expression of pure worship. The gospel song came into great popularity in the middle of the last century largely through the evangelistic ministry of Dwight L. Moody (1837-1899) and his musical associate Ira D. Sankey (1840-1908). It was an authentic expression of the highly emotional and individualistic religious experience which was typical of the American frontier of that day. Many Christians today do not realize what a comparatively recent development in religious music the gospel song actually is. Often when the great old hymns of the church, which have survived the centuries because of the magnificent depths of pure devotion expressed in them, are introduced in contemporary services the people complain. "Why don't we sing the good old songs? Why must we sing new songs which we do not know?" The "old songs" to which they refer are the comparatively new gospel songs which have been put to highly singable melodies of the general type of the popular songs of the day.

The earliest gospel songs, while mostly intensely personal, dealt with some of the outstanding values of the Christian life. Such songs as Joseph Scriven's "What a Friend We Have in Jesus," and many of Fanny Crosby's writings such as "Blessed Assurance, Jesus Is Mine," are an expression of authentic Christian experience. Some of the later gospel songs became quite banal; they had questionable doctrinal content with a dominant sentimental appeal. Many of the tunes to which these songs were sung could hardly be distinguished from those of the dance hall. In fact, some had such appealing rhythms that they have actually been used by the popular dance bands. It must be insisted that in our instruction in worship we teach believers what the difference is between good hymns of praise to God, which always are thoroughly scriptural, and gospel songs, which, while often very worthwhile, belong in a different category of religious music. Believers need to acquire and exercise discernment in the music which they use in worship so that sentimentality and shallow emotionalism will be replaced by authentic poetic and musical expression of genuine worship. A later chapter of this book will be devoted to the great hymns of the church universal.

I would not want anyone to get the impression that in suggesting that most gospel songs are not appropriate for a worship service I would want to substitute an ancient mode of musical worship not suitable to contemporary life. There are those who feel that by introducing some ancient and repetitious versicles and cramming the hour full of unrelated canticles and responses by the choir they are giving deeper meaning to a service of worship when actually about the only thing they are contributing to is its length. Of course, choral responses and many of the ancient canticles can contribute not only beauty but also meaning to a service when they are used in the proper places and for the proper purpose. Many of these musical additions to a service are beautiful. But we must never confuse the beauty of holiness with a holiness of beauty. An authentic worship service must always be directed at the specific purpose of bringing praise, honor, and glory to God Himself and then also bringing the individual worshipers into a deeper experience of the love of God, a greater understanding of His grace, and a more firm commitment to His revealed will.

We turn now to mention another respect in which music seems particularly well suited to communicate those feelings which appropriately seek expression in Christian worship. I refer to the fact that music is the channel through which the joy of the heart finds expression. "Is any merry?" asks the apostle James, "let him sing psalms" (James 5:13). The note of joy is one which we should expect to find especially prominent in our church services and therefore in our church music. One cannot fail to be impressed with the frequency with which the note of joy is sounded in the Psalms. Certainly the devout Israelite considered the worship of Jehovah to be a very cheerful thing. The songs of the temple were the outpourings of the exuberant joy that filled the hearts of the worshipers.

O come, let us sing unto the Lord:
Let us make a joyful noise to the rock of our salvation. (Ps. 95:1)

Sing aloud unto God our strength:
Make a joyful noise unto the God of Jacob. (Ps. 81:1)

Make a joyful noise unto the Lord, all ye lands. (Ps. 100:1)

I think that our joy in the Lord does not receive as much emphasis in our worship services as it should. Certainly the music of the services should be the major vehicle by which the believers' joy in the Lord is expressed. Unfortunately many of our hymn tunes do not adequately convey the impression of joyfulness. Church members have the right to demand music with a note of true joyfulness about it, music which is suited for use by those who with joy and gratitude welling up in their hearts long to sing to the Lord with cheerful voice.

Before we leave the subject of music in the church, attention must be given to the music of the choir. There are several reasons why churches that have adequate numbers of competent singers in them should have a choir, in spite of the fact that choirs can often be the source of troublesome problems in the church. Let us consider the two principal benefits of a good choir. First, a well-trained choir contributes greatly to the congregational singing. Music has a social feature which makes it specially suited to a united expression of congregational praise. Individual members of the congregation, however, may hesitate to raise their voices in song if those around them are not singing heartily. A well-trained choir can give such substantial support to the congregational singing that all who are present will be encouraged to participate in the musical praise.

A second great contribution to the service of worship which can be made by a good choir is the offering of musical praise to God which is beyond the capacities of the entire congregation. The music of the choir should always be on an entirely different musical level from the music which the whole congregation sings. We cannot expect to find much musical skill on the part of entire congregations. Therefore, if we expect all worshipers to join in the singing, music must be chosen which will be simple enough to make no great demands upon the musical ability of the individual members of the congregation. Even today, when most children get some musical education in their early schooling, only a small portion of the average congregation has the requisite musical skill to sing parts capably. An alto here, a bass there, may be quite capable, but certainly most of the congregation will do best singing the melody. The choir, however, should be capable of singing anthems which are well beyond the musical capability of the average member of the congregation. Just as the pastor and the elders should be more capable of leading the congregational prayers or preaching the sermon than the average worshiper, so the choir should be better able to provide elaborate and inspiring musical praise in which the individual worshipers can participate even as they participate in the prayers that are offered. Music is an art, and skill in the performance of music is not something with which all are endowed. The Lord does enjoin skill in musical performance, however. "Sing to Him a new song; Play skillfully with a shout of joy" (Ps. 33:3, NASB).

There are those who feel that the congregation should not take part in the musical praise, but that it should be left entirely to the choir because native talent, study, and practice are necessary in the development of skill in music, just as special study and practice are necessary for the minister who preaches the Word. However, all music need not be on a high artistic level. We would not silence the lullaby that the mother sings to her child, nor the enthusiastic chorus with which a convivial crowd makes the rafters ring at a reunion. We need not silence the congregation in offering musical praise to God. Indeed, we must encourage very enthusiastic participation in this form of worship. At the same time we must be thankful for those who can render music which because of its special beauty and the skill of its performance allows each worshiper the sense of offering up to God the best that can be given. The choir should not sing hymns as anthems. If the choir sings a hymn in which all members of the congregation could join, they should be allowed to sing. To exclude them gives an entirely erroneous impression as to what the function of the choir actually is. Just as long as men find music a natural outlet for the expression of their deep feelings of gratitude and joy, so long will the congregation be justified in claiming a right to join in songs of praise suited to their capacity. For these songs form an integral part of their worship.

The Order of Worship

Let us turn now to a consideration of the practical problems in establishing an order of worship for a congregation. Let me begin by saying that I believe it is a mistake to have a fixed order which is unchanged from week to week. While the general order may be, and perhaps should, remain much the same most of the time, the specific order of the component parts must never become inflexible. It is very easy for an order to become routine, and when anything in worship becomes routine, it ceases to be meaningful. My wife and I worshiped for some months with a congregation which had an order of worship which was not modified in any way from Sunday morning to Sunday morning except that the hymns were changed and the Scriptures which were read were varied. I found myself so familiar with the routine that I knew exactly what the minister would do and say at every point in the service. No explanations were ever given as to why the service proceeded as it did, nor was there any obvious justification for the movement from one element of the service to the next. Some very important elements of corporate worship were omitted, yet apparently no one in the congregation was aware of their absence.

In objecting to routine in worship I do not mean to suggest that we must introduce novelty simply to sustain interest. The proper, scriptural movement of the service must be sustained. Unity must be preserved no matter what variations are introduced. The dialogue between God and man should certainly be apparent. Beauty must be present, but never at the expense of truth. Restful adoration must be combined with soul-searching and inspirational preaching of God's Word.

In establishing their orders of worship some ministers have utterly failed to recognize the importance of the proper direction for the movement of the worship, while others have invented or borrowed certain captions for what they consider the principal divisions of the service. These captions are intended to indicate to the worshipers the movement of the corporate worship. They are printed in the church bulletin. Such divisions as "The Approach to God," or "The Preparation for Worship," "The Service of the Word of God," "The Service of Response to God," and other similar titles are supposed to provide a structure into which the various elements of the service fit. Surely such captions may help some to understand more clearly what is taking place in a worship service. I have noticed again and again, however, in the churches where captions are used, that the elements of the service represented by the captions involve more than what the captions suggest. For example, I recently attended a service in which the title "Worship Through Meditation" included not only the organ prelude and a choral introit, but also the call to worship; while the caption "Worship Through Praise" included the Lord's Prayer, which is not primarily a prayer of praise. In addition to the problem that giving titles to various divisions cannot accurately cover the movement of the service, there is a serious question as to whether such schematized captions can retain any vital significance when used week after week. Other problems also suggest themselves. For example, we must keep in mind that in the early portion of a good worship service there must be definite response to God on the part of the worshipers. To suggest that the "Service of Response" or the "Service of Dedication" follows the preaching of the Word of God is perhaps somewhat misleading.

Worship can hardly be structured and led so that the human spirit will fall readily into the same pattern again and again. This is so even if the minister uses printed captions to keep the people aware of the significance of the corporate acts of worship in which they are participating. The minister who prepares the order of worship will find that his own spirit does not easily adjust to conformity to a predetermined scheme each week, even if he has himself originally established the structure. This is not to say that the order of worship should be prepared without serious concern for the proper direction and movement of the common worship. Indeed we are emphatically urging just such concern. Our point is simply that we should avoid a rigid structure with neatly stated divisions which are the same Sunday after Sunday.

I am personally convinced that the minister who desires to provide the proper order for and then conduct a truly meaningful worship service must himself provide the spoken rubrics which will make it easy for every member of the congregation to understand exactly what the significance of each component part of the service is and how it relates to what has preceded it and then what will follow it. While many worshipers will be able to determine the relationship of one part of the service to another, by no means all of them will. There are frequently things which divert the attention of even the most informed worshipers. Therefore, it is important for the minister conducting the service to give such clear rubrics that the worshiper may easily reestablish his participation in the corporate movement of the service if he has been diverted. A word of caution concerning these rubrics needs to be given. Because we are all creatures of habit it will be vitally necessary for every minister who regularly conducts the services of worship in his church to guard against introducing the various elements of the service in the same way each Sunday. It would be easy for the rubrics themselves to become routine and to lose their great value. If the minister has not made adequate preparation for the service he is very apt to find himself "in a rut," saying the same things in the same way time after time. He may be unconscious of this, but the people in the congregation will not be.

It is very important that those who have recently become Christians, or those in the congregation who may have been Christians for many years but have had little or no instruction in worship, should be psychologically prepared to move smoothly from one part of the service to the next. Moreover, they must be able to fully understand the significance of what they are called upon to do. For example, if a unison confession of sin is noted as the next item in the service, it may have little meaning for them, unless the reason for it is explained briefly. With the proper brief rubric it may become exceedingly significant. Again, unless it is perfectly obvious (and this is rarely the case), a brief explanation concerning the reason a particular hymn has been chosen to be sung will always be helpful, especially for those who have very little familiarity with hymnody. Such explanations should not be little sermonettes. As such they could easily interrupt the movement of the service. They should serve only to make the singing of a particular hymn much more meaningful. If the worshipers understand that there is a special meaning conveyed in the hymn, they will sing it far more intelligently, and with deeper appreciation of what they are offering to God with the words of the hymn.

It is a serious mistake to think that a fully sufficient worship service can be thrown together in a few moments or even conducted extemporaneously. Careful planning must be involved if the glories of God's character and work are to be adequately set forth and the worshipers are to make an appropriate response. Recognizing the importance of good order, some have adopted a fixed liturgy which proceeds week after week in such a rigid way that it loses the freshness necessary for authentic worship. The answer is not a fixed liturgy; the answer comes with taking the time and making the effort to properly prepare the entire worship service so that all who participate in it may have a rich and meaningful experience.

It is really not difficult for any worshiper, even one who has recently become a Christian, to understand that when the Scriptures are read in a service God is speaking to His people. It is also easy to understand that when the minister is preaching his sermon this at least *should* be the voice of the Lord speaking through His servant. The problems arise in the other elements of the worship services. When the minister prays, when the choir sings, when a responsive reading from the Psalter is read, when the offering is given—these are some of the places where individual worshipers completely lose all sense of the divine-human dialogue. They tend to continue their participation in the service without really understanding the significance of what is taking place. This lack of comprehension emphasizes the importance of giving Christians careful instruction in worship.

6

The Order
of Common Worship

There are at least three different types of services which are appropriate for evangelical churches. John R. P. Sclater has classified two of them as (1) services of worship, and (2) services of mission, and has well stated that "the former of these are the supreme task of the Church and are ends in themselves. The latter are means to an end—namely, the extension of the kingdom."[1] I would like to add a third classification, (3) informal services for fellowship in praise and prayer. These are to be distinguished from the services of mission or services designed for evangelistic purposes because they give to believers a legitimate and spiritually helpful opportunity to share with one another the Lord's goodness, and then to pray together.

The services of mission in many churches, perhaps most

---

[1]John R. P. Sclater, *The Public Worship of God* (Grand Rapids: Baker Book House, 1970), p. 23.

churches, in recent decades have been the regular Sunday evening services. These certainly may properly be characterized by much more diversity than services of worship. There may be features in such services in which the audience may properly be considered observers or onlookers rather than participants. A service designed specially to attract and interest unbelievers cannot be planned so that the unbelievers are themselves expected to participate in corporate worship. We are concerned, however, at this time with services of common worship where each member of the congregation is presumed to be a Christian. The congregation is active as a unit in each part of the service. This makes necessary a common understanding of every movement. No provision can be made for those in the congregation who may not be believers.

The Beginning of Worship

Before a service begins, when men and women, young people and children, come to a church building to worship, they should realize that the moment they enter the doors of the church sanctuary they have come into a place of prayer. There may be exchange of greetings and even visiting while the people are in the narthex or in other parts of the church building not set aside for worship, but when they step into the place of assembly for worship all conversation should cease. If the church is looked upon as a lecture hall or an auditorium it will not be surprising if it is characteristically a place of informal chitchat until the service is well under way. A congregation which thinks of itself as an audience will certainly behave as it does in a concert hall or a theater. Strangely enough, Christians who enter their churches with a very casual attitude are imitating the Orthodox Jews, for in their synagogues there is no attempt made to maintain silence. Those who gather come and go at will, moving about and greeting their friends with happy enjoyment. They often do not even pay close attention to what is going on. Certainly Christians who have assembled to worship the holy God of creation and redemption should look upon the place of worship as a very special place and should realize the importance of leaving behind all of the trivialities of life when they enter into the house of prayer to render homage to the sovereign Ruler of the universe and the God of all grace. It is with God alone that they should occupy themselves when they gather to worship.

The conversational clatter which is so characteristic of many evangelical churches of this country before services begin and even during the prelude is certainly no proper aid to the preparation of hearts for worship. In the instruction in worship for which this book is a plea there needs to be specific emphasis given to the fact that worship is the believers' only proper pursuit in the place which has been constructed and prepared for worship. I am aware of the fact that some churches find it necessary to hold their services in a gymnasium or in a school auditorium or in some other large room which has not been built for worship. Some churches even deliberately plan for their building to be a multipurpose building with no part of it used exclusively for worship services. This will certainly increase the difficulty of getting individuals to approach the worship service with the proper sense of reverent preparation. If one who attends a worship service is not concerned with preparing his own heart for the high and holy occupation of divine worship, he should at least exercise courtesy and consideration toward those who do wish to begin quietly and reverently their own meditation and worship. Conversation can only interrupt the preparation of heart and mind of those who have begun their prayers. Those of us in evangelical Protestant churches could benefit greatly from observing the Roman and Anglican practices of quiet prayer upon entering the church, as well as a quiet moment of meditation and prayer following the benediction.

I should like to introduce our consideration of the various elements which make up an order of common worship with a few words about announcements in a worship service. I sincerely believe that it is a mistake to insert them into the middle of the service. They are especially bad immediately preceding the offering where they have appeared in entirely too many of the services that I have attended. It is rather amazing that after a rather extended series of announcements a pastor will often say, "Now let us *continue* our worship by presenting our tithes and offerings unto the Lord." The congregation has not been worshiping. It has been listening to announcements for several minutes. The worship has been interrupted. The minister might at least say, "Let us *resume* our worship." But this I have never heard.

In most churches there is a printed or mimeographed church bulletin which contains the announcements for the week as well as the order of worship. It is surely a mistake for a pastor to take the precious time of a worship service to read to the people the announcements which are already in their hands. Not only is it an insult to their intelligence, but it is an inexcusable waste of time. However, there are certain coming events in any active church which do merit brief emphasis to the congregation, and there often arise unexpected events and special needs which were not included in the church bulletin and which must be announced to the congregation. A few words of warm welcome to visitors are certainly not out of place either. It would be a mistake to arbitrarily rule out all announcements. However, because they are not a part of worship they should not be included within the service after the people have been called to corporate worship. Of course, if given before the service, announcements will be a short interruption in the personal worship of those who have been engaged in individual prayer; but if the announcements are handled expeditiously this will not be a serious break since the united worship of the congregation has not yet begun.

The most logical place for necessary announcements, then, is before the service begins. Some have placed them at the conclusion of their services. It is my opinion that this is not the best place. The impressions of the worship service, including the application of the Word of God and the sermon, should be what remain in the minds of the worshipers. It would seem best, then, to have the necessary announcements out of the way before actual corporate worship begins. If the objection should be raised that the people would not all be present if the announcements were given at the beginning, my response would be that punctuality would be encouraged by such a practice since members of the congregation normally like to know what lies ahead in the church program. They are also interested in knowing before the service important events of recent days. Perhaps even more fundamental than either of these considerations is the fact that being on time for the worship service itself is even more important than being present when the announcements are made—no church should cater to the lack of punctuality on the part of its members!

It is perfectly proper for the organ to be playing as the worshipers assemble, for an appropriate soft musical background aids in providing an atmosphere which is conducive to meditation and in preventing the noisy visiting with family and friends which all too often prevents good preparation for worship. Sometimes, if the church sanctuary is not being used for Sunday school classes or other purposes, the organ music may begin as much as fifteen minutes before the scheduled time for the service. If the announcements are to be given before the service, however, the actual organ prelude should come after them and should be comparatively brief. When the minister has completed the giving of the announcements he should indicate to the people that it is time for them to put their minds and hearts in readiness for the corporate worship. He should make some brief statement such as, "Let us now prepare our hearts for the worship of God," taking care to be brief and to avoid saying the same thing each Sunday morning. There are many ways of varying this brief reminder that during the musical prelude each member of the congregation should, in silent prayer and meditation, prepare for the high and holy privilege of common worship.

The Prelude

This musical number, whether played on an organ or a piano, is of special importance for it should provide a suitable atmosphere for the preparation of heart and mind for the exalted activity of worship which is to occupy the members of the congregation for the following hour. It should never be a showpiece in which it is evident that the one playing the instrument is concerned with a display of his technical skill. It is perfectly appropriate for the numbers used for the prelude to be listed in the bulletin together with their composers, for the sake of the musically discriminating who might have their personal meditation disturbed by hearing a composition with which they have some sense of familiarity but which they are unable to identify. However, it should always be borne in mind that the first few moments of a worship service are not a musical recital, nor are they to be considered a musical filler. They have the definite purpose of making it possible for those in attendance to attain the proper frame of mind for the common worship. Donald Kettring has properly suggested that "the last four minutes of prelude time are always quiet music so that a hush tends to descend on the church."[2] He also has proposed that the organ prelude might on occasion begin quietly and then perhaps reach close to full organ. I would hesitate to recommend much full organ in a prelude unless the organist is consciously assisting the minister in getting the people away from the habit of exchanging pleasantries during the prelude so they might learn to use the time instead for preparation for worship.

Every pastor should have a clear understanding with his organist, or pianist, as to what is expected in the musical ministry of the church. It is of utmost importance that the organist understand clearly the function of music in the service itself as well as what the purposes of the musical preludes and postludes are. A skilled musician whose talents are dedicated to the Lord can contribute much to a congregation's worship of God, but one who is concerned to display his own technical virtuosity may well provide music which is

---

[2]Donald D. Kettring, *Steps Toward a Singing Church* (Philadelphia: Westminster Press, 1948), p. 277.

a hindrance to worship. I have listened to organists perform instrumental preludes during which it would have been impossible for any sensitive listener to be aware of anything but the skillful rendition of the difficult composition. Frequent discussion between pastor and organist should provide opportunities for the expression of sincere appreciation for proficient service and also for a reminder of the necessary goal to be kept before all of those who share the responsibility for significant parts of the worship service. Unless an organist realizes that he has a genuine ministry in the service and agrees with the pastor as to what that ministry is to be, the service will not have the unity that it should have.

Let me suggest here that the playing of familiar hymns for the prelude or, for that matter, as a musical interlude during any other part of the service when quiet meditation is in order is not the best practice. When one plays hymns which are familiar to the members of the congregation it is impossible for those who are musically sensitive to keep the words of the hymn from coming into their consciousness as the music is being played. It is not wise for the music thus to interfere with meditation and prayer. Sometimes the words of only one stanza or part of a stanza will be remembered. At other times a familiar melody will be played, but the words of the hymn simply cannot be recalled. All of this is disturbing rather than serving the purpose of providing an appropriate soft musical background for quiet reflection and for communion with God. Moreover, it is not the organist's responsibility to provide the poetic substance for meditation by playing familiar hymn tunes. The prelude should not be long unless provision has been made for several minutes of instrumental music before the announcements. There is an abundance of music available which is very fitting for use at this time. Even a relatively inexperienced organist or pianist need not be concerned. Many of the great German chorale tunes, for example, are not associated with familiar words and are excellent for instrumental preludes.

When the instrumental prelude for the service has been played and the congregation has had an opportunity to prepare for worship through contemplative thought and prayer, the actual corporate worship begins. The minister sends forth a

Call to Worship

The call to worship takes the place of the ringing of the bell in the Roman Catholic mass. The spoken word is far more meaningful than the sound of a bell, although where church bells still exist it is lovely to hear one ringing out the news that a service of worship is beginning. The call to worship summons the people to a consideration of that exalted purpose for which they have assembled. The minister calls them on behalf of God, and this introduces the divine-human dialogue. We must always remember that no one is fully ready for the high and holy experience of united corporate worship. The people who gather on the Lord's Day in the house of God are a miscellaneous group of individuals much bound to the things of this earth. They have diverse interests and passions and must be welded together in a common experience in the body of Christ. They have come to the service with a wide variety of mental attitudes. Very few are actually ready to worship God when they arrive in the church sanctuary. Some have been in a Sunday school class where they have been bored by poor teaching or by a lesson which they did not feel was relevant to their needs. Some may have been upset by family friction which developed in their automobiles on the way to church. Some may be struggling with severe temptations known only to themselves. Others may have their minds occupied by important business decisions which must be made during the coming week. It would be impossible to list all of the varieties of mental attitudes with which men and women approach the weekly church service. The call to worship must, just as far as possible, secure their attention for the all-important activity of the precious hour of corporate communion with God in which it is each one's individual privilege to participate.

There are many ways in which the call to worship may be

given. Let me suggest possibly combining the very ancient
Salutation and Sursum Corda as an appropriate call to worship. Both have been used from the earliest days of the Christian church. Using them today gives a worshiping congregation a definite link with the past which they will appreciate if
they understand the antiquity of the forms.

Salutation: Minister: The Lord be with you.
             Congregation: And with your spirit.

Sursum Corda: Minister: Lift up your hearts.
             Congregation: We lift them up unto the Lord.
             Minister: Let us give thanks unto the Lord.
             Congregation: It is meet and right so to do.

As you can see, these two very brief ancient litanies combined make an excellent call to the worship of God. They
could be printed in the church bulletin and used frequently
until a congregation becomes familiar with them. I would
certainly not recommend their use every Sunday morning,
but after the congregation becomes well acquainted with
them there will be many times when the words will come to
their consciousness and provide a rich blessing and a reminder to lift their hearts in worship, even when they are not
in the house of worship.

A choral introit with the words appropriate for a call to
worship may be substituted for the minister's call at times
for the sake of variety and to avoid any meaninglessness
caused by a routine repetition. However, it must be emphasized that the minister's own words are most effective.
The minister speaks for God; when the choir sings, it is normally the response of the people. Even if the minister says
with deep feeling something as simple as, "Let us worship
God!" it will serve to remind the people in a meaningful
way of the reason for their being in the church together.

The congregation gathers to offer to God that honor and
praise of which He is worthy. The very best way to call to
mind His worth is from His own holy and infallible Word.
Actually the only way we can find out about God's worth is
from God Himself. Therefore the Scriptures are the best

source for words designed to call men to contemplate the greatness of God and to worship Him. No words of man could be better. The Book of Psalms is full of verses containing very specific calls to worship; no part of Scripture is better for this specific purpose. Let me give you a few of the very best passages to use from the Psalms:

Psalm	18:1-3a	62:1, 2	107:1, 2
	24:1-5	*84:1-4	111:1, 2
	25:1-5	89:1, 2	*113:1-3
	27:1-4	*92:1, 2	*117
	30:10-12	*95:1-3	118:1-4
	32:10, 11	*95:6, 7a	138:1, 2
	*34:1-3	*96:1-4a	*145:1-4
	34:8-10	98:1, 2	*145:8-11
	40:1-3	*100	*145:17-21
	42:11	*103:1-5	146:1, 2, 10
	46:1-3, 10, 11	104:1-5	149:1, 2
	47:1, 2	*105:1-4	*150:1, 2, 6

I have placed an asterisk (*) in front of fifteen of these selections which I consider the best for our purposes. This list is not exhaustive, of course, even from the Psalms; and there are other passages of Scripture which would be very appropriate. For example:

Isaiah	12:5, 6	Isaiah	55:6, 7
	40:28-31		61:10, 11
	42:5, 6, 10a	Jeremiah	33:2, 3
	44:22, 23	Daniel	2:20b-22

There are many others; there are actually so many appropriate verses that different ones could be used each Sunday of the year without repetition.

The selection chosen for the call to worship should always be given from memory. These passages lose something of their effectiveness when read. Of course, this means that the minister must take time for careful preparation and for memorization.

Another word of caution should be given concerning the call to worship. It must contain a clear invitation to worship. A Scripture verse which contains some significant truth is not sufficient in itself. Not long ago I was a worshiper in a large church where the minister began the service by repeating John 3:16. All would agree that this is a great verse; it is considered by many the greatest verse in the Bible. There are tremendous truths in it. However, it is not a call to worship. The use of it without comment at the beginning of a service does not serve to call the people to worship God. It would cause them rather to wonder why this familiar verse is being quoted. If one is to use such a verse in connection with the beginning of a worship service, he should add his own words to make it a call. For example, he might say after quoting the verse, "Since God has so loved us, and given us the gift of eternal life, let us worship Him with our hearts and with our voices."

When the congregation has been called to worship by the words of the Lord Himself, there must be a proper response. An opportunity must be provided for the people to do what they have been called to do. A pure act of worship must be the response. This is perhaps best offered in a

Hymn of Adoration and Praise

I will have more to say about the selection of appropriate hymns for each part of the service a little later. It should be mentioned here that this first hymn may properly be a processional hymn, but only if the church sanctuary is properly constructed to make a processional effective. If the choir loft should be in the rear, which is undoubtedly the best place for it, a processional would not be proper unless the choir could enter the church conveniently at the front and move down the center aisle to the choir loft in the rear. Any unnatural or circuitous routing of singers is best not done at all. Many churches are so constructed that a processional would be extremely awkward. If a processional is used, the congregation must be included in the singing of the hymn of praise, for this is the congregational response to the call which has been given. The response should not be assigned to the choir, for the congregation is capable of singing all of the hymns in the service.

In connection with the musical ministry of the choir let me mention one very important rule. The choir should be used to the full limit of its capacity, but it should never be expected to do more than that of which it is capable. For example, a processional well done is a magnificent opening act of corporate worship in which congregation and choir unite, but one done poorly is worse than having no processional at all. Everything in a church service should be done with such perfection that no attention is called to the method used; each of the worshipers should be conscious only of the fact that the desired result has been achieved. If a choir is not large enough for an effective processional or if its members are not skilled enough to process smoothly and gracefully while singing joyfully to supplement and lift the congregational hymn, then processionals should be discouraged.

It seems quite clear from a study of the Old Testament Scriptures that processionals were frequently used in the temple worship, as the worshipers proceeded up to the temple to offer praise and sacrifice to God. The magnificence of some of these occasions must have been very moving to the devout worshipers. There is something very uplifting and inspirational today about a competent choir singing enthusiastically as it proceeds to its place in the house of praise. If a processional is used the choice of the processional hymn is of great importance. It must be what has been referred to as "a burst of praise." It must not be simply a hymn with a good marching beat, for the processional of a choir in a church is not a march! A choir composed of well-trained singers will have little trouble in keeping in step with the music; this adds to the overall effect, but a march step is not appropriate. As Scott F. Brenner has said, "This is no time for marching around the walls of Jericho or for the fanfare of figures on parade."[3] The hymn chosen should have a four-four or a two-four tempo, not a three-four or six-eight tempo. With two or four beats to the measure the singers will have no dif-

---

[3]Scott F. Brenner, *The Art of Worship* (New York: Macmillan, 1961), p. 23.

ficulty in walking in physical harmony with the tempo of the music. Every good hymnbook (not gospel songbook) contains a number of excellent hymns which may be used for processionals. Not only are they appropriate as expressions of pure adoration and praise to God, but they also have the correct rhythm. Such hymns as "O Come, My Soul, Bless Thou the Lord Thy Maker"; "The God of Abraham Praise"; "Praise, My Soul, the King of Heaven," as well as the very familiar "Holy, Holy, Holy! Lord God Almighty" are just a few excellent examples of good processional hymns. Many more could be listed.

Most evangelical churches will not be using processional hymns, so a word about the first hymn sung by the congregation is in order. It must be just as much as the processional hymn a "burst of praise" which is a clear response to the call and a hymn of pure worship and adoration. I have observed some amazing choices of songs (I could not say hymns) for this place in morning worship services. Recently I was a visiting minister in a large evangelical congregation and to my astonishment the first song announced was "Ye Must Be Born Again." This is a fine gospel song and quite appropriate in an evangelistic service, but it could not be more inappropriate as the opening song of praise in a worship service. On another occasion I remember that the first song announced by the pastor was "Make Me a Blessing." This is a worthy prayer, but it certainly is not a song of praise to God. When ministers use such songs as these, it is evident that they have given little serious thought to what is involved in a corporate worship service.

There are also good hymns of praise and thanksgiving which are not appropriate at certain times or at certain places in the service. Let me give you an example. Not long ago, during the spring of the year, I was worshiping with a fine evangelical congregation and the first hymn which was announced was Henry Alford's great "Come, Ye Thankful People, Come." Now this is a truly great hymn, but how could a congregation unite in such words as these during the spring of the year?

> Come, ye thankful people, come,
> Raise the song of harvest-home.
> All is safely gathered in,
> Ere the winter storms begin.

Obviously the pastor or the one who chose the hymn was looking for a hymn of praise and thanksgiving, read the first line, and decided that this was a good hymn to use. I found it difficult to sing a harvest hymn with the rest of the congregation who were singing it heartily, apparently unaware that what they were singing was not suitable at that time of the year. I dropped out and picked up the singing on the words of the stanzas in which I could join heartily. Every sincere believer ought to be able to enter reverently and joyfully into every part of the corporate acts of worship. For this reason every hymn must be carefully selected for its particular place in the service.

But now we must proceed to a consideration of the next element in the service of worship, which is properly

The First Prayer: A Prayer of Adoration

It is better for the first prayer to follow the first hymn. However, if the minister offers a prayer immediately following the call to worship, he must keep in mind the importance of the dialogue between God and the congregation, and he must make his prayer a response to his call, so that he is providing the words for the congregation to use as they together with him respond to the Lord's call for worship.

Usually the first prayer which the minister leads in a worship service is referred to as "The Invocation." It need not be an invocation, but if it is so listed it should certainly be what the title suggests. An invocation is not primarily a prayer of praise and thanksgiving, although it might well contain a brief ascription of praise. This is entirely fitting at the beginning of any prayer. Nor is an invocation a prayer of intercession. Prayers of intercession belong later in the service. An invocation is a prayer in which the presence and power of God are called forth in recognition of the fact that it is only as the Holy Spirit Himself moves upon and in both the minister and the congregation that the desired end of the service will be realized.

One Sunday morning recently I was a visiting worshiper in a large independent church in a city not far from my home. After a more or less perfunctory singing of the doxology which opened the service, the pastor led in a prayer which was indicated on the bulletin as "The Invocation." I have reproduced it as nearly verbatim as possible from notes I made immediately after the prayer:

> Dear Lord, how happy we are to be here in this place of worship this morning. Grant to us the presence and power of your Holy Spirit, so that not one of us will go away from this service without having received a definite blessing from being here. This we ask in the name of our Savior. Amen.

One should never take a critical spirit to a service of worship, for if his own heart is right he can worship God in an acceptable manner no matter what the leader of the service may do. It was impossible for me, however, not to realize how much was missing from this opening prayer. It was entirely subjective, from the opening expression of happiness at being in the house of God to the closing indefinite petition for a "definite blessing" for each member of the congregation. Even the opening salutation, "Dear Lord," seemed to give no recognition of the ineffable majesty and the infinite glory of our sovereign, omnipotent God, but rather seemed to suggest an almost smug relationship on a strictly fraternal basis. The word *dear,* meaning precious or beloved or highly prized, is never used in the Bible, either in the Old Testament or the New, in addressing the living God. While this does not necessarily rule out the use of the word under certain circumstances, it would suggest that it is inadequate as the only adjective to be applied to God in the opening of corporate worship. Obviously, the one who led the service, splendid Christian and faithful pastor though I know him to be, had given no thought to the fact that the primary purpose of a corporate worship service is not to get blessing for the individual worshiper's own self, but to glorify God through the worship of His holy and adorable person. We are all basically selfish creatures. We naturally tend to seek that which brings pleasure and satisfaction to ourselves. We even tend to go to worship services essentially for our own benefit. This is why the one who leads a service of worship must continually remember to focus the attention of the worshipers upon the One who is the only true object of worship. It is true that the minister did ask for the presence and power of the Holy Spirit, but the opening statement of happiness at being in the place of worship (without any explanation of the basis of the happiness) and the expression of desire that the Spirit's presence might provide a "definite blessing" for each worshiper completely obscured the focus on God which the opening prayer should present. It is little wonder that believers are concerned more with what they receive from a worship service than what they give to it when their pastors pray after this manner.

Ministers whose responsibility it is to lead corporate worship services could learn much from studying some of the great prayers of invocation which are found in the Book of Common Prayer (Anglican or Reformed Episcopalian), the Book of Common Worship (Presbyterian), and other splendid collections which are readily available. Consider, for example, the beautiful simplicity of such a brief invocation as this:

> Almighty God, whose glory is above the heavens, praise waiteth for Thee in Zion! Out of Thy great mercy Thou hast gathered us into Thy church. Receive the adoration of our hearts, and grant that we may so honor Thee, both in spirit and in outward form, that Thy name may be glorified through the worship of our lips and of our hearts. Through Jesus Christ, our Lord.

I have mentioned above that the opening prayer need not be designated an invocation. It may properly be (and I believe it should be) a prayer of adoration in which due recognition is given to the glory of the one true and living God; to His majestic being as one God in three persons, infinite, eternal, and unchangeable; and to the wonder of His redeeming grace. A sense of awe and reverence should permeate this prayer. If we are going to call our meeting together a worship service, certainly nothing should be more important than recognizing God's worth and rendering to Him appropriate honor. This should begin with the very first hymn and the first prayer of the service. And if this prayer comes, as it should, very early in the service, it should properly contain a brief petition for the ministry of the Holy Spirit enabling the congregation to worship in a manner fully pleasing to God. It is vital in this connection to remind pastors who lead such prayers in which the congregation is to join that they must exercise care that they do not slip into habitual expressions. One pastor whom I know quite well prays almost every Sunday morning that the Lord will enable the congregation "to worship in spirit and in truth." This is indeed a very worthy petition, but like anything else which is repeated too often, it loses its significance for those who are called upon to share in its frequent repetition.

In a previous chapter I indicated my conviction that all of the prayers offered in the service should come to an end with the congregation's making the prayer its own with a unison "Amen." This practice will certainly aid any worshiper in the congregation who is not accustomed to it to realize that he is a member of a congregation which is worshiping as a corporate body.

Before we leave the subject of the first prayer it should be stated clearly that this is not the proper place for the use of the Lord's Prayer, although in many churches it follows the invocation every Sunday morning. With the exception of the opening salutation, "Our Father, which art in heaven, hallowed be thy name," and the closing words, "for Thine is the kingdom, and the power, and the glory forever," the Lord's Prayer is composed of petitions for ourselves rather than ascriptions of praise to God. It is perfectly proper later in the service in connection with the prayers of petition and intercession, but it is best not to use it in the early part of the service when the assembly of believers is responding to a call for worship of the Lord.

In connection with the subject of prayer something needs to be said about the physical posture of the congregation during the corporate prayers. I hope that no reader of these words will accuse me of being "high church," "formalistic," or "liturgical" without giving attention to both the biblical and the historical basis for what I want to suggest. I believe most sincerely that there would be much to be gained in all of our evangelical churches if we were to return to the biblically endorsed and historically approved practice of kneeling for prayer in our churches. The objection will immediately be raised that we worship the Lord "in spirit and in truth," and that an outward act such as kneeling is simply unimportant. I would be the first to agree that it is possible for a congregation to have effective and very meaningful corporate worship with the worshipers standing or even sitting for prayer, although the Bible gives us no instance of the Lord's people praying while they are seated. Careful attention should be given to every indication in the Word of God of the very best ways to worship God. The Bible is our norm, and our worship should always be judged by the standard of its teaching.

It must be admitted that the question of the relationship between the outward and inward in worship is a very difficult one. No one who studies the New Testament Scriptures carefully could deny that the emphasis in them is entirely upon that which is inward. Therefore to insist that a particular physical posture is necessary in order to pray earnestly and effectively would be absurd. That is not what is being suggested here. It is my sincere conviction, however, that something is undoubtedly lost, in spite of whatever offsetting gains there might be, when such external, physical expressions as kneeling in prayer before God are eliminated from our services of worship. It cannot be denied that putting one's whole body in a proper attitude before God simply does make a difference.

Interestingly enough, I have often, when serving as a guest minister, been invited to kneel in prayer in the pastor's study with the elders of the church before the service began. I wonder if those same elders would object if the pastor insisted that the entire congregation be called upon to kneel in reverence for the prayers of the worship service. In many of our churches today to ask the congregation to kneel would require the special provision of kneeling benches since without them kneeling would be very awkward. The physical arrangements, however, are a very minor consideration.

Here we must look again to the Scriptures. It is certainly not without great significance that the Word of God speaks so often of the children of God kneeling for prayer. In Acts 20:36 we read of the apostle Paul kneeling to pray with the Ephesian elders before he departed from them. It is tremendously impressive to read again and again in the Book of Revelation how, for example, the apostle John, the twenty-four elders, and even the angels fell down before the Lord and worshiped Him (see Rev. 1:17; 4:10; 5:8, 14; 7:11; 11:16, etc.). We cannot take the time to consider all of the Old Testament references, but such a verse as Psalm 95:6 speaks to us about the scriptural nature of this physical attitude in prayer, "O come, let us worship and bow down: let us kneel before the Lord our maker." We remember that Daniel knelt down to pray faithfully three times a day, but of even greater significance for us today is the fact that our Savior, the Lord Jesus Christ, knelt to pray (see, e.g., Luke 22:41). That this is the physical posture for prayer endorsed by the Scriptures cannot be doubted.

An additional word should be said concerning the history of kneeling in the Christian church. The Reformation did not bring a change in the universal practice of kneeling for prayer in the churches. Of course, Protestants eliminated the genuflection before the host, which is characteristic of Roman Catholic worship. We do not believe that the presence of Jesus Christ is localized upon an altar. In fact there is no altar in any true Protestant church, for an altar is a place of sacrifice, and the true sacrifice for the sins of all believers was made upon the cross of Calvary once for all. Our churches have communion tables, but no altars. As we have already noted, however, the Lord Jesus Christ has promised to be present when we gather to worship in His name, and it is appropriate that we should kneel in His presence. Until the latter half of the seventeenth century the posture for prayer in the Reformed churches of England and Scotland was kneeling. During the eighteenth century sitting for prayer became much more common after the custom of the Independents. The emphasis shifted from the corporate worship of the congregation to the sermon, which was often dull, long, and entirely lacking in evangelical warmth. The members of the congregation became spectators or learners instead of active participants in worship. It is my earnest hope that more and more of the evangelical churches of our land will return to the scriptural practice of kneeling in prayer.

Here a word needs to be included for those whose responsibility it is to lead the prayers of the congregation. They should never just bow their heads and begin to pray, nor should they raise their hands and lift their faces toward heaven and begin to pray. Such actions as these often take a congregation by surprise, even those who may be familiar with the minister's habit in this matter. It is not good for any part of a service to be a surprise to the worshipers. The pastor should say, "Let us pray," or something similar, and give every member of the congregation a moment to put himself in the spirit of prayer since he is expected to be participating personally in all of the prayers of the service. I have quite often discovered that the pastor conducting a service in which I was a worshiper was praying when I had not anticipated that prayer was to be the next thing in the order of the service. Such an experience always takes something away from full participation in corporate prayer. It should not be necessary for members of a congregation to keep their eyes on the pastor at all times in order to know what is next in the order of worship. It should also be noted here that the minister should never say, "Shall we pray?" or "May we pray?" as though he were asking permission or putting the matter to a vote of the congregation. He should also avoid florid expressions like "Let us look to God in prayer."

Following the first hymn or the opening prayer of praise

and adoration there should be an element of corporate worship which has unfortunately been omitted in a great many evangelical churches in recent decades. I refer to

The Confession of Sin

I grew up in a Presbyterian church where there was never any corporate confession and where frequently there was not even a word of confession in the prayers of the pastor. I often attend services in evangelical churches today where this element of worship is missing. While it is true that no provision of the liturgy can take the place of the inner activity of the heart, the corporate confession of sin does bring forcefully to the minds of all worshipers the absolute necessity of coming to God with the right attitude of mind and spirit. Those of us who rejoice in our heritage from the Reformation should realize that both Calvin and Knox were careful to open their liturgies with a corporate confession of sin. One of the serious weaknesses of our modern worship lies in the fact that we have failed to make clear the inflexible holiness of our God. It is true that He is the God of all grace, that He is infinite in His kindness and mercy toward us, but He is also a God of manifest righteousness who cannot look upon sin. Entirely too many ministers give the impression in their worship services that the godly life is easy, that all we must do is rest in the lovingkindness of God, knowing that He will always supply all the healing and strength that are needed. The Christian life is not as simple as that. The believer must honestly and reverently deal with sin in his life continually day by day. Before we presume to worship God, we must remember the clear teaching of the Word of God, "If I regard iniquity in my heart, the Lord will not hear me" (Ps. 66:18). Until we have truly and sincerely confessed our sin before the Lord, our worship will not be acceptable in His sight. Undoubtedly this is the reason that Calvin placed the prayer of confession at the very beginning of his prescribed service. I do not think, however, that it is inappropriate for us to first recognize and adore God, and then, because we are

aware that we are in His presence, to immediately acknowledge before Him our own unworthiness and sin, even as the
prophet Isaiah did after hearing the seraphim exalt the
holiness and power of God.

The prayer of confession can be offered in a variety of
ways. I believe it is a mistake to use the same prayer of confession every Sunday morning. Like anything else repeated
regularly, it can become quite routine and meaningless.
However, every congregation should frequently unite in unison prayers of confession. A number of very beautiful and
fitting forms for this prayer, some dating from very ancient
times, others from the Reformation period, and still others
of more modern origin, are available. The prayer of confession could be reproduced in the printed or mimeographed
bulletin provided each worshiper.

The confession of sin should never become automatic. It is
necessary for the minister conducting the service to provide a
rubric explaining very briefly but meaningfully the necessity
of each person's confessing his sins to the Lord. In order to
guard against ritualism and to achieve a desirable variety in
form, the prayer of confession should be offered in many
different ways. The minister might suggest a time of silent
prayer of confession. He might even offer various specific
items for the worshipers to confess. Another very meaningful way for a congregation to unite in corporate confession is
by the singing of a hymn of confession. If a good hymnal is
in use there will always be available a number of very fine
hymns of confession. Often these hymns will include a
prayer for forgiveness.

Still another way to observe a corporate confession is
through the unison or responsive reading of appropriate passages of Scripture. Certain Psalms are especially appropriate; for example, Psalm 25 (especially vv. 6-11), Psalm
40:11-13, and Psalm 51. If Psalms are used, it is quite acceptable to read them responsively; but sections of Scripture not
written in Hebrew poetic form should not be read responsively. They should be read in unison. Hebrew poetry has a
parallelism in structure which lends itself to responsive read-

ing, as it did originally to antiphonal singing. This parallelism is completely obscured in the King James Version of the Bible, which is the version usually found in the back portion of our hymnals. It is most unfortunate that we cannot read the Psalms responsively according to the structure of the Hebrew poetry because that structure is obscured in this translation. If the Psalms are properly printed, the leader of worship can read a line of the inspired poetry and the congregation can then respond with the next line, which is a parallel thought. Unfortunately, with the many different translations of the Bible which evangelical Christians carry today, it is next to impossible to have a responsive reading from the Bibles which the believers bring with them to the worship services. It is to be hoped that soon some of the best hymnals will have the New American Standard Version or the New International Version of the Psalms printed in them. There is little significance to be found in a congregation's reading alternate verses of the Bible with the minister. This is called "responsive reading," but there is actually no meaningful response involved. If the Psalms are properly translated, there is a genuine response when they are read according to the structure of the Hebrew poetry. The practice of reading alternate verses seems to have been adopted as a means of securing audience participation. Unison reading of Scripture would be more meaningful.

The reading of a Psalm, either as the Old Testament lesson or as a separate reading during the service, is entirely appropriate. However, if the congregation is asked to read a Psalm either responsively or in unison, very great care should be given to make the Psalm intelligible to those who will be reading it. A brief introduction is necessary for almost all of the Psalms except perhaps the most familiar ones like Psalm 1, Psalm 23, and Psalm 27. There are many Psalms which make little sense to believers who are not well instructed in the Word unless something is said concerning the meaning a worshiper should have in his mind as he reads them. In some Psalms there are verses which need a brief explanation beforehand. Nothing seems worse than to ask a congregation to participate in a meaningless reading, even though it is taken from the Holy Scriptures. Messianic passages are almost impossible to understand unless the one who reads them knows that they were written prophetically of Jesus Christ. Consider Psalm 22, for example. Unless it is introduced by a proper explanation many worshipers in the average congregation have no understanding of what they are reading. When they get to verse 12, "Many bulls have compassed me: strong bulls of Bashan have beset me round," the words are not only meaningless, but they probably seem somewhat weird. To give just one more example from the very many that one finds in the Psalms, how can the untaught Christian enter into the tenth and eleventh verses of Psalm 31, which read, "My life is spent with grief, and my years with sighing. . . . I was a reproach among all mine enemies, but especially among my neighbours, and a fear to mine acquaintance: they that did see me without fled from me"? In all probability the worshiper isn't conscious of spending his life with grief and sighing. He may be reasonably happy. Christians should be. He certainly has no sense of having had his neighbors flee from him! If the reading of this portion of Psalm 31, which begins with a beautiful statement of trust, is to be meaningful, he must have been given some brief instruction concerning David's experience which lies behind the psalm as well as its general application to those today who are suffering reproach for Christ's sake. Great care must be exercised in having a congregation read from the Psalter.

But now we must return again to the consideration of the order of corporate worship. After the confession of sin there may properly come the

Prayer for Forgiveness

Of course, the prayer for forgiveness may be properly combined with the prayer of confession and need not always be distinct from it. Mention has already been made of hymns that contain both the confession and the prayer for forgiveness. However, there will be many times that a specific prayer for forgiveness will be very appropriate and even necessary. It should never be lengthy. Here it might be very meaningful to use a prayer of one of the great Christians of a bygone age. It is vitally important for every believer to have a definite sense of continuity with the past. The gospel of the redeeming grace of God which thrills and satisfies our hearts today with its message of forgiveness, peace, and eternal life is the very same message which calmed the fears, rejoiced the hearts, and enlightened the minds of men and women who lived and served the Savior long years ago. Unless one has a sense of communion with the saints of past ages his understanding of the communion of the saints is somewhat inadequate. The use in corporate worship of the prayers of the great saints of former years is one magnificent means not only of giving expression to the same exalted sentiments and heartfelt petitions which fell from their lips, but also of realizing in a meaningful way the fact that the unchanging God who sustained our forefathers not only can but will sustain us by His grace and make us faithful messengers of His power and love.

The building in which a congregation worships God may have been erected within the last quarter century. The emphasis of the architecture may be entirely upon contemporaneity and the needs and aspirations of today. In the service of worship, however, through a proper use of prayers drawn from all ages of the past, the worshiper may be made conscious of his rich heritage and his oneness with the saints of God in all periods of the history of the church. As he unites in an ancient prayer or versicle the worshiper joins hands across the centuries with the saints of God of long ago, and in his approach to God he expresses himself in phrases hallowed by the use of many generations of the Lord's people.

Of course, the prayer for forgiveness is by no means the only prayer of the service for which a prayer of a saint of former days is appropriate. Such prayers can be used in other places in the service. I mention them in connection with the prayer for forgiveness simply because it is a proper place for their occasional use. Following the prayer for forgiveness, whether it is offered as a part of the confession or separate from it, there should always be a statement of

Assurance of Pardoning Grace

God's people, many of whom are inwardly tormented by their sense of guilt, need to be reminded that they have a gracious God who has provided a full atonement for the sins of His believing children. So if they have sincerely confessed their sins, they can be and should be assured of God's full forgiveness. Of course, we all sin daily in thought, word, and deed; and thus all of us need to be reminded of God's full pardon to the genuinely repentant.

This element in the service is not the pronouncing of absolution. That is a Roman Catholic practice; it is not the privilege of any minister to declare that anyone has been forgiven for sin. God forgives, and He alone. However, it is perfectly right and proper for worshipers to be assured of the special forgiving grace of God which is based upon the full atonement of Christ and confirmed by the promises of the Word of God.

The assurance of pardoning grace may be introduced into the service in a number of ways. The easiest, of course, is the use by the minister of some of the promises of the Bible which clearly state God's provision of full forgiveness. I John 1:9 was the most frequently used in services which I have attended, but it must not be used too often. It is possible for such a magnificent promise as this one to lose its freshness and significance if used every Sunday. Other splendid passages abound in the Scriptures; for example, Psalm 32:1-5; 85:1, 2; 86:4, 5; 103:1-3, 12; 130:3, 4; Isaiah 53:10, 11; 55:7; Ephesians 1:7.

If the confession of sin and prayer for forgiveness have been taken from the Scriptures, it would be perfectly proper to use a hymn as a means of expressing the assurance of pardon. Such a hymn as William Cowper's well-known "There Is a Fountain Filled with Blood" would be an excellent choice, especially if the minister calls attention to the stanza which says, "Dear dying Lamb, Thy precious blood shall never lose its power. . . ." This fact is the perfect basis for assurance of forgiving grace.

It is important to remember that there are many different ways in which the confession of sin, the prayer for forgiveness, and the assurance of pardoning grace may be included in the order of worship. All three could be, if circumstances dictated brevity, combined in a prayer led by the minister, but this would not normally be the most desirable method of including these important elements. Sufficient variety is available from the use of Scripture, litanies, prayers (both extemporaneous and written), and hymns so that this part of the service need never seem routine or repetitious. To maintain the sense of the divine-human dialogue it is perhaps best to have the confession and prayer for forgiveness an act of the congregation with the assurance of pardoning grace spoken by the pastor on behalf of God.

After the assurance of pardoning grace there logically follows a

Hymn of Thanksgiving

Since a later chapter of this book will be devoted to hymns, I shall take time here to say only that this hymn should be very carefully chosen to express the believer's thanks to God for the cross of Christ and the blessings which flow from the sacrifice of the Son of God on that cross, for this is indeed always at the very heart of the Christian's worship. Without the shed blood of Christ we would have no cause for assurance and hope. Good hymnals have an abundance of hymns which are appropriate for this place in the service. Following this hymn is a very good place for

The Offering

Some prefer to place the offering after the sermon as a part of the response of the congregation to the message of the sermon. Certainly if the sermon is on some aspect of stewardship, it would be most fitting for the offering to come following it. If the sermon is not concerned with stewardship, the offering is just as appropriate in the early part of the service when the emphasis is upon the praise, adoration, and worship of God. It is important that every believer should realize that the giving of an offering to God is an act of pure worship. Any other motive for making an offering is unworthy. For this reason the minister should emphasize the worship function of the offering. He should remind the congregation that, having worshiped the Lord with their prayers and with their hymns, they also have the privilege to worship Him by the giving of their tithes and offerings. The tithes are a recognition of the sovereign authority of God and the offerings are an expression of deep love and thanksgiving to Him for the riches of His salvation.

The method of receiving the offering is very important. Unless it is properly collected and brought to the front of the church the offering can easily lose the significance of an act of worship. Empty offering plates should never be resting on the communion table, nor should they be placed there when they are full. An even more regrettable practice is to have the offerings collected and then taken out of the sanctuary to be counted by the deacons or the church treasurer during the latter part of the service.

The offering should always be received as quickly and efficiently as possible (though undue haste is to be avoided). Even a very large congregation can present its offerings in a very short space of time if the deacons have been properly instructed and there are enough of them. It is easier for the members of the congregation to keep their attention upon the act of worship in which they are participating if the receiving of the offerings does not consume a large amount of time.

When the offerings have all been collected the deacons should come forward and await a short and simple prayer of dedication by the minister. He should be careful to vary this prayer from week to week. When he has concluded his prayer he should receive the plates from the deacons and set them in an appropriate place which has been provided for them.

During the offering it is appropriate for the organist to play an offertory, although it should not be a number designed to attract the attention of the congregation away from the act of worship in which they are engaged. This is also a good place in the service for a sacred solo or duet, provided the words direct the attention of the congregation to some aspect of the character or work of God for which they should praise Him and make their offerings to Him.

Ministers should be very careful about the special musical numbers which are introduced into worship services. If musicians are allowed to select their own numbers they will often display very little understanding of what the function of their music is in a worship service. The choice of display pieces which have little or no relevance to the service of worship is most unfortunate. There is a great wealth of fine sacred music available to soloists as well as those who sing in duets and quartets. Selections can always be found which fit very well into a morning worship service, but often singers left to choose their own music will select a sentimental song which does not contribute to the worship experience of the congregation. It is difficult to make some singers who perform in the services of worship in their churches understand that they are not singing to entertain, nor are they singing to display their own vocal prowess. The only purpose for an individual musical performance in a worship service is to provide musical praise to God in which all those who are listening can participate with rejoicing.

There are many songs used frequently which have absolutely no purpose or place in a service of worship. Let me give you one example. I frequently have heard singers perform the Geoffrey O'Hara number, "I Walked Today Where Jesus Walked." It depicts a sentimental, imaginary experience of a poet which simply cannot be translated into a true worship experience for a congregation assembled in the church. If it is sung well, the congregation can enjoy and appreciate the gifts and skill of the singer and can admire the beauty of the composer's melody, but music in a worship service must either be a message from God sung to the hearts of the people or an expression of praise and worship which is offered to God on behalf of the people and in which they can participate as they listen.

7

The Order of Common Worship, Continued

When the offering has been received and the deacons take their seats the first division of the service has come to a close. The minister then directs the attention of the people to the Word of God or, if it seems best, to

The Prayers of Intercession

Many pastors prefer to leave the prayers of intercession until after the sermon, and this is perfectly acceptable. However, since the people have offered their praise and thanksgiving as well as their offerings to the Lord, it is quite proper for them to approach the Lord in intercessory prayer at this point in the services. That part of the service which was particularly designed for adoration and exaltation of God has lifted the hearts of all true worshipers to the magnification of the name of the Lord. Now attention must be given to another significant corporate act, the offering up of prayers of petition and intercession. In most of our evangelical churches today this part of the service is designated the pastoral prayer, but that is unfortunate, for it suggests that the pastor is doing the praying. Of course, in many churches the pastor is about the only one who is praying at this time. His prayer is often referred to as "the long prayer." Many Christians have admitted honestly that during the pastoral prayer they often find themselves simply listening to what the pastor is saying. They also confess that they have difficulty in keeping their minds on the minister's prayer and so allow themselves to think about other things until he comes to the conclusion. It is indeed a great weakness in the evangelical churches of our day that the prayers in their services have been almost completely limited to those offered by the minister in the name of the people.

Several problems are before us in considering this part of the service. One of them is the length of most pastoral prayers. It would seem that many ministers have not realized that when they are leading a congregation of worshipers in prayer they are not demonstrating their own personal powers of intercession, but they are actually to be providing the members of the congregation with the very words with which they are to join in offering up petitions to God. If the minister takes seriously the fact that the congregation is praying with him, he will be careful about the way he prays, not with great deliberation and with frequent long pauses. He will also be careful about the length of his prayers. It takes rigid discipline to carry on an extensive ministry of intercession when the minister is alone in his own study. But it is very easy to pray a long time when he knows that a congregation of people is listening. Perhaps the greatest test of his leadership ability comes when he leads in prayer. During that time he must be self-forgetful, but at the same time fully aware of his unchanging needs as a sinful man. He must be able to ignore his own particular mood, no matter how dominating it may be, and project his consciousness of the needs of those who are gathered in the name of the Lord, so that he is properly presenting their needs to the Lord. He must remember that he is not just praying on behalf of the congregation, nor just praying for them. He is leading their prayer, providing them the means by which they can unite with him in offering up to God their corporate petitions.

It is especially important that ministers realize that the pastoral prayer, if it is called by that name, is no time for them to pray *at* their congregations. By that I mean that it is no time to give them instructions or reproof or a sharp rebuke which he feels they deserve but which he would hesitate to give directly to them in his sermon. I have listened to ministers scold their congregations in their prayers. Such a practice is entirely unworthy of the high calling of a pastor.

It is equally important for members of the congregation to realize that whenever it is time for prayer in a worship service, each of them is to participate wholeheartedly in the offering up of the prayer to God. It is not a time to sit and listen, or to think about other things. Of course, as Nathaniel Micklem has pointed out, "The mental agility required to grasp the thread of another's thought as it moves on in a prayer of any continuance, to make it one's own, and to direct it to God, is considerable."[1] Men need to understand that faithful worship is not easy. Our people need to be instructed and to understand the self-discipline which is required to make corporate worship all that it should be.

If a minister wishes to be effective in leading the prayers of his congregation he must prepare for his public prayers. This is especially true if he leads in the prayer of intercession called the pastoral prayer. He must be careful that he does not fall into sloppy habits of prayer. When I was a child, I could always tell when our pastor was getting near the end of his prayer, for he followed the same pattern Sunday after Sunday. When he prayed he intoned the words in such a solemn and affected manner that I gained the impression that, when standing in a pulpit, one found it necessary to speak to God in a way very different from the way he would

---

[1] Nathaniel Micklem, ed., *Christian Worship* (London: Oxford University Press, 1959), pp. 194-95.

speak to others in ordinary conversation. I held the minister
in high esteem, but it would never have occurred to me that I
was to participate with him in the offering up of this
strange-sounding prayer. After I was old enough to have a
watch of my own I would often time his prayers, and I found
that frequently they took as much as twelve minutes of the
service.

Pastors should be careful to see that their prayers are fresh
and relevant to the spiritual needs of their congregations.
While there are certain needs in every church which continue
week after week—the need for spiritual growth of the members, for example—certainly the prayers for these needs
should not be offered in the same way each Lord's Day.
There are new concerns which arise every week about which
prayer must be offered. Only good preparation will prevent
pastoral prayers from becoming too long and too routine.

I should like to suggest a practice which has been followed
in the chapel services at Covenant Seminary and which also
has been adopted in some of the churches pastored by our
seminary graduates. It requires some instruction for the
congregation, but I believe that it helps in a very splendid
way to give each worshiper a real sense of participation in the
time of intercession. To begin with, the leader of worship,
normally the pastor, must prepare in advance four or five
special matters for prayer about which he wants the congregation to unite. When the time comes for the prayers of intercession in the service, instead of his leading in one long
prayer he should mention one specific item, briefly pointing
out any aspect of the situation which will help the people understand it better and give them a greater sense of personal
involvement as they pray. He then leads in a brief and earnest prayer about that one matter. At the conclusion of this
brief prayer the congregation will, if properly instructed, indicate its fellowship in offering up the petition by a unison
"Amen." He will then mention the next item about which he
wants his people to join him in prayer. Again he will confine
himself to a brief specific prayer about this one item and
again the congregation will express its full agreement and as-

sent with an audible "Amen." Four or five brief prayers about very specific matters, each of which has been shared with the congregation before the prayer is offered, will certainly help the worshipers to have a real sense of personal participation in this all-important part of common worship. The "Amens" of the congregation will also be a blessing to the pastor. It is most encouraging to know that people are praying with you.

A series of brief prayers of intercession such as I have suggested could certainly be brought to a conclusion with the offering of the Lord's Prayer in unison. I would not, however, suggest that this prayer be used every Lord's Day in the morning service. When the Lord gave this model prayer in His Sermon on the Mount, he preceded it with the warning that we should not use vain repetitions when we pray. It is exceedingly difficult to pray the Lord's Prayer every Sunday morning and not have it become a vain repetition. Because it is so familiar to all of us it requires a certain discipline to offer it thoughtfully and sincerely when we are carried along in unison prayer with everyone else in the congregation. The minister who uses it every Sunday morning is, I believe, making it somewhat difficult for his people to keep from vain repetition.

Here I want to recommend to every evangelical pastor and to all Christians who are concerned about making their worship more meaningful that they study the collect (pronounced with the accent on the first syllable) as a distinctive form of prayer and become familiar with the collects which have come down to us from previous generations, many of them from the ancient church. There are many Christians who believe that there is something wrong about the reading of prayers in a public service. If careful thought is given to the matter, however, one will realize that in corporate worship the members of the congregation are actually praying with words supplied by the minister in all the formal prayers of the service. Why then should it be objectionable to unite in common prayer using the magnificent sentiments of the saints of some previous period of church history? Certainly anyone who has difficulty in expressing himself adequately in public prayer will gain much from the study of great prayers; I refer particularly to the collects which have been so firmly established in the minds and hearts of many of God's choice saints. They speak to God in phrases hallowed by many centuries of believers' usage, but they are as fresh and meaningful today as when they first poured out of the heart of some noble Christian.

Because I am sure that many evangelical believers are not familiar with the collect, I want to give a brief explanation of its origin and its form. It is a form particularly well suited for use in prayers of intercession such as we have been discussing, even though the ancient collects themselves are not used. Anyone who leads in common prayer will do well to make himself familiar with this form so he can adapt it to his own petitions. As Adrian Fortescu has well said of the collect, it "asks for one thing and one thing only, and that in the tersest language."[2]

The actual origin of the form of prayer which is called a collect is not certain. None of the earliest records of Christian worship services make mention of the collects. However, by the fourth century they appear as the first formal prayers in the liturgy, and by this time there were collects for every Sunday and holy day of the year. The word *collect* comes from the Latin word *collecta*. L. E. H. Stephens-Hodge tells us that "in the days of the Early Church, a service of Christian worship was called 'a gathering together.' . . . In Rome, after the days of bitter persecution were over, it became the custom on the Lord's Day for people to assemble at different points and then converge, in procession, upon a central church for the celebration of the Holy Mysteries. Before they set out a prayer was said—oratio ad collectam—'a prayer for the gathering together' and a litany was chanted as they went on their way to join the other worshipers."[3] While this sug-

---

[2]Adrian Fortescu, *The Mass* (London & New York: Longmans Green, 1937), p. 246.

[3]L. E. H. Stephens-Hodge, *The Collects* (London: Hodder and Stoughton, 1964), p. 18.

gests the historical origin of the word *collect,* it certainly does not exhaust nor even by any means fully indicate the significance of the word today. It is indeed a collecting or a gathering together by the pastor of the prayers of the people so that all may be offered unto God in unison. It gives corporate expression to the prayers of all who are gathered to worship.

The structural form of the collect is quite simple. It consists as a rule, but not always, of five distinct parts: (1) the invocation, (2) the acknowledgment or grounds of approach, (3) the petition, (4) the aspiration, and (5) the plea. In the invocation God is addressed, sometimes with only the words "O God" or "O Lord," but sometimes with added descriptive adjectives. The acknowledgment is a clause usually but not always introduced by a relative pronoun such as "who" or "whose." The petition is the prayer itself, expressing some deep need of the heart. The aspiration is the statement of the desired end which is sought. The plea is usually stated in the simple words, "through Jesus Christ our Lord," because it is fitting always to recognize that our only basis of acceptance with God is the merit of our Savior.

To give an example of this beautiful form of prayer let me quote perhaps the best known and certainly one of the most beautiful of all the collects. It is used in the Anglican and Reformed Episcopal service before the Lord's Supper. This is the prayer:

> Almighty God, unto whom all hearts are open, all desires known and from whom no secrets are hid; cleanse the thoughts of our minds by the inspiration of Thy Holy Spirit that we may perfectly serve Thee, and worthily magnify Thy Holy Name, through Jesus Christ, our Lord.

This prayer could not be stated more movingly nor with a greater economy of words. I heartily commend a study and a use of the collects. Although they are used every Sunday in Anglican and Reformed Episcopal churches, these denominations certainly do not have exclusive rights to them.

We return now to the order of worship. If the prayers of intercession have followed the giving of the offering, the next unit of the service will be

The Old Testament Lesson

Now the service turns specifically to the instruction of the people through the proclamation of the Word. We have already noted that a responsive reading of an appropriate psalm may well appear in the early part of the service. This should not be regarded as the Old Testament lesson, however. The Psalms are prayers and praises, and while they do contain doctrine of great importance they are not generally regarded as proclamation. That is why they fit into the early portion of the service. If one is not read, it is good to have one sung. The Old Testament lesson, however, should be proclamation from the Lord. In many evangelical churches today there is only one Scripture lesson, and it is usually the portion of Scripture from which the sermon text is taken. Although in the early church there was frequently a reading from the Scriptures of the Old Testament as well as a reading from some of the apostolic epistles which had not yet been fully formed into the collection of canonical writings we know as the New Testament, there is no indication from the early church that both Old Testament and New Testament reading are essential. Because of the great importance of the entire Word of God and the general ignorance of the Old Testament Scriptures among believers today, a worship service will be more complete if it includes both an Old Testament lesson and a New Testament lesson. It will always be helpful for the worshiper to understand that the general theme of the sermon is found in both of the major parts of the Bible. The specific sermon text may be found in one of the portions of Scripture used, but the other reading must also be selected with great care. The unity of the service must not be disrupted just to read a lesson from each Testament.

Before the reading of any portion of the Scriptures the minister should always provide a verbal rubric reminding the people of the significance of what is about to be done. He should at least say, "Let us now turn our attention to the hearing of the Word of God." In the service books of the Scottish, English, and Irish churches of the Reformed tradition the minister is directed to say, "Hear the Word of

God." This much is certainly a minimum, although it would seem that a statement just a bit longer would more clearly emphasize the importance of listening carefully to the Scriptures. Since a minister should never get in the habit of saying precisely the same thing, he should remember that there are many ways of varying even a brief introduction to the reading of the Scriptures. Before reading any passage of Scripture the minister should provide, if it is not completely obvious, the reason why that particular passage has been chosen. At the end of the lesson, he should never say, "May the Lord *add* His blessing to the reading of His Word." The Word itself is God's message, and it is always a blessing if given reverent attention. The Lord never adds blessing to its reading to make its ministry more complete.

If one uses both an Old Testament lesson and a New Testament lesson, it is good to conclude the Old Testament lesson with the singing of the Gloria Patri. We learn from L. Duschene that "it was customary as early as the fourth century to end the antiphonal singing of a psalm with the singing of the Gloria Patri."[4] This was in part because controversies had arisen in the church as to whether the God of the Old Testament was the same as the God who revealed Himself in the person of His Son, the Lord Jesus Christ. The Gloria Patri is one of the very earliest of the ancient canticles; it is easy to see how it was pressed into use in the service to affirm the identity of the God of the old with the God of the new covenant. There are many who question the authority of the Old Testament today; so it is quite fitting to use the Gloria following the Old Testament reading. However, even the Gloria Patri should not be used so often that it becomes threadbare. Therefore, I would suggest that following the Old Testament lesson would be a fine place for

The Anthem

This musical number is an appropriate offering of praise following the proclamation of the Word of God. Most evan-

---

[4]L. Duschene, *Christian Worship: Its Origin and Evolution* (London: S.P.C.K., 1927), p. 116.

gelical churches today consider their choirs an important part of their ministry. Unfortunately very few choir members have any real understanding of the function of a choir in a worship service, and few choir directors are concerned with the selection of anthem music which is appropriate for the place in the service at which it will be sung. There is a wealth of splendid music in anthem form which would be excellent following the reading of the Old Testament lesson. The pastor should, of course, always point out briefly the significance of the words which are being sung. It needs to be said most emphatically that the function of the choir is not to entertain nor is it to impress the congregation with the beauty and skill of its choral rendition. As we have already pointed out, when a choir sings an anthem in a worship service it is for the purpose of offering musical praise which is beyond the capacity of the congregation as a whole. Every member of the congregation should understand that it is his privilege as well as his duty to enter into this musical praise which the choir renders to God.

The fact that the choir is providing musical praise for all the congregation to enter into certainly dictates that every word of an anthem must be distinctly sung so that it can be clearly understood. Nothing is more frustrating to members of a congregation who desire to participate in the worship of the choir than to have the choir sing an anthem only a few words of which can be understood. In the church of God not only must words spoken be clearly understood, but those that are sung as well. The apostle Paul tells us in I Corinthians 14:26 that everything which takes place in a church service must be for the strengthening of the church. He establishes an important principle when he says in verse 19, "In the church I would rather speak five intelligible words to instruct others than ten thousand words in a tongue" (NIV). Certainly if a choir sings in unintelligible words it is the same as speaking unintelligibly.

The fact that I have suggested that an anthem follow the Old Testament lesson does not mean that this is necessarily the best place for it. Sometimes the Gloria Patri will be sung after the reading from the Old Testament. No rigid pattern regarding the development of the service should ever be set. The place that the anthem occupies in the service should be determined by the content of the anthem. The choir director should always consult with the pastor about the anthems which he proposes to use. The minister should be as familiar with anthem literature as possible so that he can make wise suggestions for particular anthems which will preserve the unity of the services he is to conduct. He should always be familiar with the words of the anthem that is going to be sung so that he can fit it into the best place in the service, and also can give the congregation a brief word concerning its message.

There are many, many excellent anthems which use the words of the inspired Psalms. When these are used it is quite fitting for the minister to suggest that the believers follow the words in their own Bibles. There are also fine anthems which fit well with the themes of sermons. These could be used just before the sermon. If they are particularly appropriate as a climactic response to the sermon they may be used immediately after the sermon. Much careful thought must be given to planning the musical ministry of the choir and placing the anthems at the proper places in the services. Most anthems are songs of praise, and therefore fit well into the early part of the service.

It is quite acceptable for an appropriate anthem to be sung during the giving of the offering. There are also some beautiful short canticles which would be particularly fitting for the choir to sing at this time. No choir director who is concerned about his ministry of music as well as his witness and work with a group of singers will be satisfied, I am sure, to be called upon to present his anthems always while the offering is being received. As Donald Macleod has said, "Since every minister must face up to the realities of the local situation and reckon with the psychological as well as theological factors in worship, his decision relating to the placing of the anthem, for example, cannot be too arbitrary. Monotony in worship originates in doing any one thing too frequently or too long."[5]

The New Testament Lesson

The New Testament lesson will frequently be the basis of the sermon, although it may include more than just the text itself. If an expository message is given, the entire lesson may be the text of the sermon. In communicating to the congregation the message and meaning of both of the Scripture lessons, the manner in which the minister reads is of great importance. He should never give the impression that he is reading just because the order of service calls for a reading from the Scripture at that time. He should convey to the congregation that what he is reading is of very great importance. He is not just reading from a textbook on ethical conduct. He should study his passage carefully and understand it thoroughly and then read it with mastery. If there are biblical names included, he should know the correct pronunciation; he should never stumble over them. If theological terms are included, it is justifiable for him to add a very brief word of definition. Before he begins the reading it is often helpful to describe the setting of the passage and put it in proper context for the congregation, but he should avoid little sermonettes at this time.

The reading of an overlong passage of Scripture is not good psychologically, for no one will remember the details of a long passage. If, however, a long passage must be read in order to include all the material which is to be covered in an expository sermon, the passage should be practiced aloud until it is very familiar to the minister who is to read it. Then it can be read rapidly, but clearly, with special emphasis given to those verses or phrases which are important for the sermon of the morning. If a narrative passage is to be read and it seems too long, certain portions of it may properly be summarized. One should do this in such a way as to preserve

---

[5]Donald Macleod, *Presbyterian Worship: Its Meaning and Method* (Richmond: John Knox Press, 1965), p. 38.

the deep reverence that should always characterize our attitude toward the Word of God. The actual reading of the Scripture portion should always be done with as much expression as is possible without being overly dramatic or sentimental. It is a challenge to those who read the Scriptures to do it well; for all too often in evangelical churches today, when the pastor begins to read the Scripture lesson, many members of the congregation settle themselves to read the church bulletin or something else which they have in hand. Careless listening to the Scriptures is often the result of indifferent reading, or a reading which is artificially solemn and unnatural.

When the lessons from the Scriptures are announced, the references should be given correctly: first the book, then the chapter, and finally the verse. If they are given in the reverse order, it is difficult for individuals in the congregation to remember the verse and perhaps even the chapter.

It is of great importance that members of the congregation should follow the reading of the Scriptures in their own Bibles or in Bibles provided for them in the pews. A well-taught congregation will be in the habit of bringing their Bibles with them, but there will always be some people present who are visitors or who for some reason have not brought their own Bibles. For this reason as well as to encourage the habit of following in the Bible not only the Scripture lessons but also the sermon, every church should provide Bibles as well as hymnbooks in the pews. There is greater benefit to be derived from Scripture reading and from listening to sermons if the people see the Word of God and hear it at the same time.

We live in a day of multiplication of new translations of the Bible. Some of them are good and some are not to be depended upon. No translation has yet fully replaced the Authorized or King James Version. Among evangelicals wide acceptance has been given to the New American Standard Version, and still more enthusiasm has been expressed for the New International Version, which is not a revision of an older version but an entirely new translation by a large group of evangelical scholars, all of whom are committed to the verbal inspiration and infallibility of the Bible. It is to be hoped that this version, which uses easy-to-understand, yet beautiful modern English, may become the standard version in evangelical churches and will be as familiar to believers as the King James Version has been for the past many years. This would make unison readings in our church services more feasible and would eliminate the problem arising from the people's following the Scripture lessons in different versions.

After the New Testament lesson has been read, an appropriate psalm or hymn may be sung, or if the anthem of the choir fits better in this place than at any other, it may be used here. For example, if the choir is singing an anthem which exalts the Word of God, it would be particularly appropriate here. The congregation could always sing a psalm which exalts the Scriptures. There are many of them. If a congregational hymn is to be sung here, it must be well chosen. It should not present the main argument of the sermon which is to follow. It should rather call attention to the fact that the congregation is to give heed to the authoritative message of the Scriptures. Such a hymn as Benjamin Beddome's great "God in the Gospel of His Son," or Frances Havergal's "Lord, Speak to Me, That I May Speak," or the well-known "Break Thou the Bread of Life," which is so often erroneously used in connection with the communion service, would be excellent at this time. There are many other suitable hymns to sing just before the Word of God is preached.

After the New Testament lesson, whether or not a hymn or an anthem is sung, the sermon should be preceded by

The Prayer for Illumination

The prayer for illumination is a brief prayer which John Calvin and Martin Bucer both placed before the Scripture lesson, as both felt strongly that the reading of the Scripture was just as much a proclamation of God's truth as was the sermon and therefore needed the illumination of the Holy

Spirit to make it meaningful. While I would certainly not take issue with their position, I nevertheless feel that because in most services the Scriptures which have been read are going to be expounded in the sermon it is quite acceptable to offer this prayer just before the preaching begins. If the Old Testament lesson follows immediately after the prayers of intercession, it would be quite appropriate to conclude the group of short prayers which have been suggested with the prayer for illumination.

Little needs to be said about the content of this brief prayer. It should be just what its name suggests. It should not contain specific petitions other than those directly related to the preaching and hearing of the Word of God.

Following this prayer would come, of course,

The Sermon

This is not a book on the theory of preaching. But in connection with preaching as a part of worship a number of things need to be said. We have decried the attitude of those who go to church simply to hear the sermon, those who speak of all that precedes the sermon in a worship service as "the preliminaries." This does not mean that we believe that the preaching of a sermon is merely a necessary accompaniment to a more important rite. We want the entire service to provide a rich, fulfilling experience of worship. While we have placed emphasis upon the other elements of the service, because in so many of our churches they have been so sadly neglected, we would not want to minimize in any sense the importance of the preaching of the Word. When we concentrate our attention upon the essential meaning of worship we realize that it is just as important that God should speak to His people as it is that they should speak to Him. Preaching, therefore, is an integral and essential part of Christian worship.

Preaching was the primary activity of the apostles. It was through their preaching that the church was brought into being. We read concerning them that "they went forth, and preached every where, the Lord working with them" (Mark 16:20). The apostle Paul tells us that Christ sent him "to preach the gospel," adding that "the preaching of the cross is to them that perish foolishness; but unto us which are saved it is the power of God" (I Cor. 1:17, 18). It is not only the preaching of the gospel or the preaching of the cross, if those messages are taken as limited to the preaching of the good news of salvation, which is the power of God. God's power is manifest through the preaching of "the whole counsel of God" (Acts 20:27, RSV), which Paul was faithful to bring to the churches which he established. The place which the apostles gave to preaching, and the place which it has occupied in Christian worship down through the history of the church, indicate that God has chosen to communicate with man not alone through His written revelation in the Scriptures, but also through the clear exposition and powerful proclamation of that Word by His appointed ministers. God speaks to man through His Word by the power of His Holy Spirit, but He doesn't speak in man's subconscious life; He rather speaks to him as a rational creature.

True preaching, of course, is the proclamation of the authoritative Word of God. The divine command to all preachers is "Preach the word; be instant in season, out of season; reprove, rebuke, exhort with all long suffering and doctrine" (II Tim. 4:2). The church of Jesus Christ is not simply a society for the study of religion made up of people of good will who are against injustice, or racism, or bad housing for the poor. These concerns should and do appeal to the minds of godly men, and they are causes in which the children of the Lord should be involved. There is, however, something more than social reforms which must occupy the minister in the church of Jesus Christ. If he is a preacher who understands the minds of men and knows their basic needs, he will never be deceived by the idea that it is unnecessary for him to preach the doctrines of the Bible. Every true Christian minister lives and carries on his work within a framework of biblical truth. His every argument and appeal are based upon the presupposition that God's whole Word is true. If he is truly concerned to make God's truth live in the lives of those to whom he ministers, he must preach biblical doctrine. It is possible to preach doctrine so that it becomes of thrilling interest to his listeners. There is nothing essentially dull about doctrine, although many ministers have the capacity to make it seem so.

It must be noted here that preaching offers the minister an opportunity unparalleled to witness the sovereign purpose of God being worked out in his congregation. This is not to say that the various other aspects of his pastoral ministry are ineffective. He can accomplish much through his counseling, his personal evangelism, his visitation of the sick and sorrowing, and just through the impact of the witness of his life. However, there is nothing comparable to the effects of Spirit-filled preaching. When a godly minister preaches, something significant happens. The building of the body of Christ, the church, is accomplished largely through preaching. "It pleased God by the foolishness of preaching to save them that believe" (I Cor. 1:21). The salvation of souls, of course, is only the beginning of the blessings which come through the faithful preaching of the Word. It is through the fervent preaching of biblical truth that believers are built up in their faith and encouraged and enabled to meet the trials and difficulties of life. We live in a society that is disintegrating around us. It is through the preaching of the whole gospel that the church is kept in existence as the only organism which is dynamically alive and able to point the way out of the distress and decay which engulf the nations of the world. It is through preaching the Word that the faithful minister upholds the moral and ethical standards which are necessary for the basic preservation of our society. Indeed preaching is at the very heart of the life of the church and must occupy a central place in its worship.

Every minister must realize that preaching is, as it has been designated, "the finest of the fine arts," because of the significant results with which it is attended. Since this is so, every minister must determine to be a master of the art of preaching. It is the most creative aspect of his office in the church and at the same time the most challenging. If he has been called to preach, he has been called to be an artist whose material is words. He is not worthy of his calling if he does not choose and arrange his words with all the precision and beauty of which he is capable. He must continually study to make himself a more skilled preacher of God's truth. Words were never cheap and unimportant to the prophets of God. "When the Hebrew prophet said, 'The word of the Lord came to me,' it was to him an overwhelming and even heart-shattering experience. When he said, *Thus saith the Lord,* he was repeating no idle formula. The Word was like a fire that burned the prairies; a hammer that broke the rock into pieces."[6] The modern minister must have the same attitude toward the Word of God as did the apostles and prophets.

Evangelicals understand that the very words of the Scriptures are God-breathed, and that the Holy Spirit never speaks otherwise today than He did when He spoke through the men of old who wrote down the Scriptures. The testimony of the Holy Spirit in the written Word is to Jesus Christ, the living Word. The one theme of the entire Bible is the incarnate Word of God, Jesus Christ the Eternal Son. As an exposition of the Scriptures, then, the sermon must be a ministry of the Holy Spirit through the Word bringing the living Christ to the people. If it is not this it may be a lifeless discussion of doctrine or it may be a presentation of Christ which is false because it is inconsistent with the revelation of the written Word and therefore is not a ministry of the living Word. It is in the sermon delivered in the power of the Holy Spirit that God deals with man on the basis of His infinite wisdom and grace. He shows man the error of his sin and the sufficiency of Christ to pardon, cleanse, guide, and enable him to live a life of holiness. Through the Word of God, as well as through the sacraments, God's infinite grace is mediated to men.

It is deserving of special notice here that the preacher is not the only one who must manifest great concern for the ser-

---

[6]E. Shillito in *Christian Worship,* ed. Micklem, p. 214.

mon. The attitude of the listener is most important. The individual worshiper should as eagerly anticipate every sermon preached by a Spirit-filled minister as he does the blessed experience of the holy communion when he receives the ministration of the body and blood of the Lord Jesus Christ. The Word and the sacraments cannot be separated from one another, nor should one ever be exalted above the other. If the individual worshiper is to go away from the house of worship with the consciousness that the Lord has spoken to him concerning some important aspect of his life and has given him the instruction that he needs, he must make sure that his ear is open to the truth of God and that he listens eagerly for spiritual food for his own soul.

There are several important rules for listening to a sermon. If a minister is well trained in homiletics and has spent adequate time on the preparation of his sermon, it will be much easier to listen to his sermon and get great benefit from it. However, even a poorly prepared sermon will have something of significance for the listener who has trained himself to get the most from what he hears in the church services which he attends. The first rule is to make sure what the text of the sermon is and to have the text open in the Bible as one listens. There may be important things which will come to the listener out of the text even though they are not particularly emphasized in the sermon. If the pastor is skilled in expository preaching he will normally use a text which is longer than just one verse. He has a right to expect that those who listen to him in the service will be following in their own Bibles his exposition of the text.

The second rule for listeners is to seek to determine what is the main thrust of the argument of the sermon. In homiletics, which is the science of preparation and delivery of sermons, preachers are taught to work out what is called a "proposition" for each of their sermons. This proposition may not be clearly stated in the sermon itself, but a good listener will seek to determine the principal idea which the minister is seeking to get across. He will look for what could be called the "sermon in a nutshell." He may discover that he can state the argument of the sermon more clearly and more succinctly than the minister does.

A third rule for good listening is to seek to determine from the sermon what action is called for in the life of the listener. Unfortunately, after many sermons with which any true believer might be in hearty agreement, it is difficult if not impossible to tell just what the minister expects the congregation to do as a result of their listening to the sermon. If the listener can determine this for himself—and this may take some careful thought—he has immeasurably added to the effectiveness of the sermon in his own life. It is easy to be critical when one listens to a sermon which does not seem to be as well prepared as it should be. It is quite another thing to set one's mind to discover important truth which may or may not come out clearly in the minister's message.

Following the sermon the congregation should be encouraged to respond appropriately to the message which has been given. This may be done in a variety of ways. In some congregations the giving of the offering has always been a part of this response. Certainly there are times when this is a very appropriate response. It is a mistake, however, always to identify the offering of our material substance as the appropriate response following a sermon. This may reduce the effectiveness of the appeal which the minister has made for another specific response to his sermon. Generally, if the sermon has been clear and forceful the congregation will express its response more satisfactorily by a

Hymn of Response

In order for the right hymn to be chosen the minister who prepares the sermon and plans the worship service must know the resources available to him in the hymnody of the Christian church. The congregation must also possess an adequate hymnbook. I have sometimes listened to good sermons which seemed to demand a particular hymn that came to mind as I listened; yet the closing hymn which was eventually announced was not only not the hymn I had in mind, but one which was completely unsuitable to express the response of the congregation. The poverty of the collection of gospel songs and a few hymns which characterizes so many of the songbooks used in evangelical churches today is to be deeply regretted since there is such a wealth of material available. It is very easy to choose a familiar song which is well liked by the members of the congregation; it is quite another thing to carefully determine that hymn which will most appropriately express the corporate response of the congregation to the message of the sermon. Unless the offering is received at this time, or the intercessory prayers have been placed at this point in the service, the service will come to a close with

The Dismissal and Benediction

Not many of our congregations today ever hear words of dismissal from their pastors at the conclusion of worship services. Normally the pastor raises his arms as a signal that he is about to offer the benediction, and the people bow their heads and consider themselves dismissed by this act. A few words of dismissal reminding the people of the challenge to serve Christ and to live for Him in this dark world of sin are of real value. This practice also has ample historical precedent. It has been part of the Irish and Scottish Presbyterian liturgies for centuries. The dismissal need not be more than a sentence or two. Such a word as, "Go in peace and serve the living God in a world of strife and turmoil," will remind each listener that his worship of God should have prepared him for a richer experience of witnessing for God in the everyday world of men.

The words of dismissal are followed by the benediction, for no worshipers should ever be sent forth to serve in their own strength. They must ever be dismissed in the name of the Lord with the assurance of the power and presence of the Triune God to accompany them always.

There are many excellent benedictions in the Scriptures. A minister should not make up his own when the inspiration of the Holy Spirit has made available ample words of benediction so that there need be no repetitive use of the same one or two.

Before bringing this chapter to a close, I want to speak of some elements which I have not included, though they are found in the worship services of many of our evangelical churches. Unless I make explanations some readers may imagine that I have not considered these popular components of the worship services of our day.

The Doxology

There are very few believers in our evangelical churches who realize that the doxology which is used to open the service in so many churches is actually the last stanza of three hymns written by the great Anglican Bishop Thomas Ken, who lived from 1637 to 1711. Two of these hymns, the Morning Hymn and the Evening Hymn, appear in every good hymnbook. The Midnight Hymn is not found in modern hymnals, for we do not have corporate worship at midnight. The final stanza of these three hymns is sung today by more English-speaking Christians throughout the entire world than any other single verse in existence. The problem arises from its too frequent repetition. Nothing that is used every Sunday can retain its freshness and deep meaning. How much better it would be to use it only occasionally as the congregational response to the call to worship, or, even better, to use the entire Morning Hymn, which begins,

> Awake, my soul, and with the sun
> Thy daily stage of duty run;
> Shake off dull sloth, and joyful rise
> To pay thy morning sacrifice.

It then concludes with the familiar stanza we refer to as the doxology. There seems to be no valid reason for extracting one stanza from a fine hymn and using it every Sunday of the year.

The Gloria Patri

I have already suggested one appropriate use for the Gloria Patri. There are others, of course. This song is of very ancient origin, and it would be a sad mistake for it to be dropped out of use entirely in any modern evangelical church. The first statement of this brief canticle, "Glory be to the Father and to the Son and to the Holy Ghost," was from the very earliest time the common doxology used throughout the churches of Christendom. The latter portion, "As it was in the beginning, is now and ever shall be, world without end. Amen," was added during the time of the Arian controversy. The Council of Nicea in A.D. 325 made a final determining decision concerning the doctrine of the Trinity, and from that time on the Gloria Patri was used as we now know it throughout the Western church. Interestingly enough I have quizzed many individuals about the meaning of the final part of this song, and have had them confess that while they sing it very frequently they do not understand exactly what the last portion means. For example, the "it" in the phrase, "as it was in the beginning," is a reference to the Trinity. The statement "world without end" with which the song concludes is an idiomatic expression meaning "eternally."

It is most fitting for the Gloria Patri to be used immediately following the Apostles' Creed whenever that great statement of faith is used in the services of worship. Since the Gloria Patri is a statement of strong theological conviction it is very appropriate when sung in connection with the Creed. It is also suitable to follow a responsive reading of one of the Psalms, or the Old Testament lesson, as previously mentioned.

The Creed

In most evangelical churches today, when a creed is used, it is the Apostles' Creed. For variety as well as for some increase in depth of theological statement it would be good to use the Nicean Creed at times. This would serve to give the people something of a sense of their heritage in sound doctrine. How thankful believers should be that in ages past faithful men fought for the truth and preserved the truth of the Scriptures in their creedal statements. These ancient creeds are much more definitive and meaningful than some of the modern creeds.

The Apostles' Creed, or, if preferred, the Nicean Creed, should be used regularly only at the time when the sacrament of the Lord's Supper is being observed. If it is used every Sunday it loses its significance. Before a communion service, however, it is not only appropriate but actually necessary. Before partaking of the Lord's Supper every believer should gladly reaffirm his faith by using the words of one of these historic creeds. Much actually depends upon the manner in which the Creed is announced and said. If communion is observed as often as twice during each month, the Creed would be frequently used and the continual recitation would always open up the possibility of overfamiliarity and listlessness. When it is time for the Creed the minister should be careful in his introductory words. He should avoid saying, "Let us repeat the Apostles' Creed," for this is exactly what many will be encouraged by these words to do, just repeat the words of the Creed. The Creed can be repeated meaninglessly. He should say, "Let us unitedly affirm our Christian faith with the words of the Apostles' Creed," or some such statement. Then he should lead out in a strong personal affirmation, being careful to avoid the tendency to race through the words and phrases. If he speaks with a measure of unaffected deliberation, giving emphasis to the strong truths of the Creed, the worshipers will be encouraged to think seriously of the things which they are affirming.

The Children's Sermon

The practice of gathering little children at the front of the church for a "sermon" of their own has become increasingly popular in some evangelical churches today. In other churches the children remain in their seats with their parents while the pastor directs a message to the little ones. Whether the children come to the front or remain in their seats the minister ignores the young people and the adults while he addresses himself exclusively to the small children.

There are several reasons why I do not recommend the inclusion of a children's sermon in a Sunday morning worship service. In the first place it brings a very distinct break in the worship experience of all the older children and adults who comprise the majority of the congregation. There can be no doubt about the fact that a group of little children gathered around the pastor at the front of the church is indeed a most interesting spectacle. It is amusing to watch them, especially those who are precocious and uninhibited and who enjoy being on display before their parents and other adults. A church worship service, however, is not a time for the enjoyment of the antics of little children, precious and important as each one of them is. This is a time for corporate worship, and no segment of the congregation should be singled out for special attention.

Another reason for calling into question this practice is that the children's messages are not essentially different from those they receive during the Sunday school hour, which usually either precedes or follows the worship service. The pastor's "sermon" for the children usually consists of a rather simple object lesson; it does not contribute to the congregation's receiving of the Word of God. I remember worshiping in a fine evangelical church where some of the people felt that they understood the pastor's message for the children better than they did his rather pedantic sermon prepared for the adults. But children's sermons, of course, are not designed to aid the adults' understanding!

There is great value in teaching boys and girls from earliest childhood to participate in the worship services of their churches. It is a mistake to give them the impression that everything in which they take part must be tailored especially for them. They have their Sunday school classes in which the instruction is on their level. There is much profit in their learning to sit quietly with their parents during the common worship of the whole family of God. If the pastor is wise in his preaching there will be much in his sermons that even the smaller children can understand and appreciate. With helpful instruction from their parents they will very early be able to participate meaningfully in common worship.

8

Hymnody in the Church

One of the major contributing factors to the superficiality of the lives of evangelical Christians in our country today is the failure of the churches to teach and use the great hymns of the church universal in their services of worship. We have reared a generation or two of Christians who prefer sentimental songs with highly questionable theology to the greatest Christian poetry which has ever been penned. For example, on a recent questionnaire which was submitted to thousands of Christians in this country in an effort to determine their favorite hymns the two ranking selections were "The Old Rugged Cross" and "In the Garden," neither of which can actually be classified as a hymn. I have already made reference to the sentimentality and bad theology of "In the Garden." While "The Old Rugged Cross" is considerably better, it certainly is not a true hymn, but a subjective and sentimental gospel song. Because of the great popularity of these two songs I realize that many readers will immediately resent any criticism of them. I can only hope that they will give careful thought to the problems of these songs. One of the features of many of our modern gospel songs which is not present in the great hymns is their boastful assertions of faithfulness to God rather than a prayerful petition for help to be more faithful. The last stanza of "The Old Rugged Cross" requires every singer to state with amazing confidence, "To the old rugged cross I will ever be true, its shame and reproach gladly bear." Nothing of this kind of sentiment is found in the Scriptures nor in the great hymns. The apostle Peter, who boasted that he would never deny the Lord, had to experience a tragic denial before he understood how utterly undependable he was in himself apart from the sustaining power of God.

The Gospel Song

In a previous chapter we have emphasized the necessity of all of our worship being "in truth," and thus without any pretense or hypocrisy. It is the gospel songs which again and again encourage us to sing statements which are untrue. Whenever "I Love to Tell the Story" is announced and a large congregation of people sings it, I find it difficult to keep from wondering how many in the congregation are affirming something that is really true in their lives. There are so many believers who cannot honestly say that they love to tell the story. Many of them have told me of their great fear of witnessing, of the difficulty they have in approaching the subject of the gospel with their unconverted friends. Is it right that such people should be encouraged to sing over and over again that they "love to tell the story," when perhaps they realize in their own minds that they have many times avoided opportunities to tell the story of the gospel? If we profess something in our songs which is not true in our hearts, is it any wonder that the result is superficiality in spiritual living?

There are many gospel songs that are splendid examples of musical witness to the grace of God. I must avoid giving the impression that I decry all gospel songs. To the contrary, I greatly enjoy singing many of them at the appropriate times. I think, for example, of the song of the outstanding musical evangelist, Charles H. Gabriel, "In Loving Kindness Jesus Came," which is sometimes titled "He Lifted Me." This is a fine song which is sung to a very singable tune composed by the author of the lyrics. It does not qualify as a hymn, of course, in spite of the words, "O praise His name," in the repeated refrain, because the motion of the song is not God-ward. The emphasis is upon the experience of the believer. This is not wrong, but a true hymn is worship and a sacred song is not necessarily worship. Moreover, the poetry of this song cannot be compared with that of some of the great hymns which treat of the same subject, the redeeming grace of God. A few of the gospel songs would qualify as hymns although they do not fully conform to all the standards of good hymns. Mrs. Annie Hawks's beloved song, "I Need Thee Every Hour," and Fannie Crosby's "To God Be the Glory" could certainly be considered hymns. But such characteristic gospel songs as Fannie Crosby's "Tell Me the Story of Jesus" and "Rescue the Perishing" are certainly not hymns. Examples of didactic sacred song, they do not express the worship of God. As David R. Breed has said, "A hymn coordinates with prayer. A sacred song coordinates with exhortation."[1]

The Hymnbook as a Devotional Guide

It is not just the poverty of the gospel song as an instrument of praise that is of serious concern. It is the woeful ignorance which Christians today demonstrate with respect to the almost inexhaustible riches of sacred song which are theirs in the great hymns which have come down through the centuries. A good hymnbook is the repository of the deepest devotion of the saints of the ages. Its treasures are priceless.

---

[1]David R. Breed, *The History and Use of Hymns and Hymn-Tunes* (New York: Fleming Revell Co., 1903), p. 336.

Yet it is a fact that in multitudes of evangelical churches today not more than about thirty or thirty-five songs are sung
in the services of a whole year, and the majority of these may
be gospel songs rather than hymns. If the reader does not
believe this statement is true, may I suggest that he collect the
bulletins of his church for a year and check on this matter.

Next to the Bible a good hymnbook is a Christian's greatest devotional guide. Yet many Christians will spend money
readily for daily devotional readings which are far inferior to
the great poetry of the hymnbook. If they possess a good
hymnal it is probably stuck away on a bookshelf somewhere
in the home and opened only rarely. James Sydnor has
reminded us that "much of the meaning of a hymn will remain unfathomed if we depend on congregational singing
alone to reveal the message. During ordinary singing, the
syllables and words pass before the consciousness at a speed
of a second or less per word. We cannot fully grasp the relationship and sequence of ideas at this speed." He therefore
makes the suggestion that "every Christian should seize the
many opportunities which are afforded for reading and con-
templating hymn texts." He adds this encouraging promise:
"Those Christians who have leisurely pondered the truths of
great hymns will find William Cowper's words true:

> Sometimes a light surprises
>   The Christian while he sings;
> It is the Lord, who rises
>   With healing in His wings.[2]

The Definition of "Hymn"

Perhaps we should proceed no further until we have made
clear what constitutes a true hymn. Augustine in a comment
on Psalm 148 gave quite an interesting definition of a hymn.
He said, "It is a song with praise of God. If thou praisest
God and singest not, thou utterest no hymn. If thou singest

---

[2]James R. Sydnor, *The Hymn and Congregational Singing* (Richmond:
John Knox Press, 1960), pp. 136-37.

and praisest not God thou utterest no hymn. A hymn then containeth there three things: song, praise, and that of God. Praise, then, of God in song is called a hymn."[3] Now, while what Augustine said is true, it is not an entirely adequate definition of a hymn. David R. Breed in his very valuable work, *The History and Use of Hymns and Hymn-Tunes,* which has recently been put back into print after being unavailable for several years, gives an excellent three-point summary of the indispensable qualities of a good hymn.[4] First, a true hymn must be thoroughly scriptural both in sentiment and in expression. Second, it must be an objective expression of praise to God and thus devotional in the purest sense. He includes in this qualification both profound reverence and liturgical propriety. The fact that it is devotional does not mean that God must always be addressed personally in any true hymn, but He must be uppermost in the thought of the singer; the motion of a true hymn is always Godward. Third, a hymn must have such lyrical quality that it must be sung in order for it to receive its best interpretation. Good hymns are far better when sung than they are when spoken even by the most skilled elocutionist. Poetic language adds to the merit of a hymn, but, according to Breed, it is not indispensable. Some of the greatest of the hymns could not be considered great poetry.

We are concerned here with the corporate worship of God. This is why we are concerned for the highest and best of musical praise when the congregation lifts its voice in sacred song. A hymn is sung praise to God for all that He is and for all that He has done in creation and in salvation. It includes praise for the believer's experience of the reality of the great events in salvation history. Because God must be worshiped in truth, every line of a hymn must be consistent with the words of the Scriptures. In the preface to his hymnbook, the great Isaac Watts said that he "might have brought some text

---

[3]*Dictionary of Hymnology,* ed. John Julian (New York: Charles Scribner's Sons, 1892), p. 640.

[4]Breed, *The History and Use of Hymns and Hymn-Tunes,* pp. 89-93.

and applied it in the margin of every verse." This is why
Watts' hymns are so thoroughly sound theologically and
have remained in constant use by worshiping congregations.

The Psalms and Christian Hymnody

As Cecil Northcott has pointed out, "Both Wesley and
Watts realized that only the Scriptures were the adequate
cradle of hymns for Christian worship. Like the Reformers
before them, who dreaded the infiltration of mere harmoniz-
ing, non-Scriptural trifles into church worship, the two modern master hymn-writers only succeeded in their revolution
by themselves being faithful to the Scriptures."[5] The influence of the Psalms on Christian hymnody must never be
overlooked. The fact that the Psalter was the principal
hymnbook for the church for the first thousand years of its
existence simply cannot be ignored. Even in the days of the
Reformation when Martin Luther was spreading the truth of
justification by faith throughout Germany and using songs
to stir the hearts of the people, he created his greatest hymn,
"A Mighty Fortress Is Our God," out of the forty-sixth
Psalm. It was the Psalms that inspired many if not most of
Isaac Watts' greatest hymns, although he added a New Testament interpretation and flavor to them.

We should sing the Psalms today. It is unfortunate that
among most of the evangelical congregations of our land the
ability to chant the King James Version of the Psalms is no
longer in existence, although some Lutheran churches still
engage in this very lovely means of worshiping God in musical praise. There are, however, in some of the best hymnbooks available today beautiful metrical versions of the
Psalms, although they are not always identified as such.
These should be introduced to singing congregations; they
should be in constant use among evangelicals. Many congregations sing the doxology every Sunday to a tune composed

[5]Cecil Northcott, *Hymns in Christian Worship* (Richmond: John Knox
Press, 1964), p. 9.

in the sixteenth century for a metrical version of Psalm 100, but they never sing the beautiful metrical version of the Psalm itself:

> All people that on earth do dwell,
> Sing to the Lord with cheerful voice;
> Him serve with fear, His praise forth tell,
> Come ye before Him and rejoice!

There are many congregations in our country who are quite familiar with the gospel song which begins, "Be not dismayed whate'er betide, God will take care of you," but who never sing the far more beautiful metrical version of Psalm 23, which treats the same subject:

> The Lord's my Shepherd, I'll not want;
> He makes me down to lie
> In pastures green; He leadeth me
> The quiet waters by.
>
> My soul He doth restore again;
> And me to walk doth make
> Within the paths of righteousness,
> E'en for His own name's sake.
>
> Yea, though I walk through death's dark vale,
> Yet will I fear no ill;
> For Thou art with me, and Thy rod
> And staff me comfort still.

I have quoted here only the three first stanzas of this metrical version of the most familiar of all the Psalms. I have done so in order that the contrast with the gospel song might be obvious. Apart from the repeated refrain, "God will take care of you," this song says,

> Be not dismayed whate'er betide . . .
> Beneath His wings of love abide . . .
> Through days of toil when heart doth fail . . .
> When dangers fierce your path assail . . .
> All you may need He will provide . . .
> Nothing you ask will be denied [?] . . .
> No matter what may be the test . . .
> Lean, weary one, upon His breast . . .

Through every day, o'er all the way;
He will take care of you.

What a difference there is between this didactic gospel song which is addressed to another believer, assuring him that in the worst circumstances of life he can expect God to provide perfect care, and the words of the Psalm, which exult in the constant grace of God as it is experienced daily in the life of the trusting saint! These two examples show clearly the contrast between the gospel song and the true hymn.

One of the problems that contemporary congregations face is that many of the gospel songs are popular because the tunes to which they are sung have an appealing rhythm and a lighthearted melody. There is nothing at all evil about beautiful melody. The creative arts should all be encouraged in the service of the Lord; however, when the words of a gospel song are mediocre to poor and the song becomes immensely popular because of its catchy tune, the worship of God is not being enhanced by its use. When I have questioned some believers concerning their special preference for certain familiar gospel songs, I have found that it is the music, not the words, which they really like. All serious Christians should examine their own preferences and perhaps they will find a need to enrich substantially their musical praise by using more of the great hymns of exalted devotion based upon thoroughly scriptural concepts rather than the more shallow sentimental songs whose appeal is largely musical.

It should be clear that I do not believe the laymen in our churches are principally to blame for the lack of use of the great hymns of the church. Their education in this all-important part of worship has been sadly neglected. Certainly some of the fault belongs to the ministers who have failed to give the members of their churches an adequate appreciation for the rich heritage of hymnody of which the church is the possessor. Perhaps the real blame rests upon the theological seminaries that have neglected the matter of practical instruction in worship, including hymnology. The evangelical church has been sadly impoverished. Interestingly enough, I have never found a congregation which did not appreciate learning about the great hymns, not only from the standpoint of their authors, but also from a study of the wonderful theological concepts that are found therein. Very few people have a deep appreciation for the great music, the great literature, or the great artistic masterpieces of the world until they are given some education concerning them. It is not strange that Christian men and women need to learn to appreciate great hymnody.

The Development of the Christian Hymn

There is so much that needs to be said concerning the hymns of the church that the limitations of this volume on worship simply do not permit. Even an adequate beginning study of the subject of hymnody cannot be attempted here. Let me encourage the reader to acquire some good books on the subject. Every church should offer classes in its Sunday school or in its weeknight education program in which interested believers could learn a great deal about this fascinating subject, learning which would in turn greatly enrich their worship. A warning needs to be given, however, in this connection. Don't be satisfied with some of the inexpensive volumes giving stories not always completely reliable concerning the origin of some of the gospel songs and hymns. What one needs to do is to get a perspective of the history of the development of the Christian hymn, beginning with the apostolic church. Then he needs to become familiar with the lives of the great hymn writers, for here were men who were indeed heroes of the faith. They walked with God; they experienced the grace of God as few men have; and they were gifted of Him to be able to translate their experiences and their devotion into singable praise which has blessed worshiping multitudes down through the centuries. Through their efforts the name of the Lord has been exalted in thousands of worship services.

Few contemporary Christians realize that very soon after the ascension of the Lord Jesus Christ and the coming of the

Holy Spirit on the day of Pentecost the Christians, who were accustomed to singing the Psalms of the Old Testament, began to sing songs which were distinctively Christian. Pliny the Younger, in a famous letter to the Emperor Trajan about the year A.D. 110, makes reference to the Christians singing hymns to Christ as God, so we know that as early as the beginning of the second century believers were worshiping God with the use of hymns which were not of Jewish origin. A number of these very ancient hymns have survived to our day. Many of these earliest Christian hymns were paraphrases of the New Testament Scriptures. The primitive church kept very close to the Scriptures in all of its worship, including its singing of praise. With the exception of the Gloria Patri none of the earliest Christian hymns are in common use in evangelical congregations of our country today, but many of them are still used in the Anglican and Roman churches. The magnificent Te Deum Laudamus, one of these very early hymns, is sometimes heard as an anthem in our evangelical churches, but those who listen are usually unaware that it comes down from the very ancient days of the Christian church.

The first Christian hymns were undoubtedly written in Greek; the poetical development of Greek song greatly influenced the form into which the early Christian hymns were cast. It was not until the hymn was developed in the Latin church that rhyme was added to the poetry and it began to more closely resemble what we have today.

With the coming of the Protestant Reformation the hymn reached a position of importance in public worship which it had never previously occupied. The Roman Church from early times never encouraged congregational singing. What singing was done in the services was the effort of choirs, especially choirs of monks. The people did sing some during their pilgrimages and on special festival occasions but this singing was not a part of their worship services. During the mass, singing was done by the priest who was officiating, but he sang in Latin and the people had no opportunity to sing in their own languages. The Reformation changed all this. The

German people have always loved to sing. Even the pope in Rome made concession to allow German congregations to sing. Martin Luther took advantage of the German interest in song and used it for the benefit of his reform movement. In England and Scotland and particularly in Wales, where the people were especially fond of singing, the Reformation also brought congregational song in the vernacular into a regular place in the liturgy (except in the Prayer Book of the Anglican Church, where Cranmer's opposition was influential in keeping vernacular song out of the liturgy).

The hymn had a prominent place in the Lutheran sector of the Reformation, but it fared differently in the Calvinist areas of Switzerland, France, Scotland, and England. Calvin felt that if the people wanted to sing, the metrical psalm was the answer: if any singing in public worship was to be done, it must be thoroughly biblical and only the Psalms fulfilled this requirement. It was a century and a half before Isaac Watts came upon the scene and broke the grip which the exclusive use of metrical psalms had upon congregations of Reformed persuasion.

Every Christian in every congregation of Reformed and Presbyterian churches today should be particularly familiar with Isaac Watts. In fact, all evangelical believers should know something of the life and labors of this great poetic genius. This godly minister who contributed so much to the enrichment of the worship of multitudes of Christians in the last three centuries is hardly more than just a name to many today, yet he shares with Charles Wesley the highest honors in English hymnody and his hymns are sung by Christians of all theological persuasion. His greatest hymn, "When I Survey the Wondrous Cross," always appears in any list of the ten greatest hymns and many of his hymns appear in every good hymnbook. He began writing hymns when as a young man he complained to an officer of the independent church in which his father was a deacon and where the family worshiped about the inferior quality of the poetry of the metrical versions of the Psalms they were singing. The officer responded that if young Watts didn't like them, he should produce something better, and he did, beginning that very week. He labored at the task until he had produced his own metrical versions of the Psalms. For some decades the more conservative congregations would not sing them because he had added a New Testament flavor to them. For example, "Jesus Shall Reign Where'er the Sun" is Watts' version of Psalm 72. However, his proposals for a truly evangelical system of praise was received enthusiastically by many; and the publication of his book, *Hymns and Spiritual Songs,* in 1707 could actually be said to mark the birth of modern hymnody. In the preface to this volume he complained rather bitterly about the view that the Psalms were the only proper vehicle of corporate praise in song: "Some of them are almost opposite to the Spirit of the Gospel; many of them foreign to the State of the New Testament, and widely different from the present state of Christians . . . Thus by keeping too close to David in the House of God, the Vail of Moses is thrown over our Hearts."

By the time Watts had published his second edition of *Hymns and Spiritual Songs* in 1709 and then ten years later his *Psalms of David, Imitated in the Language of the New Testament,* he had not only accomplished his basic purpose of bringing the Psalms into the worship of the church with a thoroughly New Testament flavor, but he had given the English-speaking people a large number of great hymns, some of which are certainly masterpieces. He had also firmly established the hymn as a thoroughly acceptable form of corporate praise.

John and Charles Wesley were born just about the time that Watts published his first hymnbook. John, whose prose is much more famous than his poetry, did write some hymns and published the first hymnbook of the Methodist movement. His brother Charles wrote some prose but became famous for the vast output of great and good hymns which characterized his life. The Wesleys prepared and published their hymns for a particular group of believers, the Methodists. They introduced something new in hymnody, the singing of hymns based upon the experience of true believers.

Thus they might be said to have been the forerunners of the modern gospel song, although their hymns met all the qualifications for good hymns and several of Charles Wesley's rank among the very greatest ever written. Every one of them bears the identifying stamp of strong personal faith, and they have won universal acceptance throughout the Christian church.

It is an interesting fact that Bishop Thomas Ken, whose life overlapped both Watts and the Wesleys, wrote a hymn which appears in several lists of the ten greatest hymns, "All Praise to Thee, My God, This Night." On at least one of these lists it is number one. Yet, it is a hymn utterly unknown in many of our evangelical congregations. One contributing reason is the fact that hymns are usually not sung in the evening service of our churches today. The last stanza, as I have already pointed out, has been lifted from the hymn and put to the tune of "Old Hundredth." It is familiar to all evangelical English-speaking Christians as the doxology. Every reader of this book could sing the doxology, yet perhaps very few could tell anything about the life of the fearless preacher of righteousness who wrote it. The tales of his courageous stand against the wicked King Charles II, to whom he was appointed chaplain, are the kind of true stories which the young people in our churches today need to hear.

Another great Anglican Bishop, Reginald Heber, made a contribution which should be mentioned in this chapter. He saw that hymn singing was becoming firmly entrenched in the worship of the evangelical Christians, so he published a hymnbook which contained at least sixty of his own compositions. It was a forerunner of all the hymnbooks that were to follow. It contained hymns designed for public worship on the Lord's Day but also hymns for all the great festivals of the church and for national occasions of thanksgiving, peril, or distress. It included translations of some of the ancient hymns, and a goodly number of metrical versions of the Psalms. From the time of its publication (1827) it could be said that psalms, hymns, and spiritual songs were usually combined in the best hymnbooks.

The United States has not produced a large number of great hymn writers. The two greatest are undoubtedly Dr. Ray Palmer (1808-1887) and Dr. Samuel F. Smith (1808-1895). Palmer was a Congregationalist while Smith was a Baptist. Both were given well-deserved honor in their own denominations. Palmer's greatest hymn was "My Faith Looks Up to Thee." This hymn is certainly as well-loved by evangelical Christians today as any hymn and it finds its place in every good hymnal. Another outstanding work of Palmer was his magnificent English version of St. Bernard's "De Nomine Jesu," the first stanza of which is

> Jesus, Thou Joy of loving hearts,
>   Thou Fount of life, Thou Light of men,
> From the best bliss that earth imparts
>   We turn unfilled to Thee again.

Dr. Smith's greatest work is his missionary hymn, "The Morning Light Is Breaking," which Breed says "has probably gone farther and been sung more frequently than any other missionary hymn." He is best known, however, for the song which might be called our national Christian anthem, "My Country, 'tis of Thee." The hymns of these two men demonstrate the very best in American hymnody.

In the early part of the nineteenth century the hymns of the Wesleys spread throughout the United States, but by that time the camp meeting of the American frontier had produced its own style of singing. Some of the great hymns were set to American folk melodies, and this produced some rather unfortunate results. For example, John Newton's great hymn, "Amazing Grace! How Sweet the Sound," is firmly fixed in the minds of most American Christians with a mountain folk tune which is not at all suited to the words of this great song. The tune is so appealing that it brought the hymn on to the hit parade, and it was sung by many popular singers over a period of many months on the radio and television. Then it dropped from use, as popular songs always do. If one were to suggest, however, especially in the Southland, using a tune better suited to the great words of this hymn, the suggestion would be treated as though it were the worst kind of heresy.

The outstanding contribution of the United States to sacred song is perhaps the gospel song, which largely grew out of camp meetings and similar gatherings and then was widely used throughout the English-speaking world in the great evangelistic campaigns of D. L. Moody and Ira Sankey and today in the huge crusades of Billy Graham. While these songs have been a blessing to multitudes, they are much more appropriate for evangelistic mission and for informal occasions than they are for the worship services of the church. I have already made clear my deep conviction that the evangelicals of this country need to be instructed in worship. Their common worship needs to be enriched, and a significant part of this enrichment could come from a better understanding and use of the great hymns of the church. A steady discipline of hymn singing and a sharper discernment of the function of the hymn in public worship would go far to make public worship much more meaningful to the individual worshiper. More important, however, than any other consideration, this would contribute to the true praise of the glory of God. What all of us need to realize is that what we sing when we are gathered together in the house of God is not just a pious song for us as individuals to enjoy (that is, if we enjoy singing), but is rather a corporate act of the whole church as it offers up to God on high its united, common worship.

The Word of God makes it clear that the church is a body. While it is composed of individual believers, each is a member of every other because each is a component part of the whole, which is the body of Christ. When the Christian church meets together for worship, then, it is not just to meet the needs of the individual members of the congregation, but it is also, and very importantly, to afford the church as the body of Christ opportunity to adore and worship the divine Head of the body. The hymn is a corporate and audible expression of that adoration. The hymn, if it is to discharge this function, must certainly have a recognizable motion Godward. It is not introduced into the service to provide individuals a means of "taking part." It is a united offering of the congregation's worship and not just an opportunity for sincere and devout Christians to conduct their personal devotions.

Choosing the Correct Hymn

We have discussed previously the fact that if a congregation is seriously concerned with offering acceptable corporate worship in which the participating worshipers are consciously united in what they are doing, there must be a structural unity in the order of worship. The choice of the correct hymn for each place in the liturgy in which the congregation unites in song is of great importance. The wrong hymn inserted in a service may disturb the structural unity even though it is a fine hymn. Not long ago I worshiped in a fairly large church where it was immediately evident that the worship of God was not really the main purpose of the Sunday morning assembly of the believers. The service itself gave the impression of having been hastily "thrown together" in order to meet the deadline for printing the bulletin for the Sunday services. Two songs preceded the sermon. The first was a gospel song, " 'Tis So Sweet to Trust in Jesus." I will make no comment on this except to say that it could hardly have been a worse choice. But the second song was Isaac Watts' great hymn, "Jesus Shall Reign Where'er the Sun," to which I have already made reference. There was absolutely nothing either before or after this hymn which provided any reason for the congregation to be called upon to sing this particular version of Psalm 72 with its strong missionary emphasis. The person who selected this hymn, and I suppose it was the pastor, had given no thought to the unity of the service and apparently had paid no attention to the contents of the songs he had chosen.

In the vast reservoir of English hymnody there are hymns for every place a hymn is to be used in the order of worship. There are hymns which are suitable for the expression of every authentic feeling, condition, or quality of the human soul in worship. How sad it is then that in the majority of the services in the evangelical churches today the hymns which are chosen seem to have been selected because of their familiarity or perhaps in order to give the individual worshiper a warm emotional uplift. As S. F. Winward has so well said, "A service is not a miscellaneous selection of items . . . arranged anyhow, as dictated by the whims of a particular individual. It is a two-way conversation between God and man with a given structure and appropriate sequence."[6]

What a shame that so many ministers in preparing the order of worship for a particular service give so little attention to selecting hymns which are fitting for the place in the service where they are to be sung and which serve to unify the service as a whole. Instead, hymns are chosen because they are well known and well liked. I have had pastors tell me that they would not dare to announce a hymn which the congregation did not know, for if they were to do so no one would sing. This attitude indicates that careful and patient instruction in hymnology needs to be undertaken. Christians are not so different from one another that the truly great hymns which have stood the test of time and are still loved by God's people in some congregations will not be loved by others if they are given an opportunity to learn to appreciate them.

Of course, the proper selections cannot be made unless ministers know the hymnbook and spend the necessary time in the preparation of their services to get the right hymn for each place in the order of worship in which a hymn is to be used. More than this, of course, if the members of the congregation are to make the proper use of their hymnbooks and to contribute to the corporate worship in the best way, they must be given adequate instruction and periodic reminders of what they should be doing when they sing a hymn in a service. Otherwise, they may feel, for example, that the hymn before the sermon is inserted to give everyone an opportunity to stretch his legs or have a welcome change of posture be-

---

[6]S. F. Winward, *Baptist Hymn Book Companion* (London: Carey Kingsgate Press, Ltd., 1964), p. 48.

fore sitting through the message from the Word of God.

Because all of worship is an offering of something to God—even our rapt attention while listening to His Word—every hymn must be placed in the service as an act of praise or prayer or as an expression of faith or dedication. As Cecil Northcott has said, "A congregation must take hymns and hymn singing seriously."[7] The hymnbook is not only the repository of the devotion of the saints of the ages, but it also provides materials, gathered from the church universal, for the offering up of the sacrifice of praise and thanksgiving. It is a prayer book as well as a songbook. It also provides a popular commentary on the creeds of Christendom. A good hymnbook gives a more balanced view of the Christian faith than do many theological volumes. Even our most popular hymns (I do not include gospel songs) provide a very well balanced view of basic Christian doctrine and the proper response of the believer to that doctrine.

All of the truly good hymns are concerned with things which do not change. They are the same in every generation. As the Word of God is unchanging, so the good hymn, which must be scriptural, deals with unchanging truth. The age in which you and I are living is not producing any significant number of good hymns. The singing of the church of the past two generations has been quite superficial. All too often the leaders of services have been overly concerned with the volume of the congregational singing. "Let's sing a little louder on the next stanza," has been heard much more frequently than, "Notice the tremendous truth concerning which you are offering praise to God."

Aside from the Bible itself there is no book which offers the devotional material found in the hymnbook, but it is not primarily for individual devotions. Its rich resources should be mastered, not by the ministers alone, but by every earnest Christian who desires to offer to God the very highest and best in the praise of His name. We are faithful to the very finest motivations for corporate worship when we are careful

---

[7]Northcott, *Hymns in Christian Worship,* p. 49.

to sing those great expressions of praise and devotion which have stood the test of time in the worship of multitudes of believers.

9

The Administration
of the Sacraments

Evangelicals recognize only two of the ceremonies practiced in the church as sacraments. They are baptism and the Lord's Supper. That which distinguishes them as sacraments is the fact that they were instituted by the Lord Jesus Christ and to each of them is attached the promise of His grace. The church can thus administer the sacraments with the confidence that the Lord who instituted them will bless their observance.

Augustine defined a sacrament as a "visible sign of a sacred thing, or a visible form of an invisible grace." Calvin, while approving of the words of Augustine, offered instead a far more extensive definition of a sacrament as "an external sign by which the Lord seals on our consciences His promises of goodwill toward us in order to sustain the weakness of our faith, and we in turn testify our piety towards Him, both before Himself and before angels as well as men."[1]

---

[1] John Calvin, *Institutes of the Christian Religion* (Grand Rapids: Wm. B. Eerdmans, 1953), Book IV, ch. 14, p. 491.

Importance of the Sacraments

Tragically, multitudes of the Lord's people do not understand the importance of the sacraments in their lives. Many adults who were reared in Christian homes have little comprehension of what is involved in the observance of the sacraments. Those who do ascribe great importance to the sacraments unfortunately often take a magical view of them, as though the mere participation in them produces some type of merit or helps to wash away sins. The sacraments are a means of grace only to those who receive them by faith; but if faith is to be exercised when the sacraments are administered, one must understand what the Word of God teaches about the sacraments.

Calvin made it clear that the sacraments were in a sense a concession which God made to the weakness that He knew was inherent in our flesh. Because God is infinite in all His attributes, unutterably majestic in His being and perfect in His holiness, while man is depraved by nature and sinful in his thoughts and actions, Calvin saw no possibility of direct communication between God and man. He insisted that because "the light of the majesty of the glory of God is not only as the brightness of the sun, but is greater than ten thousand suns,"[2] "should God institute no medium of intercourse, and call us to a direct communication with heaven, the great distance at which we stand from Him would strike us with dismay and paralyze invocation."[3] If this is true, how then has God communicated with man, and how does He do it today? Calvin's answer is that through all the history of God's dealing with man He has revealed Himself only in such terms as man was able to comprehend and receive. He never revealed Himself to man as He actually is! He veiled His being in certain signs and symbols adapted to

---

[2]John Calvin, *The Deity of Christ and Other Sermons* (Grand Rapids: Wm. B. Eerdmans, 1950), p. 234.

[3]John Calvin, *Commentary on the Psalms* (Grand Rapids: Wm. B. Eerdmans, 1949), p. 151.

man's capacity for seeing and understanding. For example, in commenting upon Moses' experience in communing with God at the burning bush, Calvin wrote, "I indeed allow, that Moses was strengthened in his faith by that vision . . . but I do not admit that it was such a view of God, as divested him of his bodily senses, and transferred him beyond the trials of this world. God at that time only shewed him a certain symbol of His presence; but he was far from seeing God as He is."[4]

The forms by which God chose to reveal Himself were not by any means always material objects such as the burning bush. Sometimes they were dreams. Sometimes they were angels. In every manifestation of His presence, however, He both veiled Himself and at the same time revealed Himself. It must be added here, too, that both in the Old Testament and in the New the Mediator of all revelation of God to man is the Lord Jesus Christ, the Second Person of the Trinity (I Tim. 2:5). That revelation in the Son of God reached its highest form in the incarnation when "the Word was made flesh" (John 1:14) and lived among men. His glory, of course, was even then veiled by His humanity. He went to the cross to bear the sins of men, and there on the cross and in His resurrection from the dead He manifested the glory of God as it has been revealed in no other event. Yet even the glory which the disciples saw when they looked upon the resurrected Savior was not itself the full glory of God. That remains yet to be made manifest to the elect when they "see him as he is" (I John 3:2).

Having seen how God communicated with man in days gone by and revealed His glory, although through a veil, we still face the question, how does God reveal Himself to man today? Clearly the answer is through the Word and through the sacraments. As Ronald S. Wallace has said in his important analysis of *Calvin's Doctrine of the Word and Sacrament,* "The Word and Sacraments are the forms of abase-

---

[4]John Calvin, *Commentary on the Epistle to the Hebrews* (Grand Rapids: Wm. B. Eerdmans, 1963), p. 179.

ment which Christ the Mediator today assumes in confront-
ing us with His grace and challenge. They are the symbols by
which He today accommodates Himself to our limited capacity for apprehending the divine and veils that in Himself with
which we cannot bear to be directly confronted . . . it is to
the Word and Sacraments that we must turn if we wish to enter into communion with Him."[5] Wallace then quotes Calvin's statement that "as men are made known by the countenance and speech, so God utters His voice to us by the
voice of the prophets, and in the sacraments takes, as it were,
a visible form, from which He may be known by us according to our feeble capacity."[6] To summarize, then, in Wallace's words, "Word and Sacrament, therefore, do not merely
take for us the place that visions and oracles and the
elaborate temple ceremony took in the Old Testament; more
particularly, they are to us what Jesus and His Word and
works were to those who received His grace during the days
of His flesh."[7]

There are spiritual realities which we do not fully apprehend simply through the hearing of the Word. The sacraments set forth the same truth which comes to us through the
Scriptures, but the truth is ministered in a different way, and
is discerned in a distinctly different manner. However, as
Wallace has reminded us, in the light of the Lord's commands and promises in connection with the sacraments, "it
follows that a sacrament can never be celebrated without at
least a clear repetition of the command of Christ to which it
owes its origin, and of the promise of Christ in the hope of
which the Church fulfills His ordinance."[8] Apart from the
Word of God the human action in the administration of the

[5]Ronald S. Wallace, *Calvin's Doctrine of the Word and Sacrament* (Grand
Rapids: Wm. B. Eerdmans, 1957), p. 22.

[6]John Calvin, *Commentary on the Gospel According to St. John* (Grand
Rapids: Wm. B. Eerdmans, 1959), p. 138.

[7]Wallace, *Calvin's Doctrine,* p. 23.

[8]Ibid., p. 135.

sacraments has no power or efficacy. There is not, however, some magical touch which the Word gives to the sacraments. In the Word are the authority and promise of the Giver of the sacraments as well as the demands made upon our lives by our observance of the sacraments. These can come to us fully only through the preaching of the Word, and thus the Word is essential when the believer comes to participation in the sacraments. He should have the Word of God ringing in his ears, and his use of the sacraments should be a token of his personal submission to the will of God revealed in the Word.

Just as the Word is essential to the sacraments, so also the sacraments are essential to give the Word its full ministry in the life of the believer and the life of the church. It is through the sacraments that God reinforces the truth and the appeal of the Word which is preached. Calvin saw them as taking the place of the miracles, visions, and special phenomena which God used in the lives of the Old Testament saints. He cited, for example, how God confirmed His promise to Abraham by pointing him to the stars of heaven (Gen. 15:5). God confirms His promises to us today in the sacraments. Because man is a physical creature, God has sympathetically given him external signs to meet that part of his being. But we must realize, of course, that just as one can listen to the Word of God without faith and gain nothing, in like manner one can partake of the physical elements of the sacraments without faith and receive no spiritual ministration whatsoever.

The man of faith recognizes that God's Word and God's act cannot be separated. What God says He does. The sacraments by their action proclaim and make real to man not only what God has done for him in the past, but also what He does for him each time he participates in the sacraments. Consider the fact that one of the greatest evidences of the love and grace of God for us poor miserable sinners is that He has joined us to our Lord and Savior in an indissoluble union (I Cor. 6:15; Eph. 4:4). This is a spiritual reality. It is not true because we have experienced it. It is not true because we feel it. It is true simply because God's Word declares it. Applying, then, this truth to the sacraments, baptism is a sign and seal making real to us our initiation into blessed union with other believers in the body of Christ, while the Lord's Supper seals and makes real to us our perseverance in this union even as we avail ourselves of the continuing efficacy of His blood and the never-failing nourishment of the Bread of Life. P. T. Forsyth has aptly said, "What makes Baptism real is God's changeless will of salvation in Christ and the Church. . . . Sacraments are modes of the Gospel (not of experience)."[9]

An adequate theology of the sacraments is beyond the purview of this book. The present chapter is concerned primarily with the services in which the sacraments are administered. In a paper on "The Sacramental Principle" published by the Christian Literature Society of India there is a statement concerning the sacraments which so beautifully summarizes what the sacraments are that we use it to conclude our brief general discussion of them:

> The Sacraments of Baptism and the Supper of the Lord are means of grace through which God works in us . . . While the mercy of God to all mankind cannot be limited, there is in the teaching of Christ the plain command that men should follow his appointed way of salvation by a definite act of reception into the family of God and by continued acts of fellowship with Him in that family. . . . This teaching is made explicit in the two Sacraments which He has given us.[10]

The Meaning of Baptism

The sacrament of baptism is the initiatory rite into the family of God. It is a sign and seal of one's identification as a member of the household of faith. I have already made reference to my book on baptism which deals with the problem

---

[9]P. T. Forsyth, *The Church and the Sacraments* (London: Independent Press, Ltd., 1964), p. 216.

[10]*The Sacraments* (Madras: Christian Literature Society, 1956), p. 1.

of the scriptural mode as well as the proper subjects of baptism.[11] I will not reproduce those arguments here. It is my hope that the fact that I espouse the Reformed and Presbyterian view of baptism and have a few comments about the conduct of the baptismal service for those who practice affusion will not prejudice the reader who has strong Baptist convictions. I do wish to reiterate my personal conviction that the mode by which baptism is administered is not what gives it validity any more than the mode by which the elements of the Lord's Supper are received give authenticity to that sacrament. There are three important components in every sacrament: (1) the scriptural words of the institution, (2) the material elements used to establish the sign, and (3) the physical action required. In the case of baptism it is clear that Matthew 28:19 is the command of Christ which authorized the sacrament, and that water was the single element used for baptism (Acts 1:5; 8:36, etc.). Differences of opinion exist only as to the physical action involved, whether the officiating minister must completely immerse the candidate in water or simply pour or sprinkle water on his head. Those of us who hold to the Presbyterian position accept as valid the baptism of those who have been completely immersed, although we believe that affusion is the more scriptural mode. We hold this view because we sincerely believe that baptism is a sign and seal of the cleansing work of the Holy Spirit rather than of the burial and resurrection of Jesus Christ. The Spirit's baptism promised by the Lord in Acts 1:5 was certainly an affusion rather than an immersion (Acts 2:3, 17, 18, 33, etc.). But if one is symbolizing the burial and resurrection of Christ with the ordinance of baptism he would certainly prefer the mode of immersion.

Without entering into a discussion of the subject of infant baptism here, let me say that those of us who believe that the Scripture not only allows for but actually requires the baptism of the infants of a covenant household do admit freely

---

[11]Robert G. Rayburn, *What About Baptism?* (St. Louis: Covenant College Press, 1957).

that much harm has been done by the careless and even superstitious practice of infant baptism. Emil Brunner, with whose view of the Scriptures I cannot agree, was nevertheless absolutely correct when he said, "The contemporary practice of Infant Baptism can hardly be regarded as anything short of scandalous." He was right in insisting that baptism is "a highly questionable arrangement where it is requested more from a consideration of custom than from conviction of faith."[12] Unless parents understand the deep significance of God's covenant and their own responsibilities under that covenant they should never be allowed to have their children baptized. Their baptismal vows should grow out of genuine faith in the covenant promises of God concerning their children.

For all too many parents the baptism of their infant children is merely an act of dedication. One could certainly not accuse them of having a superstitious attitude, but they see nothing in infant baptism beyond dedication of the infant. While it cannot be denied that there is an element of dedication, every baptism (infant and adult) is much more than merely dedication. We must remember that the initiative in both of the sacraments is with God. He has given us the sacraments and commands their observance, laying down the conditions of blessing in His Word. As Donald Macleod has said, "Baptism is the sign and seal of God's initiative taken in our behalf through His Son, Jesus Christ, and therefore the main thing is not what men do, but what God Himself has done."[13]

Because baptism is a sacrament given by the Lord to His church and is, as has already been pointed out, the ordinance of admission into the Christian community, the church, it does not have real significance if it is separated from the life and worship of the church. Therefore, baptism

---

[12]Emil Brunner, *The Divine-Human Encounter* (Philadelphia: Westminster Press, 1943), p. 131.

[13]Donald Macleod, *Presbyterian Worship* (Richmond: John Knox Press, 1965), p. 48.

should always, except in very unusual circumstances, be administered in the presence of the members of the church. It is difficult to see how one could be received into membership in a fellowship such as the church if at least some of the members of that fellowship were not present to extend a welcome and to commit themselves to the tender care of the one being received.

In the case of infants being baptized, at least one of the parents must be a sincere believer. In taking the baptismal vows parents must profess publicly their own personal faith in Jesus Christ as Lord and Savior. In addition there must be a public affirmation of faith in God's covenant promises. Parents must believe that God is not only their God but that He has promised to be the God of their children also. This means that they promise that, as God enables them, they will rear their children in the instruction and discipline of the Christian faith, trusting the Lord to bring the children to full personal faith in Jesus Christ. Infant baptism certainly does not mean that the infant is saved, but rather that the parents are trusting the Lord to bring the child to salvation and, in accord with their covenant vow, will do their required part in the clear teaching of the gospel to the child.

A significant additional part of the baptismal service for an infant is the acceptance of responsibility on the part of the congregation. In the Presbyterian tradition the members of the congregation are the child's godparents, and are accountable for his spiritual welfare. When an infant is baptized, the church of which the parents are members must receive the little one into its fellowship and promise to surround him with loving care, with tender nurture, with watchful prayer, and with an environment of active faith, so that at an early age, having had such gracious influences, he may come to confess Christ as Lord and Savior and enter joyfully into the service of His kingdom.

The Administration of Baptism

Normally baptisms will take place as part of the regular worship services of the churches, so special baptismal services do not need to be developed. In view of the weighty import of baptism in the life and growth of the individual Christian as well as in the life of the church, pastors have a strategic responsibility in this secular age to instruct their congregations in the meaning of the sacrament and the scriptural basis for its administration. Many people who have been reared in evangelical churches do not really comprehend the purport of the ordinance. A pastor should not take the time for a lengthy exposition of the doctrine of baptism every time that sacrament is included in a service, but he should preach on the subject frequently enough so that members of his congregation are well informed on the doctrine and thoroughly understand both what is taking place in a baptism and what their own participation in the service should involve. It is especially important that they should understand that they are not mere spectators.

Although, as we have indicated above, the pastor should not give an extended lesson on baptism each time the service includes baptisms, neither should he hurry through the baptism in such a way that before the people hardly realize what is taking place it is all over. He should make the sacrament of baptism as meaningful as possible. It should be introduced carefully and conducted with great reverence.

When the time has come in the service for the baptism, the pastor will call those to be baptized to the front of the church. He will then read Scripture passages which set forth the basis of the sacrament and make clear its significance. After this reading it would be perfectly proper to have an appropriate baptismal hymn sung by the congregation. There are splendid hymns which remind devout worshipers of the covenant mercies of God set forth in baptism and of the necessary response of faith.

If there are infants to be baptized, their parents will bring them to the front of the church, where the officiating minister will ask them four questions before the baptism. The meaning of each of the questions will have been carefully explained to and discussed with the parents privately in preparation for the sacrament.

1. Do you believe in one God, the Father, the Son, and the Holy Spirit, and have you personally received Jesus Christ, God's Son, as your Lord and Savior?   (Answer: We do, and we have.)

2. Do you heartily believe God's covenant promise to be your God and the God of your children, and thus present your child for holy baptism as a sign and seal of his reception into the covenant family of God?   (Answer: We do.)

3. Do you promise with the help of God to bring him up in the nurture and discipline of the Lord, to pray with him and for him, and to make every effort so to order your own life that you will not cause this little one to stumble?
(Answer: We do.)

4. Will you encourage him as soon as he is able to comprehend its significance to acknowledge personally his own faith in the Lord Jesus Christ and become a full member of the church, serving God faithfully in its fellowship?
(Answer: We will.)

Then the pastor will address the following question to the congregation:

Do you receive *(name of child)* as an infant member of this church, and promise to surround him with Christian love, to pray for him, and to set an example before him of genuine Christian faith and virtue, so that he will early in life know the reality of personal salvation and rich fellowship in the kingdom of God? (An affirmative answer may be indicated by the raising of hands.)

After these questions have been answered properly, the pastor (or another minister) will lead in prayer for the parents and for the congregation, asking God to give them the special grace needed to fulfill their vows.

If the baptism is being administered to an adult or to a young person old enough to make his own profession of faith, after the words of Scripture authorizing the sacrament have been read, as indicated above, the following questions will be asked of the candidate:

1. Do you sincerely receive and profess the Christian faith, and in this faith desire to be baptized?   (Answer: I do.)

2. Do you here and now confess your sins and repent of them, putting all of your trust in Jesus Christ as Lord and Savior?   (Answer: I do.)

3. Do you promise in the strength given you by the Holy Spirit to lead a sober and righteous life, making diligent use of the means of grace and serving the Lord faithfully in His church?   (Answer: I do)

The congregation will then respond to the following question:

Do you receive *(name)* into fellowship with you in this church and promise so to encourage him in his Christian life that he will never be ashamed to confess Jesus Christ as his Lord?

The baptismal formula itself is very simple, but it is of critical importance. Whether it is an infant or an adult baptism the sacrament is administered with the same words. There is actually only one sacrament of baptism, not two. The pastor gives the name of the person being baptized and follows it with these words: "I baptize thee [you] in [or, into] the name of the Father, and of the Son, and of the Holy Spirit. Amen." The Trinitarian formula is crucial because it not only indicates the source of the minister's authority but it also designates that marvelous spiritual union with Christ by the power of His Holy Spirit of which baptism speaks. God calls believers saints, which means they are separated unto holiness. God also calls the children of believing parents holy, but they are not holy in and of themselves. They are holy because they are united to their Holy God.

After the baptism has been administered the pastor (or the minister who has officiated) will lead in prayer. In the case of an infant baptism this prayer will be that the child may grow up in the knowledge of God and very early come to understand the reality of personal salvation through Jesus Christ. In the case of a baptism on profession of faith, the prayer will be for growth in grace that will bring spiritual maturity to the candidate.

The minister should take special care to pronounce correctly all the names of the persons being baptized. To guard against a slip of memory he should have the name of each candidate written clearly upon a card which he can hold inconspicuously. When infants are to be baptized the sacrament should be administered fairly early in the service. The baby will be less apt to be restless and to disturb the service with crying. The parents will be able to enter fully into the sacrament and then will be free to take the infant to the nursery, if one is available, and return for the remainder of the worship service.

Ministers are advised not to hold the infant during the baptism. It is something of a psychological shock for most tiny babies to be transferred quickly from the familiar embrace of their parents into the unfamiliar arms of the minister. The consequences can be quite disastrous, although this is not always the case, of course. If the minister does take an infant in his arms for baptism he should be very careful to support the little body with his chest and upper arm while he seats the baby on his forearm.

One important word concerning the actual administration of baptism by affusion is necessary here. Many times I have seen a minister who was baptizing a candidate dip his fingers in the water contained in the font and then simply place a damp hand on the head of the one being baptized. This is not an affusion! It might be identified instead as baptism by dabbing. But baptism is not to be performed by "the laying on of a wet hand"! In order for the baptism to be an act which properly sets forth the significance of the sacrament, there must be sprinkling or pouring. When this takes place, each baptized member of the congregation, upon seeing the water fall upon the head of the candidate, will be reminded of his own baptism and the cleansing power of the Holy Spirit which he has experienced. He will rejoice in the knowledge that he, too, is a member of the household of God, and will lift his heart in fervent praise and worship.

Common Errors Regarding the Lord's Supper

The central and most solemn act of the church's worship has traditionally been the Lord's Supper. It is regrettable in-

deed that this same central exercise of Christian devotion
should also be the point at which Christians divide and con-
tend, sometimes bitterly, with one another. From its institution in the upper room, when Jesus broke the loaf and distributed the bread and wine to His disciples, down to this
present day, true believers in all the centuries of the church's
existence have considered this sacrament the supreme act of
worship through which God's grace is bestowed upon men,
and men respond in a complete offering of themselves to
God. Before the Reformation, though the communion was
celebrated not only weekly, but in many places daily, the
people themselves were privileged to communicate only once
or twice a year. Only the clergy and the religious orders received communion at frequent intervals. "The Reformers,
including Calvin himself, were unsuccessful in restoring the
eucharist to its central place in the worship of the Church.
Nevertheless, they were steadfast in their teaching and purpose, as their writings show. . . . Zwingli excepted, it was the
Reformers' repeatedly declared aim to restore the eucharist
in its entirety and integrity as the principal act of Christian
worship on the Lord's Day."[14] The Reformed desired to
make both the Word and the sacraments fully accessible to
the people.

Because of the holy character of this sacrament as well as
its position of preeminence in the worship of the church
through the ages it is surprising that among evangelicals in
America today there is such a general ignorance of the essence and the implications of the Lord's Supper. This has resulted in serious misrepresentations of its significance and
misunderstandings as to what is actually involved in its observance. Among many believers today there is even a pa-
thetic indifference to the sacrament, an indifference which
leaves them unconcerned if they do not receive it with any
frequency.

Perhaps nothing is needed in the evangelical churches of

---

[14]William D. Maxwell, *Concerning Worship* (London: Oxford University
Press, 1948), p. 25.

our country today more than a theology of the sacraments. A detailed study of the subject is not, however, within the purview of this book. Nevertheless, we could not consider the conduct of the worship services in which the Lord's Supper is observed without mentioning some of the erroneous ideas held by Christians which have contributed to various abuses in the administration of the sacrament.

Perhaps the greatest mistake which believers have made regarding the Lord's Supper is to consider it merely or mainly as a commemoration. This is Zwinglianism. Huldreich Zwingli (1484-1531), one of the leaders of the Reformation, wrote two liturgical treatises setting forth his position with respect to the sacraments. Concerning the Lord's Supper he wrote, "The Eucharist or Communion or Lord's Supper is nothing else than a commemoration whereby those who firmly believe that they have been reconciled to the Father by the death and blood of Christ announce this life-giving death, that is, praise it and glory in it and proclaim it."[15] To Zwingli the Lord's Supper added nothing to the word which had been preached. It is not surprising that in the churches which hold this view there is little concern for the sacrament. But it is surprising that within the Reformed churches which trace their historical origins to John Calvin, who opposed Zwingli strongly on the sacraments, there are many who hold the Zwinglian position. It is true that our Lord said, "This do in remembrance of me" (Luke 22:19). However, it must be clearly understood that, for the Hebrew of Jesus' day, to "remember" did not mean just to recall to memory a fact, nor did it mean to look upon a memorial. For the devout Jew to remember meant to bring into actuality a past event or a previous situation. We establish memorials today, but they are only for those who have died. How could we have a memorial for one who is still alive? Yes, how could we have a memorial for the One who not only lives Himself but is our very life? The Lord's Supper has never been a solemn wake held in sorrowful remembrance of a dead person. From its

---

[15]Huldreich Zwingli, *Opera* (Zurich, 1832), Vol. III, pp. 605-606.

beginning in the early church it has been a joyful time of fellowship, dominated by thanksgiving. Its very name through the centuries has been the Eucharist, meaning thanksgiving. We thank God because Christ died for our sins, but at the same time we adore Him because He broke the bonds of death and came forth from the tomb to give us eternal life. The resurrection of Jesus Christ is an absolutely incontrovertible fact. Our hope of salvation and eternal life is solidly based upon our faith in His having risen from the dead and being alive forevermore. He is present in this world today. He is especially present in His church when that body gathers in His name. The Lord's Supper itself is His own established means of feeding His children on the rich spiritual resources of His own being. The whole Christ is really ministered in the sacrament.

That there is mystery involved in the communion which believers enjoy in the sacrament of the Lord's Supper we cannot deny. The method by which the risen Lord holds spiritual communion with His own and imparts to them the grace of spiritual nurture with the symbols of the supper we cannot fully know. But Adam Hunter has well said, "It is not in the Sacraments that confidence should be placed, but only in the God who gives grace to them. Grace comes with the Sacraments, not from them."[16]

Another serious error which has kept many from knowing the rich blessing of the proper observance of the Lord's Supper is the idea that there is some kind of magic about the sacrament which gives it an overpowering influence or an unusual effectiveness for a limited amount of time. This has led to severe restrictions on the number of times that the sacrament is observed in many churches. In fact, the church in which I was reared provided the sacrament of the Lord's Supper only four times a year. I have known many evangelical churches where it was observed once a month. This could hardly fail to suggest that there is something in the sacrament itself, perhaps some supernatural virtue, which is good for

---

[16]Adam Hunter, *The Teaching of Calvin* (London: James Clarke & Co., 1950), p. 168.

one month, or for three months, and will sustain the believer that long, but might be harmful if received more often.

Not long ago a young minister who had come to a deeper understanding of the sacraments was suggesting to his congregation a more frequent observance of the Lord's Supper. The response of one of his members was, "Well, just be careful not to have it too often!" Such an attitude indicates a belief that there is something in the act itself which produces certain consequences which might be lost with frequent performance. Yet I have never heard any Christian say, "Let's be careful not to have our pastor preach the Word too often." All Christians recognize that it is through the Word that our Savior speaks to us today, but many seem not to understand that He speaks by the sacraments also. It is the very same message. Through the sacraments Christ ministers to His children, feeding them spiritually. It is difficult indeed, in the light of the spiritual benefits which are imparted with (not *in)* the Lord's Supper, not to agree with John Calvin, who insisted that the Lord's people should have the privilege of partaking of the sacrament every Lord's Day as the climactic part of their worship services. The elders of Geneva, who refused to allow him to provide weekly communion, were like many in our evangelical churches today who do not want the Lord's gracious ministry with the sacraments too often.

A third erroneous idea concerning the Lord's Supper is that it is something entirely separate from man's normal day-by-day experience of God's grace in salvation and from his weekly, or more frequent, experiences of corporate worship. This misunderstanding is perhaps closely related to the idea of there being something magical behind the ordinance. However, it is held by some who certainly do not consciously attach any magic to the sacrament but who look upon it as something intended especially for an elite group of believers who receive very special blessing by participation in it. The very way that some churches provide the Lord's Supper in a special service following the morning worship for those who wish to remain behind and receive the sacrament suggests this attitude. Perhaps it also might suggest the idea that there are some believers who need the sacrament while there are others who do not. It is important for all of us to look upon the sacrament of the Lord's Supper as having been designed by the Lord Jesus Christ Himself for our spiritual nourishment, growth, and strengthening, and as a divinely ordained means of making more real to us continually our union with Jesus Christ in His body.

The Administration of the Lord's Supper

The order of worship prior to the observance of the Lord's Supper is not substantially different from the order suggested in Chapters 6 and 7 until after the sermon has been preached. When the minister has concluded his sermon and has offered a brief prayer, if he so chooses, he will move from the pulpit to the communion table, which will have been prepared before the service begins. He will offer a few Scripture sentences which will focus the minds of the people upon the privileges and responsibilities which are theirs in partaking of the communion. He will then extend

The Invitation to Communion

The invitation to communion includes an explanation of the most significant aspects of the sacrament and may also contain a tender warning to those whose hearts may be rebellious against the Lord. The following "Preface to the Lord's Supper," taken largely from the Book of Common Worship (Revised) is suggested in connection with the invitation:

> Dearly beloved, as we draw near to the Lord's Table to celebrate the Holy Communion of the Body and Blood of Christ, we are grateful to remember that our Lord instituted this Sacrament—
>> For the perpetual memory of His dying for our sakes and the pledge of His undying love;
>> as a bond of our union with Him and with each other as members of His mystical body;
>> as a seal of His promises to us and a renewal of our obedience to Him:

for the blessed assurance of His presence with us who are
  gathered here in His Name;
as an opportunity for us who love the Saviour to feed spiritually upon Him who is the Bread of Life;
and as a pledge of His coming again.

Seeing therefore what great benefits Christ has prepared for
us in this Communion, let us bow our knees unto the Father,
of whom the whole family in heaven and earth is named,

That He would grant us, according to the riches of His
glory, to be strengthened with might by His Spirit in the inner
man that Christ may dwell in our hearts by faith;

That we, being rooted and grounded in love, may be able to
comprehend with all saints what is the breadth, and length,
and depth, and height; and to know the love of Christ, which
passeth knowledge, that we may be filled with all the fullness
of God.

Now unto Him that is able to do exceeding abundantly
above all that we ask or think, according to the power that
worketh in us, unto Him be glory in the Church by Christ
Jesus throughout all ages. Amen.

The Communion Hymn

This hymn should be very carefully chosen. It should never
be a sentimental gospel song. It should not be morbidly subjective, but should direct the thoughts of the worshipers to
the Lord Jesus Christ and particularly to His substitutionary
atonement on the cross as well as the present efficacy of His
blood. Many excellent hymns for use at this place in the service are found in every good hymnal. Let me suggest only a
few:

"O Sacred Head, Now Wounded"	(St. Bernard)	Passion Chorale
"Ah, Holy Jesus, How Hast Thou Offended"	(Heerman)	Iste Confessor or Flemming
"Thou Hidden Source of Calm Repose"	(Wesley)	Stella
"Not All the Blood of Beasts"	(Watts)	Olmutz
"Man of Sorrows! What a Name"	(Bliss)	Man of Sorrows
"Not Worthy, Lord! to Gather up the Crumbs"	(Bickersteth)	Communion
"According to Thy Gracious Word"	(Montgomery)	Dalehurst
"Shepherd of Souls, Refresh and Bless"	(Montgomery)	St. Agnes
"Here, O My Lord, I See Thee"	(Bonar)	Morecambe
"Twas on That Night"	(Morison)	Rockingham

During the singing of this hymn the elders (or deacons in
churches which do not have elders) may bring the communion elements forward in their vessels and place them on the
communion table. This simple offertory is in line with his-

toric practice, and when understood by the congregation can be very meaningful. This ceremony can also be combined with the receiving of the money offerings of the people, in which case the pastor would announce the offering as a response following the sermon. The deacons would collect the offerings of the people and when finished would follow the elders bearing the communion elements to the front of the church. The minister would receive the communion vessels and place them on the table. He would then deposit the offering plates in an appropriate place nearby.

If the communion elements have been placed on the table before the service and covered with a white linen cloth, during the singing of the hymn two of the elders should remove the cloth and any other coverings of the elements. The other elders should gather with the pastor around the table.

The Creed

After the hymn the congregation should rise (if not already standing) and unite in affirming their faith with the words of either the Apostles' Creed or the Nicean Creed concerning the nature, life, and work of Christ.

The Words of Institution

Following the Creed, the minister should say, "Let us reverently listen to the words of institution of the Holy Supper of our Lord, as they were given to us by the apostle Paul." Then follow the words of I Corinthians 11:23-26. These verses of Scripture should have been carefully memorized and must be recited meaningfully and reverently. It should be remembered, as has been explained above, that the efficacy of the Lord's Supper depends upon the work of the Holy Spirit in ministering the body and blood of the Lord Jesus Christ with the elements, and that these essential words of institution which the Holy Spirit uses in the hearts of the faithful contain both the divine authorization of the sacrament and the promise of blessing to those who receive the elements with faith. Then follows

The Prayer of Consecration

The Scripture tells us that before the Savior broke the bread with His disciples He gave thanks. This prayer should be both a prayer of thanksgiving and also a prayer for the setting apart of the elements from their ordinary use to the holy use for which the Lord designated them. This is called the *epiklesis*. The prayer should also include the oblation, which is an offering of the worshipers themselves to the Lord who once and for all offered Himself on the cross for the sins of men. This prayer has traditionally been expressed with these words: "Here we offer and present unto Thee ourselves, our souls and bodies, to be a reasonable, holy and living sacrifice unto Thee."

The Breaking of the Bread and the Offering of the Cup

After the prayer of consecration the minister will take a loaf of the bread and holding it up so that all members of the congregation may see will say,

According to the holy example of our Lord Jesus Christ, and in remembrance of Him we do this, for in the same night in which He was betrayed the Lord Jesus took bread, and when He had given thanks, as has been done in His name, He broke it.

Here he should break the loaf in plain view of all the people.

And He gave to His disciples as I, ministering in His name, give this bread to you; and He said, Take, eat; this is my body which is given for you. Do this in remembrance of me.

The minister will then give the bread to the elders, who will distribute it to the congregation. When the elders have the vessels containing the bread in their hands and are ready for the distribution, the minister will say,

Receive the bread, and eat it in remembrance that Christ died for you and feed upon Him in your hearts by faith.

One of the elders will first serve the officiating minister. The minister must receive both the bread and the cup first. This has been the universal practice from the very earliest times. Thus the minister humbly and reverently sets the example for all of the Lord's people. It must be remembered that he is not the host at the Lord's Supper as he would be at a dinner in his own home. The Lord is the Host, and everyone, including the minister, receives from Him. When all of the people have received the bread, the elders will return the patens to the minister, who will serve them and then pause for a few moments of silence as the elders communicate.

The minister will then take the cup, and holding it in full view of the people will say,

> In the same way, after the supper, He took the cup, and gave thanks.

Here the minister or one of the elders will offer a prayer of thanksgiving for the cup and for the blood of Christ. Our Savior offered prayer before both the bread and the cup. This is our example. The minister will then continue:

> And He offered it to them, saying, Drink from it, all of you. This is my blood of the covenant which is poured out for many for the forgiveness of sins.

And when all the elders hold the cups the minister will say,

> It is the blood of Jesus Christ shed for you which preserves you unto eternal life. Drink this in remembrance that Christ died for you and be thankful.

The cup is passed in the same manner as the bread and when all have communicated the minister will offer a prayer of thanksgiving which will be followed by

The Hymn of Praise or Dedication

The Scripture tells us regarding the Lord's institution of the Supper with His disciples in the upper room that after "they had sung a hymn, they went out into the mount of Olives" (Matt. 26:30). It is appropriate, therefore, to conclude the administration of the sacrament of the Lord's Supper with the singing of a hymn which is particularly fitting, sounding the note of praise or providing an expression of dedication for those who have partaken of the sacrament. From many suitable hymns the following are suggested:

"At the Lamb's High Feast We Sing"	(Anonymous)	St. George's Windsor
"A Parting Hymn We Sing"	(Wolfe)	Schumann
"Till He Come! O Let the Words"	(Bickersteth)	Ajalon
"Jesus, I Live to Thee"	(Harbaugh)	Trentham
"Jesus, Thou Joy of Loving Hearts"	(tr. Palmer)	Quebec
"All Hail the Power of Jesus' Name"	(Perronet)	Miles Lane or Diadem
"O for a Thousand Tongues to Sing"	(Wesley)	Azmon

This hymn is followed by the benediction. The congregation should then be seated for a few moments of silent meditation before the organist begins the postlude and the people disperse.

Special Considerations

Several practical matters are of importance in connection with the Lord's Supper. They need to be mentioned because they relate very definitely to the impact of the Holy Spirit's ministry.

In the first place it must be emphasized that everything about this solemn service should be done with the utmost reverence and efficiency. The minister and the elders should always discuss the details of the actions required and have a full understanding concerning any individual responsibilities in the service so that there will be no awkward movements, no embarrassing improprieties, and no disturbing mishaps. The communion table should be prepared before the first worshipers arrive. If, as is usually the case in our evangelical churches, the elements are on the table before the service begins, all the vessels and their contents should be covered with a spotless white cloth. It goes without saying that the communion vessels themselves should always be cleaned and polished. There should be no evidence of slovenly preparation for the Lord's Supper. He is the Host. If the communion elements are to be brought in during the singing of the communion hymn, the table should be covered with a white cloth in preparation for their being placed upon it. The bringing in of the elements at this time in the service recalls the action of the early Christian church when the worshipers brought their gifts of bread and wine to the Lord for His use in the sacrament. This action has been perpetuated in the liturgy of the Church of Scotland, although it is not practiced in all of the churches.

The elements to be used in the Lord's Supper have unfortunately been the cause of considerable controversy. There are some who insist that only unleavened bread and red wine should be used because they believe that these were the elements used by the Lord in the upper room. But there is nothing essential to the sacrament in either unleavened bread or red wine. In His great discourse on the Bread of Life, which is recorded in the sixth chapter of John's Gospel, the Lord used the figure of bread many times, referring to His body. Those who heard Him would certainly have had regular bread in mind as He developed the symbolism. We do know that in some observances of the Lord's Supper in the early church regular bread was used. Not until about the ninth century did the Roman Church begin to use unleavened bread exclusively; it wanted the communion bread to be different from the people's bread.

A loaf among the Jews in Jesus' day was a round, flat, crisp cake of dough baked on the hearth. Since we do not normally use bread like this, there is no reason why our communion bread should not be the common bread of today. However, if unleavened bread is used it should be in loaves or pieces which are large enough to be visibly broken before the people. Because of the symbolism it is best not to have the communion bread cut in regular little squares which obviously were not broken. Small loaves broken by the minister and placed on the trays can be passed around to each communicant who will break off his own portion.

Red wine may have been used in the upper room. It has been used for centuries. However, some of the early Christians insisted that it should be diluted with water, thus symbolizing the blood and water which flowed from the side of Christ on the cross. With the spread of Christianity the church was established in countries where there was little or no wine available. The juice of the grape came into wide use. The Scripture does not tell us exactly what was in the cup which Jesus used in the upper room. We read simply that it was the "fruit of the vine" (Matt. 26:29; Mark 14:25; Luke 22:18). Evangelicals in this country, as well as in some parts of Europe and on the mission fields of Asia and Africa, have never been fully reconciled to the use of wine. Certainly with the increasing problem of alcoholism in our country and with the numbers of converted alcoholics attending our churches, many of whom dare not even taste an alcoholic beverage, it would seem wise to make use of grape juice, which is in plentiful supply and certainly is the fruit of the vine.

Here I must comment on a custom which has arisen in many evangelical churches of our country. It is called "simultaneous communion." The origin of this practice is unknown. It has spread rather widely, perhaps because of a lack of understanding of the real significance of the sacrament and what actually takes place when a communicant participates by faith. In churches where this practice is observed the minister directs the members of the congregation to retain the elements in their hands until everyone is served so that all may partake together. Those who defend this practice have insisted that it gives expression to the unity of believers at the table of the Lord. However, as Donald Macleod has said, "It is an affront to the basic belief that our unity around the Lord's Table is not a mechanical creation but issues from a deeper source. It rests in our risen and living Lord in whom all children of faith are one."[17] Indeed our very gathering at the table to partake together, irrespective of our past lives, our social position, or any other distinctions, is in itself sufficient witness to our unity.

The very act of holding the elements and then partaking simultaneously helps to obscure the significance of the sacrament. Feeding upon the body of the Lord Jesus Christ spiritually and drinking His blood spiritually are not corporate acts. They are individual matters. We do not receive spiritual food simultaneously with other believers. We take it individually when by faith we appropriate that truth which is

---

[17]Macleod, *Presbyterian Worship,* p. 75.

set before us in the actions as well as the words of the sacrament. The Lord's Supper is not a spectacle nor a ceremony.
The living Christ is present. He offers Himself to men. The
elements convey nothing in themselves. They are only signs
of what Christ is doing for His own. The idea of holding
them in one's hand until everyone else has them is foreign to
any true understanding of the sacrament. It is to use them for
something for which the Lord did not intend them.

When our Lord instituted the Supper, His actions and His
words were both significant, and both are essential to the
sacrament. He broke the bread. He gave it to His disciples.
He said, "Take and eat." He gave no instructions to hold the
bread. It was the same with the cup. He offered it to them,
saying, "Drink from it." He did not direct them to hold it.
In all probability He used only one cup. In large congregations today this would be impractical and nearly impossible.
We must be careful not to add to nor subtract from the significant words and actions of a divinely appointed sacrament. The custom of retaining the elements until everyone is
served "is reminiscent of a secular toast in a banquet hall.
Even at its best this practice has little to recommend it."[18]

Our very presence at the communion table preaches a sermon concerning the significance of Christ's words: "Drink
from it, *all* of you; for this is My blood of the covenant"
(Matt. 26:27, 28, NASB). By our sitting or kneeling beside
other believers to receive the sacraments we testify that we
are one with each one who is receiving the body and blood of
the Lord by faith as we are. At the communion table I acknowledge that I am a child of God, but only by His grace.
Moreover I bear witness to the fact that God's grace in Christ
is not for me alone but for everyone who believes that the
Lord has died for him and joins with me in feeding on the living Christ.

Before bringing our discussion of the sacraments to a
close, a word needs to be said concerning music during the
observance of the Lord's Supper. In far too many churches,

---

[18]Ibid.

while the elements are being distributed and the people are communicating, the organist plays a medley of familiar hymns or gospel songs. This is a poor practice for at least two reasons. First, the playing of familiar tunes always suggests the words which normally accompany them, and this can be very distracting to the worshipers, especially when poor choices are made. Upon the distribution of the communion bread I have often heard the organist commence immediately to play "Break Thou the Bread of Life." This is a good hymn, but it is not a hymn about the sacrament. It is a hymn concerning the Scriptures, the Word of God. It is not fitting as a directive for meditation during communion; and, of course, if it is played, the familiar words can hardly be kept from the minds of the listeners.

In the second place, absolute quiet is much the best atmosphere for reverent participation in the sacrament on the part of all of the people. Even very soft music can be somewhat disturbing to some members of the congregation, particularly those who are sensitive musically. In this connection Oswald Milligan has said, "Rightly used, the silence of a great congregation whilst communicating may be one of the most uplifting and inspiring influences that flow from the observance of the Sacrament. It has the inestimable advantage of providing a time when the voice of man being hushed, Christ is left free to speak His own word to the soul that waits upon Him."[19]

---

[19]Oswald Milligan, *The Ministry of Worship* (London: Oxford University Press, 1941), p. 113.

10

The Wedding Service

One of the great tragedies of our day is the fact that nearly half of the marriages performed each year in our nation end in divorce, with at least one-fourth of them being terminated within the brief space of three years! When a conscientious minister of the gospel faces this situation honestly, he realizes that it presents him with a serious problem. Divorce is by no means limited to the unchurched populace, nor even to members of nonevangelical churches. It is destroying many marriages within the evangelical Christian church and is thus striking a crippling blow against not only the church but also the basic unit of society, the home.

Serious and important efforts are being made by concerned clergymen to halt the breakdown of marriages. Ministers of all denominations have become so alarmed with the damage done by divorce that most of them have taken steps to acquire considerable skill both in marriage counseling for couples that have run into difficulties and in prenuptial instruction for those who are looking forward to marriage.

When a minister performs a marriage he is an agent of the civil government as well as the church. Because it is a civil as well as a religious contract, marriage comes under the jurisdiction of the laws of the state. Actually in our country marriage can be legalized without the participation of a clergyman and entirely apart from any religious ceremony whatever. No minister, however, is allowed to perform a marriage ceremony in the church unless the provisions of the laws of the state have been fully met. Every earnest Christian minister will recognize that his responsibility before God in uniting two people in marriage is indeed a very solemn one. He should, of course, certainly refuse to be a party to the marriage of two persons under circumstances which are contrary to the express will of God as given in the Holy Scriptures. On the other hand, when he is convinced that the proposed union has the approval of God, he is still faced with the awesome responsibility of preparing the couple for their new relationship and giving them an understanding of the significance of the marriage service itself.

It must be recognized that marriage was originally established in the Garden of Eden for the welfare and happiness of mankind as a whole, and is therefore not an institution which God intended should be limited to His believing children. Nevertheless there is very special significance in marriage for a Christian. It is designated in most wedding services as a "holy estate." The Lord Jesus Christ and the apostles took pains to emphasize its importance and its permanence and to give careful instructions concerning married life. The highest and holiest glorification of marriage came when the inspired apostle Paul used it as a figure of the relationship of Christ with His church. While marriage is not a sacrament, it certainly includes some sacramental elements, for it involves a solemn covenant between God and the two persons who are being married. It is certainly something beyond a mere physical union. When God said that the two parties to a marriage should "be one flesh" (Gen. 2:24), He certainly meant more than a mere physical union. It is a union of two personalities, a meeting of souls. Each retains his or her separate individuality, but in a very real sense the two become one, and this by their own voluntary choice.

In a series of counseling sessions every minister should make the marriage relationship intelligible in all of its various aspects. Moreover, if Christian marriage is to be what it should be, each wedding ceremony itself must be a service of worship in which bride and groom not only pledge themselves to one another but present themselves to God. This does not mean that the simple and brief liturgy found in the service books of most denominations needs to be altered. What is there is usually distinctively Christian. What is needed in most cases is an expansion sufficient to provide for a more adequate service of worship of the Triune God, so that all present, even though some be unbelievers, will recognize that in a Christian marriage God is always central. It is He who has brought the couple together; He is praised for His providence. It is His presence which will bless their life together; He is adored for His covenant blessings. It is He whose greatest gift was the offering of His Son to bring them eternal life; He is worshiped with the offering of their bodies as living sacrifices to His holy name.

All too often wedding services, even for earnest young Christians, have been governed by the social customs of the communities in which they were held or the secular pressures of friends and relatives. The congregations at many weddings seem to have come together for interests which are entirely foreign to those that are normally associated with services of worship. The nervousness anticipated by many brides and grooms has often dictated weddings so brief that little more than a couple of short prayers and the exchange of concise, summary vows was included in the ceremony. With such an important covenant as marriage being made, certainly the service should do more than establish a legal bond. A civil ceremony could do as much. But, as has been pointed out, the civil formula for marriage does not include the all-important matter of "the self-giving of two persons to God in their new oneness with each other.''[1] We are concerned, then, with a wedding service which will bring praise and glory to God and will give the bride and groom an opportunity to magnify their Savior by their willing dedication of themselves to Him.

Music for the Wedding

Let us begin with a brief discussion of the music for the Christian wedding. This is one of the first portions of the service to present itself for consideration on the part of the bride and her parents as well as the groom, if he is included in the early planning. It is of great importance that all of the music chosen for the wedding should contribute to the reverence and decorum of the service. It must be suitable for an atmosphere of worship. Much of the traditional wedding music, both vocal and instrumental, is not. It is purely secular in origin and in its associations.

There is nothing intrinsically wrong with sentimental love songs in their proper place. Such old favorites as "I Love You Truly" and "Because" are quite suitable for some occasions as are some of the contemporary love songs from musical comedies and the movies. They are most inappropriate, however, in a service of worship where the participants desire to glorify God rather than to encourage romantic affectation. Similarly the conventional wedding marches of Wagner and Mendelssohn are seriously lacking in fitness for a Christian wedding service. The "Bridal Chorus" of Richard Wagner is taken from his opera, *Lohengrin;* instead of being a joyous processional to a Christian wedding, it occurs after the wedding in an atmosphere of suspicion and hatred which ultimately brings death. Unfortunately this number also suffers from its association in the minds of many with the ridiculous parody, "Here Comes the Bride." Mendelssohn's incidental music for Shakespeare's *A Midsummer Night's Dream,* which has traditionally been used as a recessional

---

[1]Donald Macleod, *Presbyterian Worship: Its Meaning and Method* (Richmond: John Knox Press, 1965), p. 81.

march at weddings, is less objectionable, but it is still quite inappropriate because of its association.

There is an abundance of suitable music for the organist who wishes to establish the proper atmosphere of reverent worship in a musical prelude and then in a processional which will maintain the mood of reverence while providing a joyful background for the entrance of the wedding party.

For the prelude let me suggest only a few of the many appropriate compositions:

Bach, "Jesu, Joy of Man's Desiring"
Bach, "Sheep May Safely Graze"
Handel, "Aria" from Organ Concerto no. 10
Sowerby, "Carillon"
Mendelssohn, "Andante Religioso" from Organ Sonata no. 4
Edwards, "Rhosymedre" ("Lovely")

For the processional:

Bach, "Sinfonia" from Wedding Cantata no. 196
Brahms, "St. Anthony's Chorale" from "Variations on a Theme by Haydn"
Purcell, "Trumpet Voluntary"
Marcello, "Psalm 19" ("The Heavens Declare")
Clarke, "The Prince of Denmark March"

For the recessional:

Purcell, "Trumpet Voluntary" (if not used for processional)
Handel-Groves, "A Trumpet Voluntary"
Karg-Elert, "Nun danket Alle Gott"

It must be recognized also that suitable hymn tunes carefully chosen by the bride in consultation with a discerning organist can provide very fitting music for the processional. It is perfectly proper for the processional to take place during the singing of a hymn if the hymn is well selected and fits the occasion. It sometimes happens that the more difficult organ compositions (for example, some of those listed above) are beyond the skill of the organist who has been chosen. In this case, it is far better for hymn tunes to be used for the processional than for the musician to attempt music which is too difficult. The playing of very familiar hymn tunes for the prelude, however, should be avoided, even though this might appeal to some members of the congregation. The tunes which are familiar suggest to the listener the words which are

normally sung with them. These words may not be particularly apropos for the meditation of the congregation at a
wedding. There are many simple but beautiful compositions
which can be used for the instrumental prelude.

I will suggest some of the best hymns for use as processionals. It will depend upon the preference of the bride
whether the processional hymn is sung by the congregation
or simply played by the organist. Since some hymns are sung
to different tunes I am including with each of the following
hymns a suitable tune:

"Love Divine, All Loves Excelling" (Tune: Hyfrydol or
Beecher)
"Praise, My Soul, the King of Heaven" (Praise, My Soul)
"Praise to God, Immortal Praise" (Nuremberg)
"Praise to the Lord, the Almighty" (Lobe den Herren)
"The King of Love, My Shepherd Is" (Dominus Regit Me)
"Joyful, Joyful, We Adore Thee" (Hymn to Joy)
"Now Thank We All Our God" (Nun danket)

It is very important that the entire bridal party be provided
with inconspicuous copies of all the hymns which are to be
sung by the congregation, as well as any other parts of the
service, such as responsive readings or litanies, in which the
whole congregation is to take part. Hymnbooks are cumber-
some at such a time and members of the wedding party
should not be expected to carry them. On the other hand,
nothing is more unseemly in a worship service than for some
members of the congregation to be unable to participate in
the corporate worship because they do not have the necessary
materials. Conspicuously placed where all can observe its
members, the bridal party is certainly an integral part of the
worshiping congregation.

For the service a printed bulletin should be provided each
worshiper. If the service is not too elaborate the words of the
hymns and special vocal music as well as the prayer of confession and any other parts which the congregation will be invited to share can be included in it. Such a bulletin may be
adequate for the needs of the wedding party. The cover of
the bulletin should not be the same as that used for regular
church services. It should be tastefully designed with appropriate Christian symbols. On the back of the bulletin the

members of the wedding party, the musicians, and the participating ministers can be identified for the benefit of the members of the congregation who do not know them.

The Order of Worship

In the planning for the service the bride should not take it upon herself to prepare the order of worship. This should be done by the minister who is going to perform the ceremony. Often an additional clergyman who is a special friend or a relative of the bride or groom is asked to share in the service. This is quite proper. The preparation of the liturgy, however, should be the responsibility of the officiating minister. After consultation with the bride he can suggest the particular portions of the service to be assigned to the assisting clergyman.

In making the plans for the wedding service the principle of dignified simplicity should control all decision, including the decorations of the sanctuary as well as the order of worship. The wise minister will always counsel the couple to be married against elaborate displays and lavish expenditures. Floral pieces should never be so spectacular that they attract the interest of the congregation away from the worship of God.

The following order of service provides for a meaningful worship experience for both the wedding party and the congregation:

The Organ Preludes

It is quite suitable for a number of well-selected compositions to be played at this time. Wedding guests are always seated by ushers and this often takes quite a bit of time. The organist should play until all the guests who have arrived on time are seated.

Vocal Solos or Ensembles

Before the worship service itself begins, it is quite fitting to have one or more appropriate sacred numbers. If the bride or the groom has special friends who are gifted musicians, they are often asked to contribute to the wedding service in this way. There are two or three excellent places for sacred musical numbers within the service, but sometimes there is a desire for more music than would fit well into the service. This is a good place for it to be included.

Processional

Often two musical numbers are used here. One is for the bridal party, and the other is used exclusively for the bride herself as she comes in on the arm of her father. The audience should rise when the bride's music begins, as a token of honor to her.

The Call to Worship

When the entire bridal party is in place at the front of the church, the officiating minister will make it clear to all those who are present that the service is to be a Christian service of worship and not just a ceremony to unite two people in marriage.

Hymn of Praise

This hymn of praise must be an appropriate response to the call to worship. The hymn which is used need not have any special reference to marriage. It should be familiar enough so that all of the congregation can join in the singing freely.

The Scriptural Basis for Marriage

This important instruction can be given in the words of the Book of Common Worship as follows:

Dearly beloved, we are assembled here in the presence of God, to join this man and this woman in holy marriage which is instituted of God, regulated by His commandments, blessed by our Lord Jesus Christ, and to be held in honor among all men. Let us therefore reverently remember that

God has established and sanctified marriage for the welfare and happiness of mankind. Our Saviour has declared that a man shall forsake his father and mother and cleave unto his wife. By His apostles, He has instructed those who enter into this relation to cherish a mutual esteem and love; to bear with each other's infirmities and weaknesses; to comfort each other in sickness, trouble, and sorrow; in honesty and industry to provide for each other and for their household in temporal things; to pray for and encourage each other in the things which pertain to God; and to live together as heirs of the grace of life.

The charge which is still included in many wedding ceremonies that "if either of you know any reason why you may not rightly be joined together, you do now acknowledge it," as well as the similar words addressed to members of the audience who might know of reasons why the couple should not be married, seems archaic and should be omitted. These matters should all have been taken care of privately before the minister made arrangements to conduct the wedding service.

The Commitment of the Bridal Couple

Before proceeding any further the bride and the groom must commit themselves to one another and signify their desire to be made one in Christ. Then the service can continue.

The Prayer of Confession

There are a number of ways that the congregation can participate in the prayer of confession. It can be printed in a wedding service program. These programs are becoming increasingly popular. It could be a responsive reading from an appropriate Psalm found in the Psalter selections in the back of the hymnal. It could be offered by the officiating minister.

The Assurance of Pardon

Usually the assurance of pardon is a brief selection from the Scriptures.

Hymn of Thanksgiving
The Reading of God's Word
The Wedding Homily

This should be brief since the bridal party will all be standing through the entire service.

The Marriage Vows
The Ring Ceremony
Prayer

It is desirable for the bridal couple to kneel during this prayer. After the minister prays, it is suitable for a sung prayer to be offered here also.

The Declaration of Marriage
The Benediction
Recessional

The Form of the Wedding Vows

In recent years a number of earnest young Christians preparing for marriage have taken it upon themselves to write their own marriage vows. This is a practice which should be discouraged. The vows which are contained in the standard service books of most denominations are the result of years of refinement through use. Very few young people have the literary gifts to write anything which is comparable, especially in ascribing to almighty God the glory and majesty to which He is entitled. Because God is the center of all worship the vows which are taken before Him and in which He is a party must be permeated with the spirit of reverence and awe as well as love. It is all too easy for vows invented by enthusiastic young people to be lacking in those lofty sentiments and expression which are fitting for a Christian marriage and instead to mirror the sentimentality of youthful enthusiasm and the poverty of their verbal expressions.

The Rehearsal

If the wedding ceremony is to be a worship service, one of the most important steps in making it meaningful is the rehearsal. While most books on wedding etiquette indicate that the bride is responsible to direct the rehearsal it usually falls to the minister (and properly so!) to guide the proceedings. Because of his extensive experience he is best able to do so and he should be firm, in a kind way, in his insistence upon avoiding anything awkward or irreverent. From the very first contact which the minister has with the wedding party he must make them realize that while the rehearsal is held to properly prepare for a very joyous event it is also to make ready for a service of worship.

As soon as all the members of the party have arrived, the minister should invite them to be seated in the front of the church. When they have done so, he should briefly express his personal joy in the prospect of participating in such a happy occasion. Then he should give a few words concerning the distinctive character of Christian marriage, emphasizing the signal importance of the presence and blessing of the Lord in the marriage and explaining that the wedding is to be a service of worship because worship should be the first priority in every believer's life. He should then lead in a brief prayer after which the rehearsal proper begins.

The minister will ask those who are participants in the ceremony first of all to take their places at the front of the church in the positions they will occupy during the wedding. After all have located and taken note of their place, they will be asked to move to the places which they will occupy as the service begins. The bride, her father, and her attendants, along with the ushers, will be in the rear of the church. The minister, the groom, and his best man will be just outside a door leading into the chancel or pulpit area. Without any music all members of the wedding party will move in their proper order to their previously designated places at the front of the church. After this has been successfully accomplished the recessional is practiced. Then both the processional and the recessional are rehearsed with the music a time or two until everyone feels comfortable about the procedures.

When the members of the bridal party have completed this, the minister will excuse all of them except the four principals. He will then carefully go over in detail the steps in the marriage service itself, including the exchange of vows, the ring ceremony, and all other particulars. When this has been completed he should offer a brief prayer of thanksgiving and dedication for the bride and groom, asking God for special blessing upon the wedding service. He will not have an opportunity to be with them both just before the wedding begins.

Certain matters should be kept in mind by those making the arrangements for the wedding so that there are no hindrances to worship during the service. Care should be exercised on the day of the wedding that all the preparations of the sanctuary—flowers, candles, and pew reservations—are completed at least an hour before the time for the service to begin. Under no circumstances should photographers be allowed to take pictures during the wedding service. It is a time for reverent worship of God. Solemnity should always attend the taking of marriage vows before the sovereign Lord of the universe. The flash of a photographer's bulb can be nothing but distracting; even if he is using fast film without a flash his necessary movements to get the right angles for his pictures are sure to be disturbing. There is time for pictures following the service.

11

The Funeral Service

That there should be an easily distinguishable difference between the funeral of a true Christian and that of an unbeliever is evident to anyone who has an understanding of what it means to be a Christian. Unfortunately, however, in no other services of the evangelical churches of our land are there so many evidences of pagan influences as there are in funeral services. So many things which have characterized the funerals of Christians in this century have pointed more clearly to a last attempt to give recognition and honor to a human being than they have to a serious expression of faith in God. There has been little evidence, even in the funerals of devoted Christians, of the fact that God's salvation means that "to depart, and to be with Christ . . . is far better." (Phil. 1:23). In fact, as Joseph McCabe has written concerning Christian funerals, "most funeral services bear little relation to that sense of victory which throbs on every page of the New Testament since Christ rose from the dead."[1] My own personal testimony is that I was already graduated from theological seminary and was in my first pastorate before I ever heard a congregation sing a hymn of triumphant resurrection victory at a funeral, and I had attended many of them.

There are several typical features of funeral services which do not bring honor to the Lord. One of these is the music which is most often used. Regrettably, much of it is either overly sentimental or gives an utterly unscriptural view of death and of the life hereafter. Gospel songs with syrupy music are often chosen instead of the great hymns which give expression to the triumph of the Lord's victory over death and the grave. Why should not the funeral of a sincere believer resound with the congregation's singing of such a great paean of praise as Henry Alford's "Ten Thousand Times Ten Thousand"? This hymn was sung at Alford's own funeral in the great Canterbury Cathedral. Actually there are many fine hymns which would be particularly fitting for the funeral service of a Christian.

Another deplorable practice still carried on in many church funerals is the procession before the open coffin to "view the remains." Now, it is quite possible that among the friends and loved ones of a departed believer there would be some who would gain some satisfaction or comfort from a last tender look at the body which was left behind when the soul departed to be with the Lord, but this look should certainly be taken in private at the mortuary. Provision is always made for visitors to come to the mortuary. For members of the congregation to parade before an open casket elaborately outfitted with quilted satin lining certainly is not a Christian ritual. It smacks of morbid curiosity, not of Christian compassion. The expensive coffins which themselves bear testimony to the refinements of the mortician's art more than they do to the faith of the one who has died are

---

[1]Joseph McCabe, *The Power of God in a Parish Program* (Philadelphia: Westminster Press, 1959), p. 73.

certainly uncalled for. They represent an expense which can hardly be justified.

One of the most objectionable features of Christian funerals is the excessive floral display which characterizes so many of them. It is indeed a pity that so many believers have not found a more permanent and comforting way of expressing their sympathy at the departure of a friend than the sending of elaborate bouquets, many of which will be wilting and fading by the time they are placed upon the grave. There they will certainly quickly die. The custom of making funerals the occasions for elaborate displays of flowers is certainly contrary to the spirit and message of the New Testament. Commercial interests, of course, have encouraged the expenditure of large sums of money on flowers for funerals, but Christians who are concerned about their stewardship should certainly discourage this practice. Every evangelical church should have its own memorial fund to which contributions can be sent by friends and family of deceased believers in lieu of floral tributes. Many times the bereaved family will have special missionary or benevolent causes to which they will ask that memorial contributions be sent. This should always be encouraged. The church's memorial fund provides for those who have not made known any benevolent project of special interest. Even though individual contributions might seem small to the donors, when they accumulate even for one funeral they often provide a very worthwhile amount to support a Christian enterprise, and thus they go on bringing benefit and blessing long after the funeral is over.

Because the habits and customs of many years are deeply ingrained in the lives of the people, the minister who wishes to take positive action to make his funerals more definitely Christian must exercise a great deal of loving tact as well as compassionate consideration of his people. The traditions of a community are not easy to break and the minister who desires to restore a Christian witness to ceremonies which have been secularized if not paganized must patiently teach the people to see their responsibilities as sincere believers. If they love the Lord Jesus Christ and believe His Word their funerals as well as all other parts of their activity must bear witness to their faith. There are many Christians who have never had any instruction concerning some of the most puzzling issues which confront them. Death itself should be the subject of faithful instruction from the pulpit. Grief is encountered in every family, yet few are adequately prepared for it when it strikes. Every conscientious minister has an important task to discharge in instructing his people in the ways that believers honor God when calamities come in their lives.

It would be wise for the governing boards of churches to cooperate with their pastors in the preparation of detailed statements of policy concerning the conduct of funerals in the church. If such policy statements are made available to the members of the congregation and the principles behind them are explained fully at a time when no funeral is being planned, there will be no resentment when the regulations are brought to the attention of a family faced with preparation for a funeral.

The Place of the Service

It was customary until a few years ago for many funeral services to be conducted in the home of the deceased. Today one rarely hears of a funeral service in a private home except in some rural areas where the custom still lingers. There is certainly nothing objectionable about this practice. In our day, however, the majority of the services are conducted in the funeral chapels which are provided by the morticians, although a great many are held in churches.

There are a number of factors which influence the decision as to the place of the service. One of these, of course, is the spiritual condition of the one who has died. His profession of the Christian faith or the lack of it is deeply significant. Of course, it certainly is not possible for any human being to pass final judgment upon the soul of one who has departed this life. However, those men and women who have never made any profession of faith during their lifetime may be presumed to be unbelievers when they die. It would seem unwise for such individuals to be given a Christian funeral in a church building. It must always be remembered that the church carries on its ministry before a watching world. Keeping that witness free from glaring contradictions is very important.

At the same time no minister should ever refuse to conduct a funeral simply because the deceased person was apparently an unbeliever. It is possible for any minister to conduct a brief service which will honor God, make clear the gospel of God's grace to the living, and still give no appearance of encouraging those present to believe that the one who died without faith has entered into heavenly rest. A funeral is no time to touch the mourning hearts with further shafts of pain, but neither is it a time to compromise the message of the Word of God. The chapel of the funeral home provides an excellent place for the funeral of an unbeliever. It is also a perfectly proper place for the funeral of a sincere Christian. Individual circumstances may dictate that it is the best place. The actual procedures for the service in a funeral chapel are quite simple as everything is conveniently arranged for both the members of the family and their friends who come to the service.

The Service in the Church

The home church is and will remain the most appropriate place for a Christian funeral or memorial service. Two factors are causing the memorial service increasingly to replace the funeral in many evangelical churches. One is the more general acceptance of cremation. The other is the increasing custom of having private burial services with only the family and the closest friends present, followed by a public service in the church. In either case the body of the deceased is not present and the service takes on the nature of a memorial. There is less emotional stress in this type of service; the absence of the physical remains seems to make it easier for all who are present to concentrate their attention upon eternal spiritual values and the biblical teaching of Christian hope through the resurrection of Jesus Christ.

When Christian funerals include the presence of the body, the minister must be careful to arrange with the funeral director all of the details concerning the bringing of the coffin (together with a limited number of flowers) into the church sanctuary as well as its removal at the close of the service. It is important that there should be no confusion to disturb the spirit of reverence. Some modern church buildings do not readily lend themselves to convenient placing and removing of a coffin for such a service.

Normally the minister in charge of a funeral service will meet the funeral director and the pallbearers at the front door of the church and will precede the coffin down the center aisle to its place at the front of the sanctuary. The congregation will rise when the coffin is brought into the church as a token of respect and sympathy. After the casket has been properly placed, the minister will proceed to the pulpit platform and will be seated until the time for the service to begin. The congregation should sit down when the minister takes his place.

The service should begin with appropriate sentences of Scripture which will focus the attention of the congregation upon the victory of the Christian faith which has been obtained through the death and resurrection of the Lord Jesus Christ. The Word of God contains many splendid verses which can be used to open the service. These opening sentences of Scripture are followed by a prayer. It should be a brief petition for the special ministry of the Holy Spirit in the service, asking that God will be glorified and the assembled congregation edified and comforted by His Word. This first prayer is not the best time to offer thanksgiving for the life of the one who has died, nor to intercede especially for the bereaved family. Those prayers will come a little later after the congregation has given heed to the message from the Bible.

A suitable hymn of worship should follow the first prayer. Such a hymn as Bishop How's "For All the Saints Who from Their Labors Rest" is addressed in praise to Christ and directs the thoughts of those singing to the triumph of those who belong to Him. Another particularly fine hymn for this place in the service is Christian Gellert's "Jesus Lives, and So Shall I." The singing of such hymns, of which there are many, will focus the attention properly upon the Christian's hope and victory in Christ.

After the singing of the hymn the minister should read the Scripture portion or portions upon which he will base his homily. The Scripture and the brief message together should not encompass more than fifteen or twenty minutes. In a memorial service it could be somewhat longer, but a funeral service in the church with the body present should normally last no longer than half an hour.

The message is followed by a special prayer with petitions appropriate for the occasion. The prayer should include thanksgiving for the life, witness, and work of the one who has died, especially if he or she has been an active Christian serving the Lord in the church. This portion of the prayer, while it should never enlarge upon the good qualities of character of the one who has departed this life, does make unnecessary any eulogy in the service.

Following the prayer another hymn should be sung. This hymn may properly be directed to some of the joyful anticipations of the Christian in the next life. Hymns like "The Sands of Time Are Sinking" or Isaac Watts' "There Is a Land of Pure Delight" would be fine. Sentimental and unscriptural songs such as "Beautiful Isle of Somewhere" must assuredly be avoided. This hymn closes the service in the church if it is anticipated that most of the congregation will be going to the cemetery. If most of the people will not be attending the graveside portion of the service, the benediction may be given at the conclusion of the service in the church. Otherwise it will conclude the brief service at the grave.

Service at the Cemetery

When the funeral procession reaches the cemetery, it is customary for the minister again to precede the casket as it is carried by the pallbearers from the hearse to the grave. He will stand at the head of the grave and will conduct a very brief service because this is a time of particularly severe emotional strain. When all of the people are standing or sitting near the grave, he will begin with a few comforting Scripture passages and follow them with a brief committal of the body to the grave, giving renewed expression to the hope of the resurrection. The service concludes with a prayer and the benediction. As soon as the service comes to an end, the minister will move to speak a personal word of comfort to the family after which the friends in the congregation will be free to do so also.

Supplement

Aids for the Preparation of
Corporate Worship Services

Calls to Worship

1. You are not a God who takes pleasure in evil;
     with you the wicked cannot dwell . . .
   But let all who take refuge in you be glad;
     let them ever sing for joy! *(Ps. 5:4,11)*

2. The Lord is my rock, my fortress and my deliverer;
     my God is my rock, in whom I take refuge.
   He is my shield and the horn of my salvation, my stronghold.
     I call to the Lord who is worthy of praise. *(Ps. 18:2-3a)*

3. They who seek the Lord will praise Him—
     may your hearts live forever!
   All the ends of the earth will remember and turn to the Lord
     and all the families of the nations will bow down before
       Him,
   For dominion belongs to the Lord
     and He rules over the nations. *(Ps. 22:26b-28)*

4. Ascribe to the Lord, O mighty ones,
     ascribe to the Lord glory and strength

Ascribe to the Lord the glory due his name;
  worship the Lord in the splendor of His holiness.

(Ps. 29:1-2)

5. Sing to the Lord, ye saints of his;
      Praise his holy name. *(Ps. 30:4)*

6. Love the Lord, all his saints!
      The Lord preserves the faithful,
        but the proud he pays back in full.
    Be strong and take heart,
        all you who hope in the Lord. *(Ps. 31:23-24)*

7. Rejoice in the Lord and be glad, you righteous;
      sing, all you who are upright in heart! *(Ps. 32:11)*

8. Sing joyfully to the Lord, ye righteous;
      it is fitting for the upright to praise him . . .
    Sing to him a new song;
        play skillfully, and shout for joy
    For the word of the Lord is right and true;
        he is faithful in all he does.
    The Lord loves righteousness and justice;
        the earth is full of his unfailing love. *(Ps. 33:1-5)*

9. I will extol the Lord at all times;
      his praise will always be on my lips.
    My soul will boast in the Lord;
        let the afflicted hear and rejoice.
    Glorify the Lord with me;
        let us exalt his name together. *(Ps. 34:1-3)*

10. I waited patiently for the Lord;
      he turned to me and heard my cry.
    He lifted me out of the slimy pit,
        out of the mud and mire;
    He set my feet on a rock
        and gave me a firm place to stand.
    He put a new song in my mouth,
        a hymn of praise to our God.
    Many will see and fear
        and put their trust in the Lord. *(Ps. 40:1-3)*

11. Send forth your light and your truth,
      let them guide me;

Let them bring me to your holy mountain
  to the place where you dwell.
Then will I go to the altar of God,
  to God, my joy and my delight.
I will praise you with the harp,
  O God, my God. *(Ps. 43:3-4)*

For Ascension Sunday

12. God has ascended amid shouts of joy
       the Lord amid the sounding of trumpets.
     Sing praises to God, sing praises;
       sing praises to our King, sing praises.
     For God is the King of all the earth;
       sing to Him a psalm of praise. *(Ps. 47:5-7)*

13. God says to us:
     "Be still, and know that I am God;
       I will be exalted among the nations,
       I will be exalted in the earth." *(Ps. 46:10)*

14. All mankind will fear;
       They will proclaim the works of God
       and ponder what He has done.
     Let the righteous rejoice in the Lord
       and take refuge in him;
       let all the upright in heart praise him! *(Ps. 64:9-10)*

15. May the peoples praise you, O God;
       may all the peoples praise you.
     May the nations be glad and sing for joy,
       for you rule the peoples justly
       and guide the nations of the earth.
     May the peoples praise you, O God;
       may all the peoples praise you. *(Ps. 67:3-5)*

16. Sing to God, sing praise to his name,
       extol him who rides on the clouds—
     his name is the Lord—
       and rejoice before him.
     A father to the fatherless, a defender of widows,
       is God in his holy dwelling. *(Ps. 68:4-6a)*

17. Sing to God, O kingdoms of the earth,
       sing praise to the Lord,

To him who rides the ancient skies above,
   who thunders with mighty voice.
Proclaim the power of God
   whose majesty is over Israel,
   whose power is in the skies.
You are awesome, O God, in your sanctuary;
   the God of Israel gives power and strength to his people.
Praise be to God. *(Ps. 68:32-35)*

18.   Among the gods there is none like you, O Lord;
         no deeds can compare with yours.
      All the nations you have made
         will come and worship before you, O Lord;
         they will bring glory to your name.
      For you are great and do marvelous deeds;
         you alone are God. *(Ps. 86:8-10)*

19.   The heavens praise your wonders, O Lord,
         your faithfulness too, in the assembly of the holy ones.
      For who in the skies above can compare with the Lord?
         who is like the Lord among the heavenly beings?
      In the council of the holy ones God is greatly feared;
         he is more awesome than all who surround him.
      O Lord God Almighty, who is like you?
         You are mighty, O Lord, and your faithfulness
            surrounds you.

(Ps. 89:5-8)

20.   It is good to praise the Lord
         and make music to your name, O Most High,
      To proclaim your love in the morning
         and your faithfulness at night. *(Ps. 92:1-2)*

21.   Come, let us sing for joy to the Lord;
         let us shout aloud to the Rock of our salvation.
      Let us come before him with thanksgiving
         and extol him with music and song.
      For the Lord is the great God,
         the great King above all gods. *(Ps. 95:1-3)*

22.   Come, let us bow down in worship,
         let us kneel before the Lord our Maker;
      For he is our God

and we are the people of his pasture,
the flock under his care. *(Ps. 95:6-7)*

23. Sing to the Lord a new song;
      sing to the Lord all the earth.
    Sing to the Lord, praise his name;
      proclaim his salvation day after day.
    Declare his glory among the nations,
      his marvelous deeds among all peoples.
    For great is the Lord and most worthy of praise;
      he is to be feared above all gods.
    For all the gods of the nation are idols,
      but the Lord made the heavens.
    Splendor and majesty are before him;
      strength and glory are in his sanctuary. *(Ps. 96:1-6)*

24. Ascribe to the Lord, O families of nations,
      ascribe to the Lord glory and strength.
    Ascribe to the Lord glory and strength;
      bring an offering and come into his courts.
    Worship the Lord in the splendor of his holiness;
      tremble before him, all the earth. *(Ps. 96:7-9)*

25. Let those who love the Lord hate evil,
      for he guards the lives of his faithful ones
      and delivers them from the hand of the wicked.
    Rejoice in the Lord, you who are righteous,
      and praise his holy name. *(Ps. 97:10, 12)*

26. Sing to the Lord a new song,
      for he has done marvelous things;
    His right hand and his holy arm
      have worked salvation for him.
    The Lord has made his salvation known
      and revealed his righteousness to the nations . . .
    All the ends of the earth have seen
      the salvation of our God. *(Ps. 98:1-3)*

27. Exalt the Lord our God
      and worship at his holy mountain,
      for the Lord our God is holy. *(Ps. 99:9)*

28. Shout for joy to the Lord, all the earth.
      Serve the Lord with gladness;

come before him with joyful songs.
Know that the Lord is God.
It is he who made us, and we are his;
we are his people, the sheep of his pasture.
Enter his gates with thanksgiving
and his courts with praise;
give thanks to him and praise his name.
For the Lord is good and his love endures forever;
his faithfulness continues through all generations.

(Ps. 100)

29. Praise the Lord, O my soul;
all my inmost being, praise his holy name.
Praise the Lord, O my soul,
and forget not all his benefits.
He forgives all my sins
and heals all my diseases;
He redeems my life from the pit
and crowns me with love and compassion.
He satisfies my desires with good things,
so that my youth is renewed like the eagle's. *(Ps. 103:1-5)*

30. Praise the Lord, O my soul.
O Lord my God, you are very great;
you are clothed with splendor and majesty. *(Ps. 104:1)*

31. Give thanks to the Lord, call on his name;
make known among the nations what he has done.
Sing to him, sing praise to him;
tell of all his wonderful acts.
Glory in his holy name;
let the hearts of those who seek the Lord rejoice.
Look to the Lord and his strength;
seek his face always. *(Ps. 105:1-4)*

32. Praise the Lord.
Give thanks to the Lord, for he is good;
his love endures forever.
Who can proclaim the mighty acts of the Lord
or fully declare his praise? *(Ps. 106:1-2)*

33. Give thanks to the Lord, for he is good;
his love endures forever.

Let the redeemed of the Lord say this—
   those he redeemed from the hand of the foe,
Those he gathered from the lands,
   from east and west, from north and south. *(Ps. 107:1-3)*

34. Praise the Lord.
   I will extol the Lord with all my heart
      in the council of the upright and in the assembly.
   Great are the works of the Lord;
      they are pondered by all who delight in them.
   Glorious and majestic are his deeds,
      and his righteousness endures forever.
   He has caused his wonders to be remembered;
      the Lord is gracious and compassionate. *(Ps. 111:1-4)*

35. The fear of the Lord is the beginning of wisdom;
      all who follow his precepts have good understanding.
      To him belongs eternal praise. *(Ps. 111:10)*

36. Praise the Lord.
   Praise, O servants of the Lord,
      praise the name of the Lord.
   Let the name of the Lord be praised,
      both now and forevermore.
   From the rising of the sun to the place where it sets
      the name of the Lord is to be praised.
   The Lord is exalted over all the nations,
      his glory above the heavens. *(Ps. 113:1-4)*

37. Praise the Lord, all you nations;
      extol him, all you peoples.
   For great is his love toward us,
      and the faithfulness of the Lord endures forever.
   Praise the Lord. *(Ps. 117)*

38. Give thanks to the Lord, for he is good;
      his love endures forever.
   Let Israel say:
      "His love endures forever."
   Let the house of Aaron say:
      "His love endures forever."
   Let those who fear the Lord say,
      "His love endures forever." *(Ps. 118:1-4)*

39. Our help is in the name of the Lord,
        the Maker of heaven and earth. *(Ps. 124:8)*

40. Those who trust in the Lord are like Mount Zion,
        which cannot be shaken but endures forever.
     As the mountains surround Jerusalem,
        so the Lord surrounds his people
        both now and forevermore.
     Praise ye the Lord! *(Ps. 125:1-2)*

41. Lift up your hands in the sanctuary
        and praise the Lord.
     May the Lord, the Maker of heaven and earth,
        bless you from Zion. *(Ps. 134:2-3)*

42. Praise the Lord.
     Praise the name of the Lord;
        Praise him, you servants of the Lord . . .
     Praise the Lord, for the Lord is good;
        sing praise to his name, for that is pleasant. *(Ps. 135:1, 3)*

43. I will praise you, O Lord, with all my heart;
        before the "gods" I will sing your praise.
     I will bow down toward your holy temple
        and will praise your name
        for your love and your faithfulness,
     for you have exalted above all things
        your name and your word. *(Ps. 138:1-2)*

44. I will exalt you, my God the King;
        I will praise your name for ever and ever.
     Every day will I praise you
        and extol your name for ever and ever.
     Great is the Lord and most worthy of praise;
        his greatness no one can fathom.
     One generation will commend your works to another;
        they will tell of your mighty acts. *(Ps. 145:1-4)*

45. My mouth will speak in praise of the Lord.
        Let every creature praise his holy name
        forever and ever. *(Ps. 145:21)*

46. Praise the Lord.
     Praise the Lord, O my soul.

I will praise the Lord all my life;
I will sing praise to my God as long as I live.
Blessed is he whose help is the God of Jacob,
    whose hope is in the Lord his God,
the Maker of heaven and earth,
    the sea and everything in them—
    the Lord who remains faithful forever. *(Ps. 146:1-2, 5-6)*

47. Praise the Lord.
How good it is to sing praises to our God,
    how pleasant and fitting to praise him!
He determines the number of the stars
    and calls them each by name.
Great is our Lord, and mighty in power;
    his understanding has no limit. *(Ps. 147:1, 4-5)*

48. Young men and maidens,
        old men and children,
Let them praise the name of the Lord,
    for his name alone is exalted;
    his splendor is above the earth and the heavens.
Praise the Lord. *(Ps. 148:12-13, 14b)*

49. Praise the Lord.
Sing to the Lord a new song,
    his praise in the assembly of the saints.
Let Israel rejoice in their Maker,
    let the people of Zion be glad in their King. *(Ps. 149:1-2)*

50. Praise the Lord.
Praise God in his sanctuary;
    praise him in his mighty heavens.
Praise him for his acts of power;
    praise him for his surpassing greatness.
Let everything that has breath praise the Lord. *(Ps. 150:1,2,6)*

51. A time is coming and has now come when the true worshipers shall worship the Father in spirit and truth, for they are the kind of worshipers the Father seeks. God is spirit, and his worshipers must worship in spirit and in truth. *(John 4:23-24)*

52. Therefore, brothers, since we have confidence to enter the Most Holy Place by the blood of Jesus, by a new and living

way opened for us through the curtain, that is, his body, and since we have a great priest over the house of God, let us draw near to God with a sincere heart in full assurance of faith, having our hearts sprinkled to cleanse us from a guilty conscience. *(Heb. 10:19-22)*

53.   Let us consider how we may spur one another on toward love and good deeds. Let us not give up meeting together, as some are in the habit of doing, but let us encourage one another — and all the more as you see the Day approaching.

(Heb. 10:24-25)

54.   I will tell of the kindness of the Lord,
          and deeds for which he is to be praised,
          according to all the Lord has done for us —
      yes, the many good things he has done
          for the house of Israel
          according to his compassion and many kindnesses.

(Isa. 63:7)

55.   Seek ye the Lord while he may be found;
          call on him while he is near.
      Let the wicked forsake his way
          and the evil man his thoughts.
      Let him turn to the Lord, and he will have mercy on him,
          and to our God, for he will freely pardon. *(Isa. 55:6-7)*

56.   The Lord is in his holy temple;
          let all the earth be silent before him. *(Hab. 2:20)*

57.   Come to me, all you who are weary and burdened, and I will give you rest. Take my yoke upon you and learn from me, for I am gentle and humble in heart, and you will find rest for your souls. For my yoke is easy and my burden is light.

(Matt. 11:28-30)

58.   Thus saith the Lord . . . "You must observe my Sabbaths. This will be a sign between me and you for generations to come, so you may know that I am the Lord, who makes you holy." *(Exod. 31:13)*

59.   *For evening worship:*
      Praise the Lord, all you servants of the Lord
          who minister by night in the house of the Lord.

Lift up your hands in the sanctuary
    and praise the Lord.

60.   *For the Communion:*
Christ, our Passover lamb, has been sacrificed. Therefore let
us keep the Festival, not with the old yeast, the yeast of malice
and wickedness, but with bread without yeast, the bread of
sincerity and truth. *(I Cor. 5:7-8)*

61.   Give thanks to the Lord,
    call upon His Name.
Make known His deeds among the nations;
    proclaim that His Name is exalted. *(Isa. 12:3)*

62.   Sing praises to the Lord, for he has done
    gloriously;
Let this be known in all the earth.
Shout and sing for joy, O inhabitant of
    Zion,
For great in your midst is the Holy One
    of Israel. *(Isa. 12:5-6)*

Before Confession

1.   The Lord is in his holy temple;
    The Lord is on his heavenly throne.
He observes the sons of men;
    His eyes examine them.
The Lord examines the righteous,
    but the wicked and those who love violence
    his soul hates.
For the Lord is righteous,
    he loves justice;
    upright men will see his face. *(Ps. 11:4,5,7)*

Let us confess our sins—

2.   Lord, who may dwell in your sanctuary?
    Who may live on your holy hill?
He whose walk is blameless
    and who does what is righteous,
Who speaks the truth in his heart

and has no slander on his tongue,
Who does his neighbor no wrong
and casts no slur on his fellow man. *(Ps. 15:1-3)*

Let us confess our sins—

3. Who can discern his errors?
Forgive my hidden faults.
Keep your servant also from willful sins;
may they not rule over me.
Then will I be blameless,
innocent of great transgression. *(Ps. 19:12-13)*

Let us acknowledge our transgressions—

4. Who may ascend the hill of the Lord?
Who may stand in his holy place?
He who has clean hands and a pure heart,
and does not lift up his soul to an idol
or swear by what is false.
He will receive blessing from the Lord
and vindication from God his Saviour. *(Ps. 24:3-5)*

Let us confess our sins and ask God for a pure heart—

5. *Minister:* I said, I will confess my transgressions unto the
Lord.
People: And Thou forgavest the iniquity of my sin.

6. O Lord, open my lips,
and my mouth will declare your praise.
You do not delight in sacrifice, or I would bring it;
you do not take pleasure in burnt offerings.
The sacrifices of God are a broken spirit;
a broken and contrite heart,
O God, you will not despise. *(Ps. 51:15-17)*

7. O Lord, you have searched me
and you know me.
You know when I sit and when I rise;
you perceive my thoughts from afar.
You discern my going out and my lying down;
you are familiar with all my ways.
Before a word is on my tongue
you know it completely, O Lord. *(Ps. 139:1-4)*

(In the light of God's complete knowledge of our thoughts and actions, let us confess our sins)

8.   This is what the Lord says,
     My people have committed two sins:
     They have forsaken me,
         the spring of living water,
     and have dug their own cisterns,
         broken cisterns that cannot hold water. *(Jer. 2:9a, 13)*

9.   Let the wicked forsake his way
         and the evil man his thoughts.
     Let him turn to the Lord, and he will have mercy on him,
         and to our God, for he will freely pardon. *(Isa. 55:7)*

10. Even now, declares the Lord,
         return to me with all your heart,
         with fasting and weeping and mourning.
     Rend your heart
         and not your garments.
     Return to the Lord your God
         for he is gracious and compassionate,
         slow to anger and abounding in love. *(Joel 2:12-13)*

11. If we claim to be without sin, we deceive ourselves and the
     truth is not in us. *(I John 1:8)*

Corporate Confessions of Sin
(in unison)

FORM #1   Almighty and most merciful Father; We have erred
and strayed from Thy ways like lost sheep. We have followed too
much the devices and desires of our own hearts. We have offended
against Thy holy laws. We have left undone those things which we
ought to have done. And we have done those things which we ought
not to have done; and there is no health in us. But Thou, O Lord,
have mercy upon us, miserable offenders. Spare Thou those, O
God, who confess their faults. Restore Thou those who are penitent; According to Thy promises declared unto mankind in Christ
Jesus our Lord. And grant, O merciful Father; for His sake; That
we may hereafter live a godly, righteous, and sober life; To the
glory of Thy holy name. Amen.

FORM #2   Most holy and merciful Father; We acknowledge and confess before Thee; Our sinful nature prone to evil and slothful in good; And all our shortcomings and offenses. Thou alone knowest how often we have sinned; In wandering from Thy ways; In wasting Thy gifts; In forgetting Thy love. But Thou, O Lord, have pity upon us; Who are ashamed and sorry for all wherein we have displeased Thee. Teach us to hate our errors; Cleanse us from our secret faults; And forgive our sins for the sake of Thy dear Son. And O most holy and loving Father; Help us we beseech Thee; To live in Thy light and walk in Thy ways; According to the commandments of Jesus Christ our Lord. Amen.

FORM #3   Almighty God, who art rich in mercy to all those who call upon Thee; Hear us as we come to Thee humbly confessing our sins; And imploring Thy mercy and forgiveness. We have broken Thy holy laws by our deeds and by our words; And by the sinful affections of our hearts. We confess before Thee our disobedience and ingratitude, our pride and willfullness; And all our failures and shortcomings toward Thee and toward fellow men. Have mercy upon us, most merciful Father; And of Thy great goodness grant that we may hereafter serve and please Thee in newness of life; Through the merit and mediation of Jesus Christ our Lord. Amen.

FORM #4   Lord God! Eternal and Almighty Father. We acknowledge and confess before Thy holy majesty, that we are poor sinners; conceived and born in guilt and in corruption, prone to do evil, unable of ourselves to do any good; who, by reason of our depravity, transgress without end Thy holy commandments. Therefore we have drawn upon ourselves, by Thy just sentence, condemnation and death. But, O Lord! With heartfelt sorrow we repent and deplore our offences! We condemn ourselves and our evil ways, with true penitence beseeching that Thy grace may relieve our distress.

Be pleased then to have compassion upon us, O most gracious God! Father of all mercies; for the sake of Thy Son Jesus Christ our Lord. And in removing our guilt and our pollution, grant us the daily increase of the grace of Thine Holy Spirit; that acknowledging from our inmost hearts our own unrighteousness, we may be touched with sorrow that shall work true repentance; and that Thy Spirit, mortifying all sin within us, may produce the fruits of holiness and of righteousness well-pleasing in Thy sight; Through Jesus Christ our Lord. Amen.

FORM #5 O Thou whose chosen dwelling is the heart that longs for Thy presence and humbly seeks Thy love: we come to Thee to acknowledge and confess that we have sinned in thought and word and deed; we have not loved Thee with all our heart and soul, with all our mind and strength; we have not even loved our neighbor as ourselves.

Deepen within us our sorrow for the wrong we have done, or for the good we have left undone. But Thou, O Lord, art full of compassion and gracious, slow to anger and plenteous in mercy; there is forgiveness with Thee. Restore to us the joy of Thy salvation; bind up that which is broken, give light to our minds, strength to our wills and rest to our souls. Speak to each of us the word that we need, and let Thy word abide with us until it has wrought in us Thy holy will. Amen.

FORM #6 Almighty God, our heavenly Father,
we have sinned against you and against our fellow men,
in thought and word and deed,
in the evil we have done
and in the good we have not done,
through ignorance, through weakness,
through our own deliberate fault.
We are truly sorry and repent of all our sins.
For the sake of your Son, Jesus Christ, who died for us,
forgive us all that is past;
and grant that we may serve You in newness of life
to the glory of Your Name. Amen.

Scriptural Confessions

These confessions from the Psalter may be used as responsive readings with the minister reading the first line and the congregation the second, or they may be read in unison. The pronouns marked with an asterisk (*) are singular in the original Hebrew.

7.   Remember, O Lord, your great mercy and love,
        for they are from of old,
     Remember not the sins of our* youth
        and my rebellious ways;
     According to your love remember us,
        for you are good, O Lord . . .

For the sake of your name, O Lord,
　　forgive our iniquity, though it is great . . .
Turn to us and be gracious to us,
　　for we are lonely and afflicted.
The troubles of our hearts have multiplied;
　　free us from our anguish.
Look upon our affliction and our distress
　　and take away all our sins. *(Ps. 25:6,7,11,16-18)*

8.　O Lord, do not rebuke us* in your anger
　　or discipline us in your wrath.
For your arrows have pierced us,
　　and your hand has come down upon us.
Because of your wrath there is no health in our bodies;
　　our bones have no soundness because of our sin.
Our guilt has overwhelmed us
　　like a burden too heavy to bear . . .
All our longings lie open before you, O Lord;
　　our sighing is not hidden from you . . .
We confess our iniquity;
　　We are troubled by our sin.
O Lord, do not forsake us;
Come quickly to help us,
　　O Lord, our Saviour. *(Ps. 38:1-4,9,18,21-22)*

9.　Do not withhold your mercy from us*, O Lord;
　　may your love and your truth always protect us.
For troubles without number surround us;
　　our sins have overtaken us, and we cannot see.
They are more than the hairs of our heads,
　　and our hearts fail within us.
Be pleased, O Lord, to save us;
　　O Lord, come quickly to help us. *(Ps. 40:11-13)*

10.　Have mercy on us*, O God,
　　according to your unfailing love;
According to your great compassion
　　blot out our transgression.
Wash away all our iniquity
　　and cleanse us from our sin.
For we know our transgressions,
　　and our sin is always before us.

Against you, you only have we sinned
and done what is evil in your sight,
So that you are proved right when you speak
and justified when you judge. *(Ps. 51:1-4)*

11.   Cleanse us* with hyssop, and we will be clean;
wash us, and we will be whiter than snow . . .
Hide your face from our sins
and blot out all our iniquity.
Create in us pure hearts, O God,
and renew a steadfast spirit within us.
Do not cast us from your presence
or take your Holy Spirit from us.
Restore to us the joy of your salvation
and grant us a willing spirit, to sustain us.
The sacrifices of God are a broken spirit;
a broken and contrite heart,
O God, you will not despise. *(Ps. 51:7,9-12,17)*

Note: This section and the previous section from Psalm 51 may be
used together as one confession if preferred.

Assurances of Pardoning Grace

1.   If you, O Lord, kept a record of sins,
O Lord, who could stand?
But with you there is forgiveness;
therefore you are feared. *(Ps. 130:3-4)*

2.   The righteous cry out, and the Lord hears them;
he delivers them from all their troubles.
The Lord is close to the brokenhearted
and saves those who are crushed in spirit. *(Ps. 34:17-18)*

3.   Evil will slay the wicked;
the foes of the righteous will be condemned.
The Lord redeems his servants;
no one who takes refuge in him will be condemned.
(Ps. 34:21-22)

4.   Praise the Lord, O my soul;
all my inmost being, praise his holy name.

Praise the Lord, O my soul,
    and forget not all his benefits.
He forgives all your sins
    and heals all your diseases. *(Ps. 103:1-3)*

5. The Lord is compassionate and gracious,
        slow to anger, abounding in love.
    He will not always accuse,
        nor will he harbor his anger forever;
    He does not treat us as our sins deserve
        or repay us according to our iniquities.
    For as high as the heavens are above the earth,
        so great is his love for those who fear him;
    As far as the east is from the west,
        so far has he removed our transgressions from us.
                                        (Ps. 103:8-12)

6. O Israel, put your hope in the Lord,
        for with the Lord is unfailing love
        and with him is full redemption.
    He himself will redeem Israel
        from all their sins. *(Ps. 130:7-8)*

7. The Lord delights in the way of the man
        whose steps he has made firm;
    Though he stumble, he will not fall,
        for the Lord upholds him with his hand. *(Ps. 37:23-24)*

8. O you who hear prayer,
        to you all men will come.
    When we were overwhelmed by sins,
        you atoned for our transgressions.
    Blessed is the man you choose
        and bring near to live in your courts! *(Ps. 65:2-4a)*

9. Praise be to the Lord, to God our Saviour,
        who daily bears our burdens.
    Our God is a God who saves;
        from the Sovereign Lord comes escape from death.
                                        (Ps. 68:19-20)

10. You showed favor to your land, O Lord;
        you restored the fortunes of Jacob.
    You forgave the iniquity of your people

and covered all their sins.
You set aside all your wrath
and turned from your fierce anger. *(Ps. 85:1-3)*

11. I will listen to what God the Lord will say;
he promises peace to his people, his saints—
but let them not return to folly.
Surely his salvation is near those who fear him,
that his glory may dwell in our land. *(Ps. 85:8-9)*

12. You are kind and forgiving, O Lord,
abounding in love to all who call on you. *(Ps. 86:5)*

13. Praise the Lord, O my soul,
and forget not all his benefits.
He forgives all my sins
and heals all my diseases;
He redeems my life from the pit
and crowns me with love and compassion. *(Ps. 103:2-4)*

14. The Lord is compassionate and gracious,
slow to anger, abounding in love,
He will not always accuse,
nor will he harbor his anger forever;
He does not treat us as our sins deserve
or repay us according to our iniquities.
For as high as the heavens are above the earth,
so great is his love for those who fear him;
As far as the east is from the west,
so far has he removed our transgressions from us.
(Ps. 103:8-12)

15. If you, O Lord, kept a record of sins,
O Lord, who could stand?
But with you there is forgiveness;
therefore you are feared. *(Ps. 130:3-4)*

16. I wait for the Lord, my soul waits
and in his word I put my hope.
O Israel, put your hope in the Lord,
for with the Lord is unfailing love
and with him is full redemption.
He himself will redeem Israel
from all their sins. *(Ps. 130:5, 7-8)*

17. The Lord is faithful to all his promises
         and loving toward all he has made.
     The Lord upholds all those who fall
         and lifts up all who are bowed down. *(Ps. 145:13b-14)*

18. Surely he took up our infirmities
         and carried our sorrows,
     yet we considered him stricken by God,
         smitten by him and afflicted.
     But he was wounded for our transgressions,
         he was crushed for our iniquities;
     the punishment that brought us peace was upon him,
         and by his wounds we are healed. *(Isa. 53:4-5)*

19. We all, like sheep, have gone astray,
         each of us has turned to his own way;
     and the Lord has laid on him the iniquity of us all. *(Isa. 53:6)*

20. It was the Lord's will to crush him and cause him to suffer
         and though the Lord makes his life a guilt offering,
     he will see his offspring and prolong his days,
         and the will of the Lord will prosper in his hand.
     After the suffering of his soul,
         he will see the light of life and be satisfied;
     by his knowledge my righteous servant will justify many,
         and he will bear their iniquities. *(Isa. 53:10-11)*

21. Come now, let us reason together,
         says the Lord.
     Though your sins are like scarlet,
         they shall be as white as snow;
     Though they are red as crimson,
         they shall be like wool. *(Isa. 1:18)*

22. If we confess our sins, he is faithful and just and will forgive
     us our sins and purify us from all unrighteousness.
                                                    (I John 1:9)

23. My little children, I write this to you so that you will not sin,
     but if anybody does sin, we have one who speaks to the
     Father in our defense—Jesus Christ, the Righteous One. He is
     the atoning sacrifice for our sins, and not only for ours but
     also for the sins of the whole world. *(I John 2:1-2)*

24. He himself bore our sins in his own body on the tree, so that we might die to sins and live for righteousness; by his wounds you have been healed. *(I Peter 2:24)*

25. To him who loves us and has freed us from our sins by his blood, and has made us to be a kingdom and priests to serve his God and Father—to him be glory and power for ever and ever! Amen. *(Rev. 1:5b-6)*

26. Here is a trustworthy saying that deserves full acceptance: Christ Jesus came into the world to save sinners. *(I Tim. 1:15)*

27. All the prophets testify about him that everyone who believes in him receives forgiveness of sins through his name. *(Acts 10:43)*

28. God so loved the world that he gave his only begotten Son that whosoever believeth in him should not perish but have everlasting life. *(John 3:16)*

29. Because Jesus lives forever, he has a permanent priesthood. Therefore he is able to save completely those who come to God through him, because he always lives to intercede for them. *(Heb. 7:24-25)*

30. Christ did not enter a man-made sanctuary that was only a copy of the true one; he entered heaven itself, now to appear for us in God's presence. Nor did he enter heaven to offer himself again and again, the way the High Priest enters the Most Holy Place with blood that is not his own. Then Christ would have had to suffer many times since the creation of the world. But now he has appeared once for all at the end of the ages to do away with sin by the sacrifice of himself. So Christ was sacrificed once to take away the sins of many people.

(Heb. 9:24-28)

Before the Offering

1. Let us remember the word of the Lord Jesus, how he himself said, "It is more blessed to give than to receive."

(Acts 20:35b)

2. Remember this: Whosoever sows sparingly will also reap sparingly, and whosoever sows generously will also reap gen-

erously. Each man should give what he has decided in his heart to give, not reluctantly or under compulsion, for God loves a cheerful giver. *(II Cor. 9:6-7)*

3. You know the grace of our Lord Jesus Christ, that though he was rich, yet for your sakes he became poor, so that you through his poverty might become rich. *(II Cor. 8:9)*

4. Honor the Lord with your substance (NIV, wealth) with the firstfruits of all thine increase. *(Prov. 3:9)*

5. And do not forget to do good and to share with others, for with such sacrifices God is pleased. *(Heb. 13:16)*

6. Freely you have received; freely give. *(Matt. 10:8)*

7. Bring the whole tithe into the storehouse, that there may be food in my house. Test me in this, says the Lord Almighty, and see if I will not throw open the floodgates of heaven and pour out so much blessing that you will not have room enough for it. *(Mal. 3:10)*

8. Therefore, as we have opportunity, let us do good to all people, especially to those who belong to the family of believers. *(Gal. 6:10)*

9. A generous man will himself be blessed,
   for he shares his food with the poor. *(Prov. 22:9)*

10. Give unto the Lord the glory due his name.
    Bring an offering and come before him. *(I Chron. 16:29)*

11. Bring an offering for me from each man whose heart prompts him to give. *(Exod. 25:2b)*

12. This is what the Lord has commanded: Take from what you have an offering for the Lord. Everyone who is willing is to bring to the Lord an offering. *(Exod. 35:4b-5)*

13. No man should appear before the Lord empty-handed: each of you must bring a gift in proportion to the way the Lord your God has blessed you. *(Deut. 16:17)*

14. How can I repay the Lord
    for all his goodness to me?
    I will fulfill my vows to the Lord
    in the presence of all his people. *(Ps. 116:12,14)*

Before a Hymn of Praise

1. I will give thanks to the Lord because of his righteousness
   and will sing praise to the name of the Lord Most High.
   (Ps. 7:17)

2. I will praise you, O Lord, with all my heart;
   I will tell of all your wonders.
   I will be glad and rejoice in you;
   I will sing praise to your name, O Most High. *(Ps. 9:1-2)*

3. I will sing to the Lord
   for He has been good to me. *(Ps. 13:6)*

4. Sing to the Lord, you saints of his;
   praise his holy name. *(Ps. 30:4)*

5. My tongue will speak of your righteousness
   and of your praises all day long. *(Ps. 35:28)*

6. I (we) will praise you forever for what you have done;
   in your name I (we) will hope, for your name is good.
   I will praise you in the presence of your saints. *(Ps. 52:9)*

7. Be exalted, O God, above the heavens;
   let your glory be over all the earth. *(Ps. 57:5)*

8. I will praise you, O Lord, among the nations;
   I will sing of you among the peoples.
   For great is your love, reaching to the heavens;
   your faithfulness reaches to the skies.
   Be exalted, O God, above the heavens;
   let your glory be over all the earth. *(Ps. 57:9-11)*

9. I will sing of your strength,
   in the morning I will sing of your love;
   For you are my fortress,
   my refuge in times of trouble.
   O my Strength, I sing praise to you;
   you, O God, are my fortress, my loving God.
   (Ps. 59:16-17)

10. Because your love is better than life,
    my lips will glorify you.
    I will praise you as long as I live,
    and in your name I will lift up my hands.

My soul will be satisfied as with the richest of foods;
    with singing lips my mouth will praise you. *(Ps. 63:3-5)*

11.   As for me, I will always have hope;
    I will praise you more and more.
My mouth will tell of your righteousness,
    of your salvation all day long,
    though I know not its measure.
I will come and proclaim your mighty acts,
    O Sovereign Lord;
I will proclaim your righteousness, yours alone.

(Ps. 71:14-16)

12.   I will sing of the love of the Lord forever;
    with my mouth I will make your faithfulness known
        through all generations.
I will declare that your love stands firm forever,
    that you established your faithfulness in heaven itself.

(Ps. 89:1-2)

Before Prayer

1.   Know that the Lord has set apart the godly for himself;
    The Lord will hear when I call to him. *(Ps. 4:3)*

2.   Give ear to my words, O Lord,
    consider my sighing.
Listen to my cry for help,
    my King and my God,
    for to you I pray.
Morning by morning, O Lord, you hear my voice;
    morning by morning I lay my requests before you
    and wait in expectation. *(Ps. 5:1-3)*

3.   Those who know your name will trust in you,
    for you, Lord, have never forsaken those who seek you.

(Ps. 9:10)

4.   May the words of my mouth and the meditation of my heart
    be pleasing in your sight,
    O Lord, my Rock and my Redeemer. *(Ps. 19:14)*

5.   The righteous cry out, and the Lord hears them;

he delivers them from all their troubles.
The Lord is close to the brokenhearted
   and saves those who are crushed in spirit. *(Ps. 34:17-18)*

6. The eyes of the Lord are upon the righteous,
       and His ears are open to their cry. *(Ps. 34:15)*

7. Cast your cares on the Lord
       and He will sustain you;
       He will never let the righteous fall. *(Ps. 55:22)*

8. Trust in him at all times, O people;
       pour out your hearts to him,
       for God is our refuge. *(Ps. 62:8)*

9. The Lord is righteous in all his ways
       and loving toward all he has made.
    The Lord is near to all who call on him,
       to all who call on him in truth.
    He fulfills the desires of those who fear him;
       he hears their cry and saves them. *(Ps. 145:17-19)*

10. Come and pray to me, and I will listen to you. You will seek
    me and find me when you seek me with all your heart.
                                        (Jer. 29:12-13)

11. Because of the Lord's great love we are not consumed,
       for his compassions never fail.
    They are new every morning;
       great is your faithfulness. *(Lam. 3:22-23)*

12. Ask and it will be given to you; seek and you will find; knock
    and the door will be opened to you. For everyone who asks
    receives; he who seeks finds; and to him who knocks, the
    door will be opened. *(Matt. 7:7-8)*

13. If you then, though you are evil, know how to give good gifts
    to your children, how much more will your Father in heaven
    give the Holy Spirit to those who ask him! *(Luke 11:13)*

14. Do not be anxious about anything, but in everything, by
    prayer and petition, with thanksgiving, present your requests
    to God. And the peace of God, which transcends all under-
    standing, will guard your hearts and minds in Christ Jesus.
    (Phil. 4:6-7)

15.   We do not have a high priest who is unable to sympathize with our weaknesses but we have one who was tempted in every way, just as we are—yet was without sin. Let us then approach the throne of grace with confidence, so that we may receive mercy and find grace to help in time of need. *(Heb. 4:15-16)*

16.   This is the assurance we have in approaching God: that if we ask anything according to his will, he hears us. And if we know that he hears us—whatsoever we ask—we know that we have what we asked of him. *(I John 5:14-15)*

Before Reading the Scripture

1.   Blessed is the man
        who does not walk in the counsel of the wicked
     or stand in the way of sinners
        or sit in the seat of mockers.
     But his delight is in the law of the Lord,
        and on his law he meditates day and night. *(Ps. 1:1)*

2.   As for God, his way is perfect;
        the Word of the Lord is flawless.
     He is a shield
        for all who take refuge in him.
     For who is God beside the Lord?
        and who is the Rock except our God? *(Ps. 18:30-31)*

3.   The law of the Lord is perfect,
        reviving the soul.
     The statutes of the Lord are trustworthy,
        making wise the simple.
     The precepts of the Lord are right,
        giving joy to the heart.
     The commands of the Lord are radiant,
        giving light to the eyes.
     The fear of the Lord is pure,
        enduring forever.
     The ordinances of the Lord are sure,
        and altogether righteous.
     They are more precious than gold;
        than much pure gold;

They are sweeter than honey,
    than honey from the comb.
By them is your servant warned;
    in keeping them there is great reward. *(Ps. 19:7-11)*

4.   Teach me your way, O Lord,
    and I will walk in your truth;
Give me an undivided heart,
    that I may fear your Name. *(Ps. 86:11)*

5.   Blessed are they who keep his statutes
    and seek him with all their heart. *(Ps. 119:2)*

6.   I will praise you with an upright heart
    as I learn your righteous laws.
I will obey your decrees. *(Ps. 119:7-8)*

7.   Praise be to you, O Lord;
    teach me your decrees.
I rejoice in following your statutes
    as one rejoices in great riches.
I delight in your decrees;
    I will not neglect your word. *(Ps. 119:12,14,16)*

8.   Give me understanding, and I will keep your law
    and obey it with all my heart.
Direct me in the path of your commands,
    for there I find delight.
Turn my heart toward your statutes
    and not toward selfish gain.
Turn my eyes away from worthless things;
    renew my life according to your word. *(Ps. 119:34-37)*

p.30 On Corporate dimensions in Worship

p.176 Scriptural Calls to Worship

p.192 Scripture of Promise of Forgiveness

p.281 On Wedding Rehearsals